Learning the Media

Learning the Media

An Introduction to Media Teaching

Manuel Alvarado
Robin Gutch
Tana Wollen

MACMILLAN

First published 1987 by
THE MACMILLAN PRESS LTD
Houndmills, Basingstoke, Hampshire RG21 2XS
and London
Companies and representatives
throughout the world

ISBN 0–333–30521–3 hardcover
ISBN 0–333–30522–1 paperback

A catalogue record for this book is available from the British Library.

Printed in China

Reprinted 1987, 1988, 1992 (twice), 1993

Remembering Bill Bonney

FILM-PERCEPTION
OF THE WORLD

The most fundamental point: use of the camera as a cinema-eye more perfect than the human eye for exploring the chaos of visual phenomena filling the universe . . .

> MAKE WAY
> FOR THE
> MACHINE!

. . . I am cinema-eye – I am a mechanical eye. I, a machine, show you a world such as only I can see.

From now on and for always I cast off human immobility, I move constantly, I approach and pull away from objects. I creep under them, I leap onto them, I move alongside the mouth of a galloping horse, I cut into a crowd, I run before charging troops, I turn on my back, I take off with an air-plane, I fall and rise with falling and rising bodies . . .

. . .

My mission is the creation of a new perception of the world. Thus I decipher in a new way a world unknown to you.

Dziga Vertov

Contents

Acknowledgements

We would especially like to thank Dave Stewart and to acknowledge the following people for their critical encouragement: David Barrat, Jim Cook, Jenny Grahame, Steven Kennedy, Netia Mayman, John Morey, John Mullan, Jim Pines, Keith Povey, Philip Simpson and Sarah Turvey.

The two John Sturrock photographs and the Mike Goldwater photograph are reproduced courtesy of Network Photographers; the BARB ITV area map is reproduced courtesy of the Broadcaster's Audience Research Board Limited who hold the copyright; Christine Fitzmaurice's drawing of Terry Wogan is reproduced courtesy of the artist and of *Radio Times*; the Guinness advertisement is reproduced courtesy of Guinness Brewing; René Magritte's *Time Transfixed* (1932) (Oil on Canvas) ($57\frac{3}{4}'' \times 38\frac{1}{2}''$), The Art Institute of Chicago, is reproduced with the permission of The Art Institute of Chicago; two photographs from *The Visit* are reproduced courtesy of the ILEA English Centre; the Andrew Kolesnikow photograph and editorial copy are reproduced courtesy of *Homes and Gardens* and *Syndication International*; the feature on Dynasty outfits (which is editorial copy and *not* an advertisement) is reproduced courtesy of *Weekend* magazine; the Volvo advertisement is reproduced courtesy of Volvo Concessionaires Ltd and Abbot, Mead Vickers Ltd; the review of *C.A.T.S. Eyes* by Margaret Forwood is reproduced courtesy of *The Sunday People*; the photograph of the Notting Hill Carnival is reproduced courtesy of Popperfoto; the still from *Sanders of the River* is reproduced courtesy of London Films; the photograph of Neil and Glenys Kinnock at the Notting Hill Carnival is reproduced courtesy of *The Guardian*; Roderick Edbon's photograph of Frank Bruno and Susan Penhaligon and the photograph of Shirley Strong are copyright 1986 *TV Times* and are reproduced by permission of Transworld Feature Syndicate

UK Ltd; we would like to thank Steve Bell for his 'IF' cartoon from *The Guardian*; Thomas Gainsborough's 'Portrait of Miss Haverfield' is reproduced by permission of the Trustees, The Wallace Collection, London; the advertisement 'Playmates' is reproduced courtesy of A & F Pears Ltd; the front cover of *Mother* is reproduced courtesy of *Mother*, IPC Magazines; the advertisement 'Famine Knows No Borders' is reproduced courtesy of *International Christian Relief*; the article 'Let's Play Strikes . . .', dated Friday, 26 April 1985, is reproduced courtesy of the *Daily Mail*; the front page of *The Sun* is reproduced courtesy of *The Sun*; the stills from *Rebel Without A Cause* and from *Mildred Pierce* are reproduced courtesy of Warners; the still from *Sunset Boulevard* is reproduced courtesy of Paramount; Rod Morrison's photograph of Miss Elizabeth Wright is reproduced with the permission of *Help the Aged*; Graham Finlayson's photograph of Nazarré is reproduced courtesy of *The Observer*; the publicity still and poster of *The Eyes of Laura Mars* are reproduced courtesy of Columbia.

Manuel Alvarado
Robin Gutch
Tana Wollen

Introduction

'There is only one thing that can kill the movies, and that is education' – Will Rogers

The media are everywhere in our society. No longer constrained by geographical boundaries, technological limitations or the scarcity of radio frequencies, the new delivery systems of satellite, cable and video allow the universal, and virtually instantaneous, distribution of televisual and filmic productions. The only potential barriers left are those of state regulation, and even then it is unclear how they are going to stop (should they wish to) the bombardment from above (satellites) or from below (video piracy and smuggling).

Thus are the universalist aspirations and potentialities of the mass media – dreamt of since the early days of cinema – finally realised! Nevertheless, this trans-nationalism is achieved primarily in terms of *distribution*: both production and consumption are matters which remain culturally and geographically specific. The international markets and trade routes established by Hollywood cinema are being successfully followed by the American TV companies, but the development of the new technological systems of distribution has encouraged an increasing determination of other media organisations to break into these markets.

This has led to two related developments. On the one hand international entrepreneurs such as Rupert Murdoch, Robert Maxwell and Sergio Berlusconi have moved rapidly into satellite and cable systems, but they make their profits almost solely through the purchase and distribution of already existent, and largely American, films and television programmes. On the other hand, production houses such as the major West European TV companies and organisations such as Brazil's TV Globo are investigating the possibility of creating new international outlets

1

for their work and also seeking new possibilities for co-production finance for the generation of new work.

Researchers and research organisations around the world are monitoring and reporting on these developments, and the already published work in this field constitutes a valuable data base for those teachers who recognise the increasing significance of teaching about the new technologies of the international media. However, it is still, and will continue to be, of prime importance for students and teachers to know and learn about the complex of elements – economic, technological, institutional, legal, political, cultural, aesthetic – which constitute the production processes of films and television programmes and also to understand *how* such cultural artefacts produce meaning, *how* people and issues are represented, and *how* audiences are constructed and constituted.

This learning enables us to recognise how the media function, how they form significant parts of our 'cultural capital'[1] and incessantly constitute fundamental topics on the political agenda of all nations. In the 1980s the convergence of what already seemed to be more traditional forms of information, education and entertainment can happen instantly via telecommunications systems, computers and television screens installed in homes, offices, schools and community centres. The proliferation of mass media forms will undoubtedly mean noisier and more intense struggles for everyone's attention.

Education has also had to struggle for the attention of its own audiences in school and college classrooms. This has sometimes involved teachers appointing themselves as moral guardians, contesting the media and their baleful influences, especially on the young and on the male working class. At other times teachers have used the media to lend chalky traditions a hi-tech gloss. These essentially contradictory engagements between education and the media still take place, but the last twenty-five years have seen more rigorously considered media studies develop in further and higher education and in primary and secondary schools. There are various kinds of media studies and each commands a particular history of emphases and approaches; some of these are described in the next chapter. To discover a discrete and coherent subject discipline across such a range of social formations, even in English-speaking countries, would be a vain hope. Nevertheless, learning about the media is gradually becoming institutionalised in school and college courses across Europe, the USA and Australia, and UNESCO has been monitoring these for possible implementation in the Third World.[2]

There are different reasons why learning about the media is considered to be important, and we hope our own will become clear in this book. We have not suggested things to do in the classroom so much as we have tried to explain theoretical arguments for the provision of sound pedagogies. Although our rationales are intended to be prescriptive, we would not presume that there are right or wrong ways of teaching about the media throughout the variety of classrooms in which the readers of this book will find themselves working. The arguments here, we think, hold as well for primary education as they do for colleges and polytechnics. Pedagogical hints can come in handy, but there are always particular group dynamics to consider, specific course objectives to meet and the perennial limitations of time, resources and willing to be overcome! Teachers are extremely versatile in the uses they make of materials and suggestions, and the very transience of the media material which their students learn about encourages already practised skills. We hope that as readers question the bases and tenets of our arguments, so ways of mediating them to classroom audiences will also be considered and debated.

In Britain media education has grown unevenly but apace. Its various developments have been due almost exclusively to the activity and enthusiasm of classroom teachers and advisers, and so it has yet to gain the widespread political support and resourcing which computing, for instance, has been given. Learning about the media has been taking place in Media Studies in secondary schools since the 1960s and has also become an important component of English, Social Studies and Humanities. In recognising the media's ubiquity, some have sought to defend students from media influences in their teaching, while others have argued for the validity of studying forms of popular culture which the media have made so widely available. Media Studies has challenged curricula, even though there are still schools and colleges where the subject option is still unavailable.

By making explicit the connections between what we know and how we come to know it, Media Studies has made learning the media an important part of any subject on the timetable. The learning of English has begun to take account of how language is determined and determining; in Social Studies and the Humanities films and videos can no longer be used as simple audio-visual aids which reveal the state of the world, but have themselves become subjects of educational inquiry. To learn about the ways in which our knowledge is mediated is to connect disparate parts of the curriculum.

In Scotland elements of media study are now compulsory parts of 16+ education, and there are moves to make learning about the media part of the core curriculum for 10–14 year-old students.[3] In England and Wales curriculum developments are still diverse and unwieldy in spite of current 'rationalisation'. Media Studies is not one of the twenty areas of knowledge designated as 'subjects' by the Secretary of State, although there are several GCSE Media Studies syllabi available.[4] Aspects of media study are valid components of some English and Humanities GCSE syllabi, and learning about media institutions could quite legitimately become a core element of *CPVE* (Certificate of Pre-Vocational Education) courses.[5] Video production has been a central part of some *TVEI* (Technical and Vocational Education Initiatives) courses, especially in Wales, and there is a growing network of primary school teachers who are working to make learning the media part of the primary core curriculum.[6]

In England and Wales teachers are using a variety of curriculum spaces where learning the media can take place. We have tried to recognise this variety, the diversity of course requirements and objectives. Nevertheless we also recognise that education institutions are the main agencies for the transmission of an effective dominant culture, and that the selective processes of education go too often unremarked. Our intention here is to explain why we think learning about the media is important so that teachers can, if they wish, use the rationales provided to inform the content, structure and pedagogy of their courses, however varied these may be. We aim to describe the kind of education that learning the media could gain.

It is a further contention of this book that the accounts and analyses we offer, while drawing primarily on the British media context for examples, possess an international significance. Obviously, it is impossible to make assertions and arguments which are totally universal, in the same way that it is impossible

for the media to make totally universal television programmes –
much as Lorimar Productions would like this to be the case with a
production such as *Dallas*! Nevertheless, we contend that the
conceptual issues we examine and explicate have a pertinence in
many countries and cultures of the world. Certainly, this book
was written with that intention kept firmly in mind.

So what are the structuring principles around which this book
has been organised? We should make it clear from the outset that
by the term 'mass media' we understand books, magazines and
newspapers; radio, records and tapes; photographs and posters;
films, cinema, television; and the new delivery systems of cable,
satellite and video – that is to say, all those media which are
capable of providing both information and pleasure, and which
are capable of being either mechanically or electronically
reproduced many times over. Throughout this book, however, we
shall focus more on the audio-visual media largely because of the
increasing power of those media in terms of political relationships
and *pervasiveness of address*.

The first chapter will offer brief guidance to the arguments and
rationales in the chapters which follow. It will also offer, as a case
study, an assessment of the present positions of media education
in British curricula and will outline a history of how those
positions came to be occupied. The arguments and accounts
offered may better reward perusal after the rest of the book has
been read.

The book is then organised into four sections which can be
identified as follows.

Section 1. Chapter   focuses on the importance of teaching
detailed empirical wo: about the structure and ownership of the
media. In this cha┌ ɔr we describe some of the complex
relationships betweer he broadcasting institutions' structures of
finance, ownership ɛ d control and the media artefacts they
produce. We are no' :oncerned to demonstrate an economistic,
'demystifying' account of how broadcasting institutions give shape
to their particular genres and narratives, nor are we concerned to
show that audiences are simply duped by the institutional
processes which interpellate them.[7] There is no single social
group possessing true consciousness or knowledge, rather there is
a constant struggle for the dominance of some meanings over
others. Dominant meanings will certainly seem most natural to

those for whom maintenance of the status quo is a top priority, but that very maintenance will also depend, in our view, on the relations of dominance being accepted as apparently natural by those socially and economically subordinated. By teaching about media institutions it is these complex and contradictory relationships that are at stake.

Information about the ways in which broadcasting institutions organise and are organised is often inaccessible to teachers for whom research opportunities are painfully constrained by the routines and demands which schooling makes.[8] Another difficulty with this area is the constant updating required if facts are to be kept accurately. Since this book's conception Robert Maxwell's Pergamon Press has bought the Mirror Group; United Newspapers has bought controlling shares in Fleet Holdings; BET and Thorn-EMI may be about to jettison Thames TV, and TV-AM shares will probably be floated on the stock market.[9] In this kind of publication we could not be expected to maintain detailed factual accuracy, but our arguments insist, nevertheless, that however fickle the losses and gains of entrepreneurs or multinationals, the basic structures of ownership and control remain.

Media institutions, and teaching about them, are complicated. We have deliberately chosen to take a limited view of 'institutions' in terms of their more industrial arrangements to prevent the concept becoming universally determining and therefore impossible to pin down in teaching. However, political and cultural contexts of particular industrial arrangements – from censorship to advertising – are also described, in the hope that this will provide greater opportunity for pedagogic flexibility. In this sense the arguments and teaching strategies proposed in Chapter 2 relate closely to those in Chapter 9, 'Audiences'.

Section 2. The next two chapters form a unit in that they are concerned to explicate the two most central critical concepts for any media analysis – those of 'Realism' and 'Narrative'. As such these chapters are intended to provide frameworks within which more textual exercises and formal analyses can take place. Both chapters concentrate on how media artefacts are dominantly constructed in realistic and storytelling modes – to the extent that such modes begin to appear as the natural, the only ways of relating fact or fiction. We concentrate on how realism and dominant forms of narrative seal ideological cracks through which alternative endings and contradictory 'reals' could erupt. It is not our intention, however, to assume that either realism or narrative are at fault and that there are somewhere (if only they could be found!) particular aesthetic codings and narrative constructions which could get it all right for everybody all of the time. The Surrealists blew fuses on that one! We would simply wish teachers to emphasise how different media forms construct narratives if only to enable students to construct narratives for their own, perhaps very different purposes.

Section 3. The problems of realism and narrative lead us on from, to some extent formal, to more *content*-oriented questions concerning what determines patterns of representations in the media. Who is represented, by and for whom, and how? The next four chapters concentrate on the issues which surround media representations and which involve discussion about the changing and recurring taxonomies by which the media enable us to categorise, to make sense of the world. Questions of power relations are, of course, crucial here. Dominant groupings are engaged advantageously in the struggle for ideological consent because their representations of those they contest can be circulated widely. We concentrate on four kinds of representation in which we perceive such struggle constantly taking place: class, gender, race, and age. They are never exclusive categories, and we would hope that teachers will be able to raid the borders our headings have erected. They are intended to provide useful labels denoting specific kinds of inequality, enabling students, we hope, to begin to deal with them intellectually and forcefully rather than submit to confusion and despair.

Section 4. All the chapters in this book lead to the final one. 'Audiences'. Without audiences to watch, read or listen, the media would not exist. In the construction and maintenance of audiences the media might therefore be seen as purely serving their own interests. There are truths in this assertion, but they are not whole truths. Members of groupings within a wide variety of audiences may have knowledge of themselves and of the media artefacts they enjoy, which is quite different from any ideas producers may have of either. How the different media fulfil different uses and fuel different pleasures is still a regrettably under-researched area.[10] At worst audiences have been conceived of as a unified mass, or at best as individuals positioned by specific textual mechanisms and determined by psychoanalytic structures, such as the Oedipal complex, which are deemed universal. We cannot begin to make good this lack of research here, but our final chapter aims to encourage teachers to pose questions about the range of meanings which different audiences may bring to any text and emphasises the possibilities of audiences determining the meanings they find, rather than sinking into the intellectual passivity which the media are generally supposed to induce. If students can at the very least be taught how to realise that the world may not be such an immovable place, then they have been engaged in an education of some validity.

1 Histories

The primary purpose of this chapter is to provide an account of how the media gained a position within the educational curriculum and in particular the secondary school. Like all histories, ours displays its own set of emphases and exclusions. We do not discuss the growth of audio-visual educational technology in schools as it is precisely this form of using the media as a neutral educational aide that we aim to contest. Any such history is virtually dependent on the existence of books, journals and official reports. Certainly, uncovering the history of teaching and learning about the media is considerably harder to trace than the history of the media themselves. Doubtless there have been innovative teachers discussing with their students the development of new media such as photography and newspapers. Unfortunately the variety and vitality of the media education that has been taking place in classrooms over the last sixty years cannot be recreated. Moreover, we felt that such an account could not be secured by a simple chronology but instead had to recognise an intricate patterning of constantly shifting relations between the economic and the political, the social and the cultural, the aesthetic and the technological at any given moment. In so far as space allows, our accounts will be bound by our understanding of how media institutions and educational prerogatives have evolved within these broader parameters.

Accordingly we have distinguished four interrelated traditions of media education – sociological, cultural, 'skills' and political – whose chronological interaction constitutes the evolution of media education up to 1987. We hope these conceptual distinctions clarify what was at stake in that history, and that they indicate how the meaning of the term *media education* has itself been the site of cultural and political struggle to determine *whose* knowledge about the media should be produced and learned, *how* students should be learning the media, and for whose ultimate benefit.

Sociological

Until comparatively recently the development of sociological knowledge about the media has been primarily at the instigation of media institutions and state agencies. The USA was the leader in the new 'mass communications' research, as advertising agencies, the government and the media themselves sought to find out if the media were affecting the audiences that were being created – and if they were, in what ways. The emerging disciplines of sociology and psychology, eager to secure firm institutional bases, competed for these lucrative contracts. Newspapers and radio wanted to prove to advertisers that they were reaching larger audiences more effectively than their rivals. Advertisers wanted to check they were getting value for money. Sophisticated quantitative methodologies were created to deliver this information. The US government was more interested in finding out the propaganda efficacy of the new media. Studies were commissioned to investigate whether the USA had entered the First World War because of Allied propaganda, while the Second World War stimulated further research on propaganda techniques. The methodology was derived from behavioural science and aimed to reproduce laboratory conditions in which media 'effects' on human 'guinea pigs' could be measured. One typical experiment was to discover how effective government propaganda films had been in indoctrinating and training American soldiers to have the 'right attitudes'. After the war this type of empirical research expanded into American universities and, despite developing more sophisticated methodologies, has remained the dominant paradigm for the study of the media in America. Yet the 'knowledge' it produces is mainly instrumental rather than educational; it is designed to add to the power of the media, advertisers and government over their audiences rather than to 'empower' those audiences in learning about the media. The USA model has also been exported around the world in the general expansion of media research, a phenomenon which disturbed a 1975 UNESCO Report:

It need not be emphasized that heavy reliance on outside funds, particularly those supplied by media industries and government, is not a phenomenon unique to the United States, but occurs wherever mass communication research is conducted on any scale. But because of the wealth of the United States, its media industries and its government agencies probably have more funds available to use for research, if they wish, than anywhere else. Moreover, since American media research has been so influential all over the world, it is possible that the intellectual situation of American mass media research will recur to some extent everywhere. Indeed, a fair amount of mass media research undertaken in other countries, particularly in the Third World, is initiated by visiting American professors, sometimes with the aid of funds from the United States. This increases the probability of American research methods being exported overseas, often without due consideration for different social and economic systems and day-to-day conditions in different countries. (Mary Katzen, 1975)

The American approach to the sociological study of the media was initially influential in British media sociology, and remains prevalent in much of the seemingly never-ending research about the supposed effects of 'TV violence'. Before 1960 there had only been a few reports on children and the cinema, while the BBC's Listener Research Department produced data about programme audiences. However, in the wake of fears about juvenile delinquency being caused by television, the Home Office set up a Television Research Committee in 1963 with a predictable set of objectives:

> to initiate and co-ordinate research into the part which television plays or could play, in relation to other influences, as a medium of communication and in fostering attitudes, with particular reference to the development of young people's moral concepts and attitudes and the processes of perception through which they are influenced by television and other media of communication. (Katzen, 1975, p.80)

The initial research project was a study of television and childrens' morals, carried out at the London School of Economics, but

fortunately the Committee had widened its terms of reference by
1966 to include investigating 'the possibility that the media were
working against instead of in support of an active "participatory"
democracy'.[1] In 1966 the Centre for Mass Communications
Research was established at Leicester University and also the
Centre for Television Research at Leeds University.

Mass communications research in Britain has mainly remained
within the broadly empirical tradition of American social science,
but the degree of institutional autonomy enjoyed by British
universities in the 1960s enabled a more critical, sometimes
Marxist-influenced, sociological tradition to emerge. James
Halloran, Graham Murdock and Philip Elliott's book
Demonstrations and Communications – A Case Study (1970)
analysed how the media's preconceived framework of 'student
violence' determined the reporting of a 1968 anti-Vietnam
demonstration despite the actual event being almost totally
peaceful. However, it was the Glasgow University Media Group
whose research created most controversy. By taping all news
broadcasts over a set period of time and then rigorously comparing
the broadcasters' coverage of industrial events with other accounts
and explanations available at the time, the Group claimed to
have proved that the routines of 'news manufacture lead quite
consistently to a highly partial and distorted view of relations
within industry and within society generally' (Glasgow University
Media Group, 1982). While contemporary commonsense wisdom
about the media at the time accepted that the press was 'biased',
the publication of *Bad News* in 1976 severely questioned the
claims of the broadcasting institutions to provide an unbiased and
neutral portrayal of society in their news programmes. The
empirical evidence of a bias against strikers in industrial news
reporting – not one striker in the Glasgow dustcart drivers' strike
was interviewed in 102 news bulletins – and against left-wing
perspectives generally – they had found a routine adoption of
the Labour government and British Leyland management's
explanations of Leyland's troubles being due to strikers rather
than lack of investment – caused outrage amongst broadcasters.
The Director General of the BBC suggested that, rather than
modify BBC industrial news coverage, 'a programme like *Analysis*
should tackle the ideology of sociologists'.[2]

The steady increase in such academic challenges during the late

1970s to the broadcasting institutions to provide their audiences with an authoritative and non-partisan knowledge encouraged Media Studies to be taken more seriously by the media institutions. Granada had previously funded a seven-year fellowship at Leeds University in 1959, but broadcasters in Britain, unlike their US counterparts, had never shown much interest in stimulating the academic study of the media. However, the BBC and the ITV companies changed their attitude in the early 1980s and contributed considerable finance for a Chair in Media Studies at Stirling University, which is currently occupied by Alastair Hetherington, a former Controller of BBC Scotland. In 1986 he produced a book showing that television coverage of the 1984–5 coal dispute was admirably objective, a finding hotly disputed by other researchers (Alastair Hetherington, 1985). Martin Harrison, at Keele University, also produced a study refuting the claims of the Glasgow Group's studies, ITN blowing off the dust from their 1970s archive transcripts specially for him. Again his published reassessment of the evidence was vehemently contested when it appeared at the beginning of last year (Martin Harrison, 1985). These developments are of considerable significance for media education generally, as it is clear that broadcasters are recognising that widespread media research and education can constitute an ideological challenge to their own legitimacy. One broadcaster warned his colleagues in 1985:

> Alongside the need to provide high-quality material and a critical base against which to judge it, broadcasters must *engage actively with educators and others in the debate about TV and radio and their role in society, providing accurate and comprehensive information on all aspects of the subject from the standpoint of the practitioners.* They may do this through writing, through speaking, by discussions, and through encouraging research, but if they do not do these things then they leave the field wide open to tendentious and ideologically simplistic arguments which are bad scholarship and a disservice to real education.
>
> The work of the Glasgow Media Group which seems to inform some media studies is a case in point. One does not object to polemic, especially if it appears to make some telling points, but polemic dressed as academic research is more

difficult to take. The tone of the volumes so far produced is biased and arrogant, the very qualities being attributed to the broadcasters. Yet this very work is being quoted endlessly as if it had some 'scientific' validity. (John Cain, 1985, original emphasis)

The growth of sociological knowlege about the media has inevitably had most significant impact within higher education institutions. Yet the production of empirical knowledge about the ownership and working practices of media institutions by analysts such as Philip Schlesinger, Philip Elliott, Graham Murdock and Jeremy Tunstall has provided a welcome source of information for teachers in the secondary schools and FE colleges. It has had rather less impact on the secondary curriculum, although media sociology now forms a component within Sociology courses and the 'A' level in Communications Studies. But inevitably its abstraction makes it rather remote from the experience of secondary students, which partially explains why studying the media in schools has mainly been generated from an engagement with media texts, the tradition of media education which we have designated as the cultural.

Cultural

The emergence of the media in the school curriculum has only been achieved by a long and continuous cultural struggle. First there has been the struggle to make educational institutions overcome their fear that the popular pleasures offered by the media did not threaten their own cultural legitimacy and social function. This was not an easy task when, as Pierre Bourdieu suggests,

The school is required to perpetuate and transmit the capital of consecrated cultural signs, that is, the culture handed down to it by the intellectual creators of the past, and to mould to a practice in accordance with the models of that culture a public assailed by conflicting, schismatic or heretical messages – for example, in our society, modern communication media. Further it is obliged to establish and define systematically the sphere of orthodox culture and the sphere of heretical culture. (Pierre Bourdieu, 1971)

Second there has been the struggle – and this is still with us – to ensure that the media's culturally heretical force should contest educationally the cultural definitions of schooling and not merely be deployed to reinforce them. Early popular cinema was perceived as a positively demonic heresy:

> Before these children's greedy eyes with heartless in-discrimination horrors unimaginable are . . . presented night after night . . . Terrific massacres, horrible catastrophes, motor-car smashes, public hangings, lynchings . . . All who care for the moral well-being and education of the child will set their faces like flint against this new form of excitement.
> ('Cinematography and the Child', *The Times*, 12 April 1913)

Anxieties about the moral influences and effects (invariably bad) of commercial films have been the strongest determinants of media teaching initiatives. An early American article about film in schools written in 1913 was significantly entitled 'Making the Devil Useful' (see Ronald Polito, 1965). American interest in teaching commercial cinema in the 1930s was a direct result of the moral panic about Hollywood which occurred in the USA in the 1920s – the same panic that led to the establishment of the Hays Office to censor films. An interesting feature of this panic was that it was the drug and sex scandals of Hollywood, the *context* provided by the media themselves rather than the actual film *texts* which fuelled this populist fear. As the USA became drawn into the Second World War in 1941, the movement to educate students to 'appreciate' what had been designated as 'better' commercial films effectively ground to a halt as the key issues were transformed into questions about the possibilities of instruction *through* film and not education *in* film.

Countering the 'harmful' influences of 'popular' films by teaching, discriminating good taste and moral sense seemed to be an educational prerogative in film teaching on both sides of the Atlantic, although we would not wish to draw too many parallels. Ironically a major impetus for media education in Britain was a fear of the Americanisation of British – or rather English – culture through Hollywood films, American popular music and advertising styles. Cultural Jeremiads were legion. F. R. Leavis lamented: 'The American stage of our developing industrial civilisation was upon us' (F. R. Leavis, 1974). Together with Denys Thompson, another literary critic and teacher, Leavis attempted to intervene before the deluge with the extremely influential *Culture and Environment* (1933), arguing for the values of an artisanal and organic 'culture' against the mass production 'culture' of the mass media. Media texts entered the classroom in order that they might be used in a defensive discriminatory training *against* the media: 'Alerted critically to false values', students 'could be led to better things'. In fact they were echoing the values of one of Leavis's favourite *bêtes noires*, the BBC, which shared many of their Arnoldian assumptions. In 1929 a BBC Report was compiled on 'the ramifications of the Transatlantic octopus' which expressed concern that 'the national outlook and, with it, character is gradually becoming Americanised'.[3] Interestingly there is a convergence of concern between what was to become the dominant educational discourse for several decades and the already dominant national media and cultural institution. Both only introduce their audiences to 'popular culture' in order for them to be weaned on to a healthier cultural diet. The BBC's music policy of the time was preoccupied with broadcasting only sufficient popular music to be able to 'lift' the listeners' 'present standard of musical appreciation' to where it could appreciate classical music, which was, of course, 'better, healthier music'.

This social anxiety over which forms of pleasure should be culturally sanctioned did permit more positive interpretations, from which the task of education could be represented as creating a hierarchy of taste within the cinema. Stanley Reed had been converted to teaching 'film appreciation' by a publication issued by the Board of Education in 1929.

In the *Handbook of Suggestions for Teachers* which he was given at College, there was a sentence which urged that teachers should endeavour to raise children's standards of taste and judgement in respect of the cinema. The Board's attitude was echoed by the Ministry and now those who advocate the teaching of film appreciation had a further argument in that the Department Committee on Children and the Cinema had advocated 'some specific training, for older children at least, in film appreciation, either in or out of school, but certainly as part of the general educational process'. (Stanley Reed, 1950b)

The 'film appreciation' rubric allowed alternative emphases and assumptions. One significant tradition of film education emerged during the late 1920s and early 1930s out of the activities of the London Film Society (founded in 1925 to create a forum for the serious discussion of film) and the British Documentary movement, which was forming around the dominant personality of John Grierson. The educational task was to protect children from the distracting influences of Hollywood by teaching them to understand how the cinema worked. Alan Lovell has described this position as follows:

> The workings of the cinema were to be understood on the basis of aesthetic principles derived from Eisenstein (an Eisenstein both simplified and abstracted from the cultural context of the Soviet Union in the 1920s) by way of Grierson. The basic principles were that editing was the key act in the creation of a film; that a direct analogy could be made between film and language such that a shot equalled a word, a sequence a sentence, and so on; and that the cinema was inherently a realistic medium. These principles led to the valuing of the Soviet films of the 1920s [and] British documentary films of the 1930s. (Alan Lovell, 1971)

The moral commitment to an aestheic of social realism meant that this position partially overlapped with the Leavisite insistence on 'discrimination', but its educational and, for the time, novel value was in its recognition of the necessity of making specific features of the medium itself worthy of study.

How many people there were like Stanley Reed teaching both film appreciation and film making in the 1930s is difficult to tell, but we assume it was very few. The Second World War brought such work as existed to an end. The documentarists were co-opted into the war effort to make propaganda films. As in the USA, official funding and encouragement was given to education –

or propaganda – through, rather than about, film. But activities seemed to be renewed remarkably quickly after the war. This was in part due to the production of the 1944 Education Act, which hugely expanded the domain of secondary schooling with a concomitant need for a massive programme of teacher training, resulting in a fairly sudden explosion of educational debate. 1950 seems to have been a watershed in the history of teaching about film, for that year saw the following:

1. the publication of *School Film Appreciation* on 1 February;
2. the appointment of Stanley Reed as the BFI's first Film Appreciation Officer on 3 April;
3. the formation of the Society of Film Teachers (SFT) at the University of London Institute of Education. December saw the publication of the Society's first journal, *The Bulletin*;
4. the publication in May of what is usually referred to as the Wheare Report.

The Wheare Report, or to give it its official title, *The Report of the Departmental Committee on Children and the Cinema*, was initiated in 1947. Fuelled by a fear of the cinema and by worries about the threats it posed to children, the Committee considered and reported on the effects of attendance at the cinema on children under the age of 16, with special reference to attendance at children's cinema clubs and whether, in the light of these effects, any modification to the existing system of film classification and the general administration of the clubs was desirable. The report devoted four paragraphs to film appreciation work in schools (220–4 in Section 7) and made the following recommendation (26):

> The work being undertaken in some schools, youth clubs and school film societies, in educating children to view films with discrimination should be encouraged. Special attention should be given to providing better facilities for the training in film appreciation of teachers and youth service leaders.

With the assimilation of the remnants of the Documentary movement into television, teaching about film in order to alleviate 'pernicious' media effects became educational common sense.

Discrimination continued to be the operative educational term, but the hows and wherefores became more telling subjects for debate, not least because there were so many more films to discriminate between.

> The object of teaching film appreciation is not so much to discourage children from going to bad films as to encourage them to select better ones and to derive a deeper enjoyment from their film-going. In this work the way has been made easier by the marked improvement in the quality of films produced today, as compared with those made as recently as 15 years ago. It is too little realised that the film industry has already responded to the demands of a more mature cinema public and that the best way of accelerating this process, while appreciating the advances so far made, is so to increase the power of discrimination that still higher standards will be sought. (Janet Hill, 1951, p.61)

There were renewed attempts to formulate what is often referred to as the 'film grammar' approach, which better represented the position of those who strove to find a more precise analytic method. Drawing on traditional forms of linguistic analysis and on the principles of parsing in particular, the 'film grammar' approach never really gained much support. Quite obviously, however connotatively rich a word or a sentence might be, the complex plenitude of images and sounds, amplified and extenuated by camera angles and movement, lighting, colour, framing and editing, was straitjacketed by such prosaic analytical attempts. We should remember, however, that teaching and discussion would have to take place after just one screening of a film and without any visual resources to assist students in describing the flickering images already fading from memory for quotation, analysis and debate.

By 1959 'film appreciation' was being questioned. Regarded as too passive a term to describe the learning and teaching actually taking place in classrooms, H. R. Wills advocated its replacement by 'intelligent viewing'. He wrote: 'We must help them to really *appreciate*, i.e. estimate the worth of what they see' (H. R. Wills, 1959). The unhelpful emphasis and repetition only led back to the concept of discrimination. But by this time there was a more persistent plea for the recognition of (some) films as Art. This was partially an attempt to recuperate film within the Leavisite

canon of art being the organic expression of the individual
sensibility. Directors such as Renoir, Welles and Ford could be
seen as true artists in film, straining against the inorganic and
industrial processes of production, the Hollywood machine.
European directors such as Bergman and Wajda aspired to the
'poetic truth' of art cinema. Both the 'film grammar' and the 'art'
approaches made requisite more detailed attention to film texts
themselves, but neither offered ways of discovering how films
functioned within the political and social worlds inhabited by the
children being taught. For film was losing its heretical powers and
was about to be deployed by educationalists to ward off
new demons who were encroaching upon schools from the
phantasmagoria of popular culture.

The world that students now occupied was also drastically
changed. Neither they nor their parents, according to Harold
Macmillan anyway, had ever had it so good. The seemingly
inexorable thrust of 1950s consumerism had transformed the
relationship of the working class to leisure. Not only were the
traditionalists anxious now, the Left, too, was worried as its
traditional forms of addressing its working-class audience declined
in popularity and relevance. Richard Hoggart charted the
corruption of collective working-class culture by the new mass
consumer culture in the influential *Uses of Literacy* (1957), while
the Communist Party agitated against the decadence of American
horror comics. Most significant of all was the explosive escalation
of domestic television sets owned. One alert teacher commented:

> Television will ultimately develop into an art form in its own
> right capable of being judged by its own standards of criticism,
> as the cinema and the theatre are. And, when it is more
> widespread, it will become in the dramatic field as much a
> rival, but no more, of the cinema and the theatre as they are of
> one another. But as a medium for the expression of ideas and
> as a social force it will have no rival. (Andrew Millar Jones,
> 1948)

But this positive approach was rarely echoed. Commercial
television had captured 57 per cent of the audience by 1957 in a
cultural onslaught on the BBC which Lord Reith likened to the
spread of smallpox and bubonic plague. The BBC's curriculum

was being decisively rejected; how could the inherited academic grammar school curriculum compete? These anxieties were mediated into schools through an influential National Union of Teachers Conference in 1960 on 'Popular Culture and Personal Responsibility'[4] and the Newsom Report of 1963, which was specifically concerned with the 'less academically gifted' child. Newsom was concerned with the possibility of schools having 'a seriously depressed class of pupils on their hands' (para. 251) and the media were clearly seen as a factor in this alienation:

> The culture provided by all the mass media, but particularly film and television, represents the most significant environmental factor that teachers have to take into account. The important changes that take place at the secondary stage are much influenced by the world offered by the leisure industry which skilfully markets products designed for young people's tastes. (para. 475)

'Relevance' to these new worlds, as teachers perceived them, became not so much an educational criterion but an attempted solution to what might be termed a crisis of cultural and educational address. Film and television were perceived as 'relevant' to education simply because they modernised classroom activities. The Newsom Report gave teachers who used film and television official benediction by advocating their use to open educational windows on to new and strange worlds. This remains the most prevalent use of video and television in classrooms to this day. Apparently, television can show, in ways that teachers can't, what the world is *really* like. Even as recently as 1984 the Hargreaves Report (1984) recommending widespread curriculum changes in secondary schools lists 'mass media and leisure' as only one of sixteen areas to be covered by 'Personal and Social Development'.

One problem was the rigid academicism of a traditional grammar curriculum defining valid knowledges for students who had themselves been defined as 'secondary modern kids'. Some saw the 'kids' as the problem; Peter Harcourt argued that screen education developed in secondary modern schools and technical colleges because it was felt that the 'dull' most urgently needed education in discrimination (Harcourt, 1965). Others saw film and television offering possibilities for more thematic approaches, enabling the personal needs of students to determine a more general education:

> With slower groups, the study of the cinema has been less a critical discipline and more a powerful force for general growth, a source of discussion on personal and social issues, an imaginative extension of experience, and aid to both oral and written fluency. With groups of mixed ability the balance has been a better one, although always shifting, between the objective demands of the study of an art and the personal needs of the students. (Jim Kitses and Ann Mercer, 1966)

In fact Kitses and Mercer's *Talking About The Cinema* set out a relatively new concern: to understand *how* a film communicates rather than simply judging a film on moral or technical grounds.

> With swifter, more homogeneous groups the emphasis has been on a quite precise training in response and judgement. Working outside the pressures of the examination system has made it possible for us to view the teaching of film and the teaching of young people as a whole activity. We have not had to conceive of the needs of students to express thoughts and feelings, to think through the world, as being something outside the subject, something hampering the 'true' work of studying films, learning how they are made and how to appreciate them. (Kitses and Mercer, 1966, p.6)

The companion volume, *Talking About Television* by A. P. Higgins (1966), adopted a generic approach to television and only dealt with the thematic as a final chapter and with textual analysis not at all – undoubtedly because of the technical impossibility of recording programmes. Film extracts were especially valued in 'topic' teaching, and extensively encouraged in the late 1960s by the Schools Council Humanities Curriculum Project.[5] In teaching about 'young people', 'war' and 'personal relationships', the desire to 'heighten awareness of how cinema communicates' and 'to stimulate critical awareness and independent judgement' meant that both the content and the form of a film were open for analysis and discussion.

However, these initial concentrations on film and television as *mediating* forms consequently rendered the notion of discrimination, as Denys Thompson conceived of it, politically and pedagogically problematic. Nevertheless Thompson persisted (in *Discrimination and Popular Culture*, 1965) to assert that everything 'acquired at school in the way of aesthetic and moral training is contradicted and attacked by the entertainment industry'. Arguments which countered Thompson's most influentially were those posed by Stuart Hall and Paddy Whannel in their book *The Popular Arts* (1964). This covered many aspects of the mass media for the first time in a serious and sustained way. It dealt with cinema, television, pop music, paperback and magazine fiction, comics, the press and advertising, initiating the possibilities for media studies rather than teaching discretely film or television. The book's approaches were concurrent with the thematic ones of its time, but it nevertheless recognised the importance of detailed textual analyses. It was concerned with evaluation, but its perspectives differed from most critical writing at the time:

> In terms of actual quality (and it is with this, rather than with 'effects', that we are principally concerned) the struggle between what is good and worthwhile and what is shoddy and debased is not a struggle *against* the modern forms of communication, but a conflict *within* these media. Our concern is with the difficulty which most of us experience in distinguishing the one from the other, particularly when we are dealing with the new media, new forms of expression in a new, and often confusing, social and cultural situation. (Stuart Hall and Paddy Whannel, 1964, p.15)

By publishing *Talking About The Cinema* and *Talking About Television*, Paddy Whannel, as Head of the BFI Education Department, had expanded the Institute's work as both initiator and supporter of media teaching in the classroom. The comparative lack of published material about film and television was, in Whannel's view, a problem which had to be overcome if the media were to be taken seriously by educational institutions. In the late 1960s the only institutions of higher education which taught film were art colleges, (Hornsey being the most famous example) and the teacher training colleges at Bulmershe in Reading and at Bede in Durham. Like secondary modern schools and technical colleges, these institutions were less bound by constraining exam syllabuses and by traditional notions of what kind of study befitted academies. However, if teachers of film and television were to come in from out of the cold curriculum peripheries, then a more clearly defined place for their study had to be fought for within academic education. This involved building

> a serious body of critical and historical writing on the cinema
> . . . As the study of the cinema becomes established within academic education there must be built up a literature of quality. It is true that the teacher in the secondary school does not work at such a level of complexity and sophistication. But he [sic] needs the study for himself. He needs to feel behind his teaching the weight of a properly constituted tradition. (Paddy Whannel, 1969)

Teachers at that time still felt the lack of written material on which they could draw for teaching purposes. Having weathered the onslaught of Lindsay Anderson and his magazine *Sequence, Sight and Sound* continued to be conventional and uninspiring as source material for teachers, not least in the magazine's resolute refusal to take American cinema seriously: 'The Americans have discovered, described and measured; the Continentals – especially the French and Italians – have analysed and theorised; the British have moralised' (*Times Literary Supplement*, 17 December 1964).

The strategic imperative was clearly to disrupt the hegemony which by now Leavisite views held in educational institutions, not least because English teachers were in the vanguard of the progressive reforms of the curriculum taking place in schools. 'English' and all that that 'innocent' subject denomination implied had to be dislodged from its centrality in the humanities if film education was to progress further. Alan Lovell comments:

> The assumptions about film education derived from Leavis's ideas were attacked from a number of directions. The contradictions inherent in adapting those ideas, which had been

derived from a study of literature, to the study of the cinema became apparent; it was difficult to accept Leavis's basic hostility to technology and commercialism if one were to take the cinema at all seriously; the account of cultural history as a process of decline, with the new media as important agents in the process, was hardly consistent with an enthusiasm for the cinema. Sociological studies of the effects of the media challenged the assumption that the cinema was a decisive moulder of moral and social values; this challenge was of central importance since the cinema's supposed influence on children's attitudes had been the key justification of all film education. (Alan Lovell, 1971)

The central critical thrust came from a magazine called *Movie*, which existed on a tiny financial base. Heavily influenced by the valorisation of American cinema in the *Cahiers du Cinéma* magazine, which was the critical forum for the film-makers and theorists of the French *Nouvelle Vague* film movement, *Movie* attempted to supersede the evaluative and moralistic approach so prevalent in Leavis and his followers. The *Movie* critics (with the partial exception of Robin Wood) insisted on a more formalist concentration on the text alone (in this they were similar to Leavis's 'scrutineering' approach) in order to create an analytical vocabulary adequate to describe the complexity of film:

the value of a film depends on the film itself . . . For talking about one small section of a film in great detail . . . we have been accused of fascination with technical *trouvailles* at the expense of meaning. The alternative which we find elsewhere is a *gestalt* approach which tries to present an overall picture of the film without going into 'unnecessary' detail, and usually results in giving almost no impression of what the film was actually like for the spectator. (Ian Cameron, 1962)

Movie was also responsible for popularising in Britain the notion of the director as 'author' – the *auteur* – of the film. Whatever the shortcomings of the *auteur* theory, it did enable popular films by Hitchcock, Hawks, Fuller and others to be seriously discussed. For the first time there was a convergence of critical and popular taste as opposed to a divergence, with obvious educational benefits in the teaching of film.

By the end of the 1960s *Movie*, together with the BFI and the Society for Education in Film and Television's periodical *Screen Education* and *Yearbook*, had built a formidable critical literature.[6] The exhilarating proliferation of film studies courses in American universities was a further boost to academic respectability, and Britain's first university lectureship was set up in 1969 at the Slade School of Fine Art in London University. Film had entered the Academy.

During the 1960s those advocating the teaching of film had been on the defensive. But in the 1970s film theorists went on to the attack, armed with an increasingly formidable theoretical arsenal drawn from the writing and teaching of the post-1968 Parisian intellectual milieu, most notably the work of Roland Barthes, Louis Althusser, Christian Metz and Jacques Lacan. The rationale for this new development was the dissatisfaction felt by many involved in the debate about film and education that they lacked a critical method that really illuminated the nature of film; that, despite the intervention of the now declining *Movie*, there was still a preoccupation with values without a systematic critical theory to uphold such discussion, put crudely, everyone was arguing over the *meaning* of films without having adequately analysed *how* those meanings were produced. In 1971 *Screen* (SEFT's new journal) declared the first engagement with the need to construct new critical methods and attitudes to art and education:

> Educational and critical practice has for too long remained unconscious and unaware of itself. The development and criticism of theoretical ideas is required to make meaningful, to provide a context for, what has in the past remained at the level of anecdotal accounts of teaching experience. *Screen* will aim to go beyond subjective taste-ridden criticism and try to develop more systematic approaches over a wider field. Criticism is but one element in the study of the cinema which also involves locating film in a specific system of production and consumption and of seeing it in relation to the other arts and to the culture which it reflects and reflects upon. Above all film must be studied as a new medium, a product of this

century and of the machine, and which as a new medium and a new mode of expression challenges traditional notions of art and criticism and the system of education which still in part is tied to these notions. (*Screen*, vol. 12, no. 1, Spring 1971)

Instead of valuing and handing down a cultural heritage, the editorial asserts both the need to construct more precise and systematic analytic methods and to locate these within a materialist understanding of the world. At the same time, the fundamental importance of constructing a body of theoretical work was recognised as prerequiste to a better understanding of both critical and educational practice. *Screen* became and remained until the late 1970s a journal of screen theory. Articles from *Cahiers*, post-1968, were used, but from the start *Screen* drew upon a wide range of French work concerned with structuralism, semiotics, Marxism and psychoanalysis.

'*Screen* theory', as it was later dubbed, provided the focus for radical university teachers of English attempting to loosen the still persisting stranglehold of Leavisism on the discipline. English entered the 1980s looking less secure than at any time since it had itself tried to displace Classics as the dominant humanities discipline at the turn of the century, with the very category of 'the literary' being challenged as a critical concept of any validity beyond the historical. This was a far cry from the days when studying film was a clandestine activity sneaked into the English lesson or lecture.[7]

While *Screen* had taken film theory into the portals of academe, Film Studies had become quietly established as a subject within the schood curriculum. The Associated Examining Board set up a GCE 'O' Level Mode 3 in Film Studies in 1972, which quickly expanded into several other consortia. Yet paradoxically, just as film had seemingly established its place within the curriculum, it began to seem outmoded and orthodox. The rapid decline in the number of cinemas in Britain coincided with the consolidation of television as the hegemonic medium in British popular culture. Teachers and students responded by developing ideas that had originated in Film Studies for studying the other more pervasive, and therefore assessible, media forms. Newspapers, comics and magazines were obvious classroom material, but then so was television as video recorders became ubiquitous. Courses in TV Studies, Media

Studies and Communication Studies were developed in schools and FE colleges. This growth of interest and enthusiasm produced its own theoretical and pedagogic developments. SEFT had already begun a new journal, *Screen Education*, in 1971 which had considerably broadened the concerns of *Screen* by engaging with the shifting political and educational conjuncture of the 1970s through articles on subjects as diverse as pop music, gender representations in advertising and magazines, to 'the Great Debate' and incipient cuts. Len Masterman's *Teaching About Television* (1980) was particularly influential in terms of the attention it paid to theories of pedagogy and to practical work in the classroom. All in all it was a long way from 'teaching film for seven years without a projector'![8]

Yet this upsurge in knowledge and enthusiasm from teachers and students alike coincided with a shift in educational politics in the mid-1970s, orchestrated by James Callaghan's 'Great Debate' speech in 1976. David Lusted noted how the variety of forms of media education could only be accounted for by the 'ever-increasing knowledge of the media from its committed theorists and teachers' having to accommodate and survive within 'the increasing inhibition on spaces in which media education can be practised' (Lusted, 1982). We now turn to the one expanding area of media education over the last six years which involves a potentially very different understanding of media education from that of the tradition charted above.

'Skills'

The main emphasis of our account has been on media education as cultural process. However we should mention the existence of a differing mode of media education which, while obviously possessing a cultural dimension, has been more concerned with the acquisition of media or communication 'skills'. It is worthy of consideration because it is becoming increasingly widespread following the setting of more 'vocationally relevant' objectives for education'.

Given the enormous expansion of the media industries, it is unsurprising that educational institutions throughout the world have created vocational courses to train students for work in the media. Barely a single university in the USA does not have a journalism school or a film school attached to it. There have been far fewer such developments in the UK, where, as with the rest of industry, the media industries have tended to train their workforces themselves. London University set up a diploma course in journalism in 1919, which closed in 1939. Journalism training was not reintroduced to British universities until the Centre for Journalism Studies was established at Cardiff University in 1970. Postgraduate film-making courses have been run at Bristol and the Royal College of Art in London since the late 1950s. The National Film School was set up in 1970 specifically to cater for the needs of the film industry, while several polytechnics and fine arts colleges have also developed courses involving a fruitful combination of training and theoretical study.

Vocational education in the strict sense has played almost no part in the secondary and FE sectors in Britain. However, the acquisition of media 'skills' has played a limited role in secondary education. Some of the technical and communication skills which teachers have perceived being used in the media have been abstracted from their institutional context to be used by students to reproduce, on a small scale, media products such as 8mm films, videotapes, magazines and radio audiotapes. This approach has had two distinct emphases – the 'expressive' and the 'vocational'.

In 1963 the Newsom Report recommended film-making as an 'interesting and useful' activity for students' self-expression, especially for the more disaffected pupil. Unconsciously influenced perhaps by the dominant critical view of the time that film should be recognised as an art form for individual self-expression, teachers introduced 8mm film-making into schools as an exciting extension to the general shift in English teaching away from the analytical towards an encouragement of the expressive. This pedagogic approach was given a boost in the 1970s when advances in video technology seemed to offer the promise of everyone becoming a communicator, producing their own DIY television show.

It is a unique educational tool. First you get *instant replay*, unlike movie film. While some machines are more instant than others, none involves the elaborate and time-consuming loading, unloading and processing procedures of film. Next, it's a personal medium – that is it places immense power in the hands of the people, *any* people, who are pressing the buttons. The power to recreate and order experience, to amuse, terrify, impress, convince – all are available not just to specially trained and approved media people, but to you and the children you teach. (A. Padfield, 1976)

While obviously welcoming any interest in the media within education, the 'expressive skills' approach received a critical reception from media educators. In 1968 Douglas Lowndes had warned that film-making in schools would only prove genuinely educational if used as a critical tool by teachers and students to foster their critical understanding of film and cinema. A video generation later Len Masterman also warned of how students' early excitement quickly wanes, with students finally only 'learning' their own 'inferiority' when comparing their own productions to those of the media and making little conceptual advance in the process. Having recommended that video was best used in practical exercises to interrogate the dominant television practices, he quotes Hans Magnus Enzensberger:

It has long been clear from apparatus like miniature and 8mm cine cameras, as well as the tape recorder, which are in actual fact already in the hands of the masses, that the individual, so long as he remains isolated, can become with their help at best an amateur but not a producer . . . The programmes which the isolated amateur mounts are always only bad, outdated copies of what he in any case receives. The poor, feeble and frequently humiliating results of this licensed activity are often referred to with contempt by the professional media producers. On top of the damage suffered by the masses comes triumphant mockery because they clearly do not know how to use the media properly. (Hans Magnus Enzensberger, 1970)

Over the last few years the teaching of 'expressive' media skills has increasingly become an integral part of an overall media education rather than being an isolated mode of aesthetic expression. Vincent McGrath, who spent two years on a Sony/ILEA fellowship developing video education in primary schools, comments on how media teachers have to adopt a more interventionist role than their Plowden training has prepared them for:

> Any work involving both children and the creative process can raise problems. Whilst primary teachers will address themselves wholeheartedly to the teaching of skills in, say, mathematics, they suddenly become strangely vague about a child's creative output. It is as though this process is so precious that the role of the teacher suddenly becomes that of awe-struck bystander . . . switch on the recorder, put in standby mode, focus the camera and the children will then be in a position to create something unique.
>
> From the very beginning the Research Fellowship set out to devise projects that were 'directed' and it was hoped that the children would not only learn which knobs to 'twiddle', but would also gain insights into the process itself. This meant of course that the children had to take a lot on trust, in that it wasn't until the tape was completed that the real process of deconstruction began.
>
> For example, a tape was made called 'Ghost Story'. It was different but it wasn't until the tape was shown that the questions really started to flow: 'Why are there no close ups?'; 'Why are there no exciting chases?'; 'Why isn't there any spooky music?'; 'Why isn't there any flashy editing?'; 'How can you have a ghost story that isn't spooky?'
>
> Such questions clearly demonstrate that children's (and adults') expectations of a Ghost Story is firmly based upon the viewing of literally hundreds of films/television productions. To make a 'Ghost Story' tape with children that ostensibly breaks the Rules is perhaps a way of enabling the children to uncover those conventions that would otherwise be impossible to explain. (Vincent McGrath, 1986)

All teachers will be familiar with the general shift of educational objectives in a 'vocationally relevant' direction, conventionally accepted as beginning with James Callaghan's 1976 Ruskin College speech demanding that educators pay more attention to the 'needs of industry'. Following the change of government in 1979, this re-orientation accelerated as anxieties increased in official quarters about the state's ability to maintain social stability – a concern revealed by some interviews carried out with high-ranking DES officials by Stewart Ranson:

> When young people drop off the education production line and cannot find work at all, or work which meets their abilities and expectations, then we are only creating frustration with perhaps disturbing social consequences. We have to select: to ration the educational opportunities so that society can cope with the output of education' . . . 'We are in a period of considerable social change. There may be social unrest, but we can cope with the Toxteths. But if we have a highly educated and idle population we may possibly anticipate more serious social conflict. People must be educated once more to know their place. (Stewart Ranson, 1984)

Ranson concludes that 'the state is developing modes of control in education which permit closer scrutiny and direction of the social order'. The chief instrument in this process has been the Manpower Services Commission which, lavishly funded by the Department of Employment, steadily colonised much of further education and also made inroads into the school curriculum through the Technical and Vocational Education Initiative. The effects on media education have been complex and difficult to chart, as 'vocationalisation' has both stimulated an expansion in media courses yet has also strengthened a competing paradigm of media education from that described in the previous section which is usually designated as *communications*.

'Communications' or 'Communications Studies' are theoretically based on a paradigm of the communication process which is derived from American mass communication theorists such as H. D. Lasswell, who were involved in the propaganda experiments discussed earlier. Lasswell conceptualised a model (Lasswell, 1948) which asks of any communication act 'Who says what by what means to whom and with what effect?'. This was developed by Shannon and Weaver (1949) who, using information theory developed for experiments in telecommunications engineering, produced a diagrammatic model (shown in Figure 1.1).

The message source – let's say the authors of this book – encode (write) their message (the book's content) and transmit it

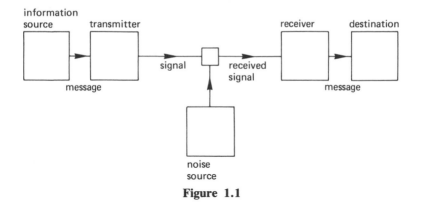

Figure 1.1

through a channel (the published book) which is then decoded by the message receiver (you, dear reader). If you happen not to decode our message correctly this will be because of noise – coffee spilt on the page, bad encoding on our part, etc. Whatever its merits for telephony, the weakness of the model is of course that a film by Stephen Spielberg and a scribbled note passed by one student to another when teacher's back is turned are represented as the *same* communication act in essence. Obviously, such a model is going to have difficulty in accounting for the institutional and symbolic complexity of the media. When teaching about the media within this framework teachers have considerable freedom to carry out valuable work with students, but, in a changing conjuncture such as that delineated above, it has to be difficult to resist a degeneration from teaching about mass communication to teaching about communication in a job interview – after all, it all involves communication. Communication *studies* become communication *skills* which are abstracted from the context of critical study of the media in the interests of being 'relevant' to a future industrial role, though not in the media industries. 'The subject is an aid . . . in industry, to the conveying of information in a wide variety of forms. A student who has successfully completed a Communications Studies course at 'A' Level is bound to be better equipped in his [sic] approach to the writing of letters, handbooks, manuals and other documents' (Associated Examining Board, 1977).

The description above is from the guidelines to teachers issued by the Associated Examining Board (AEB) when it introduced its 'A' Level in Communications Studies in 1978. While the AEB was concentrating on the prestige end of the FE and sixth-form market, the Business Education Council and the Technical Education Council (BEC and TEC), who were responsbile for rationalising the multifarious nature of technical and vocational education in the late 1970s, developed General and Communications Studies modules in their courses which permitted a certain amount of media education. However, these were steadily encroached upon by the Manpower Services Commission and its YTS courses, which inflected Communication Studies more into the area of social and life skills, which were far more limiting. The erosion of the 'liberal' residue in the vocational FE curriculum was accompanied by the spread of 'pre-vocational' education into secondary schools through TVEI and the Department of Education and Science's own Certificate of Pre-Vocational Education. Some media teachers saw this as the hijacking of media education:

> It is the domesticating and enslaving, rather than the liberating potentialities of 'communications' which are now being given full reign in TVEI and CPVE schemes, and even within Advanced level communications courses with their demands for regurgitative and reproductive skills, rather than critical abilities. (Len Masterman, 1985)

Yet outright condemnation is clearly both impractical and futile for media teachers who need to develop whatever curriculum space is left in the ever-centralising 1980s as sites for future, more progressive development in another conjuncture. Moreover, the 'new vocationalism', whatever the intentions of its instigators to return us to a stratified education system, does provide an opportunity to transform liberal education's traditional distinction between an academic 'conceptual' curriculum for some and 'skills' for others – a mode of education which has persisted long after comprehensivisation despite good intentions and many achievements. As one of us has argued elsewhere, the conceptual and technical skills developed by media education provide such a dialectical advance:

> The *dual* educational potential of Media Studies is challenging

and exciting. It throws into critical relief the distinction between the theoretical and the practical, the academic and the technical, because it requires both deliberative thought and technical dexterity. It begins to span the great divide between the mental labour of the individual which is given such high esteem in our society and the manual labour of many which is so poorly rewarded. (Tana Wollen, 1985c)

Political

While teachers have been engaged in appropriating school curriculum space for study of the media, other forms of media education have developed simultaneously outside the educational institutions. These should be mentioned because there has been considerable cross-fertilisation of ideas, and restricting our understanding of media education to the realm of the school and the academy weakens its potential as a force for social transformation. The media's representations of the crucial political and social issues of the day require serious and detailed analysis as far as all members of our society are concerned. With the fragmentation of social consensus, this is now recognised by both Left and Right, but the Left's stake in media education has a longer history.

An early social democratic interest was declared by Grierson, who believed that the educational function of film was crucial in a democracy where government was responsive and accountable: 'It is worth recalling that the British Documentary group began not so much in affection for film *per se* as in affection for national education', he once claimed.[9] Not only could documentary realism's accuracy, and therefore educational validity, oppose the formation of false values in young people and children from Hollywood escapism, but it would also be invaluable education for adults, because 'under modern conditions, the citizen could not know everything about everything all the time'.[10] Therefore film, due to its mass appeal, was the ideal medium to educate the new 'John Citizen' in an understanding of how mass society worked and 'his' role within it.

This attempt to educate *through* those films which could apparently inform the audience more honestly was shared by the

more oppositional film movement which was founded in 1929 by
the Federation of Workers' Film Societies (FWFS). This was set
up 'to arouse working class interest in films of special importance
(see Trevor Ryan, 1983). These films were almost all from Soviet
Russia, and in order for some of them to be screened film
societies had to be formed to circumvent the British Board of
Film Censors' banning of some of the films being screened in a
public cinema. The FWFS collapsed within a few years, but its
work was taken up by Kino Films, who started up in 1933.
Loosely allied to the Communist Party's educational and Popular
Front activities, Kino expanded steadily throughout the 1930s, and
was joined by other production and distribution networks such as
the Progessive Film Institute and the Workers' Film and Photo
League. Like Grierson, they were committed to an aesthetic of
realism that would provide an antidote to the capitalist 'dope' of
the commercial cinema. This both entailed the production of
'workers' newsreels' to counter the 'bourgeois newsreels' and the
screening of Russian and other Left films such as those celebrating
the Spanish Republic's struggle against fascism in a wide range of
clubs, education classes, community centres and sometimes even
sympathetic cinemas. But Kino also encouraged film appreciation
and analysis to stimulate both the informed discussion of the films
they were showing and interventions against the exhibition of
reactionary films through demonstrations.

These pioneering forms of Left media education did not survive
the Second World War. But their belief in the political importance
of challenging the dominant representations of the media re-
emerged in the development of the independent film movement
in the late 1960s which was part of that decade's political
upheavals. In 1966 the London Film Makers' Co-Operative was
set up, followed by the Cinema Action Group in 1968, Amber
Films in 1969, the Berwick Street Collective and Liberation Films
in 1972, and then Four Corner Films and the Newsreel Collective
a few years later. The influence of 'cultural politics' and the
concerns of the *avant-garde* film-makers in the London Co-Op
meant that the new film workshops and collectives differed from
Kino in significant ways. Although they too produced and
screened films that opposed the meanings of the products of the
commercial cinema (and now also television) they were equally
concerned with subverting the *form* as well as the content of the

dominant media (see Simon Blanchard and Sylvia Harvey, 1983). Sharing many of the theoretical positions becoming fashionable in *Screen*, and in particular a Brechtian distaste for realism, the discussions of the films screened inevitably involved media education about the practices of dominant film and television in order 'to change people's perceptions of political, social or personal situations, often with the aid of new film forms' (The Other Cinema, formed in 1970). In 1974 the Independent Film-makers' Association was formed to develop a unified policy for this sector of film production which later incorporated the rapidly expanding independent video movement. Also during this period a feminist film movement emerged with the formation of the London Women's Film Group in 1972 'to disseminate women's liberation ideas, and for women to learn the skills denied them in the industry' (see Annette Kuhn, 1982). The Cinema of Women (COW) was set up in 1979 to distribute films which 'seek to disrupt the social, political and economic domination of men' (Annette Kuhn, 1982).

With the exhaustion of consensus politics in the 1970s, the labour movement as a whole became ever more preoccupied with the media as a possible explanation for some of its growing ideological difficulties. The main focus of the widespread informal media education that was disseminated during this period was with media content rather than form, but it did irrevocably put the media on the political agenda. Academic research such as that done by the Glasgow Media Group confirmed what many on the Left already felt about the media's hostility to their perspective. This upsurge in concern over the media reached a new peak following the 1979 election defeat of the Labour government, which a TUC Report, *A Cause for Concern*, partially attributed to the medias' coverage of the 'winter of discontent'. Some journalists and other media workers were also now dissenting from many of their colleagues' practices. The Campaign Against Racism in the Media (CARM) had already been formed in 1976 by sixty NUJ members appalled at a particularly racist *Sun* headline which provided a crucial focus for the fight against media racism in the ensuing years. In 1979 the Campaign for Press and Broadcasting Freedom ('Broadcasting' was added in 1983) was founded to provide a broad Left forum of trade unionists, Labour Party members and sympathetic media workers to agitate for major structural changes in the media institutions and for a Labour Party media policy which would implement them. Finally, publishers such as Pluto Press and the Comedia Publishing Group steadily increased the stock of critical but accessible books about the media.

The overall impact of this diffused form of media education is impossible to assess, but certainly consciousness of the 'consciousness industries' has never been higher – and not just on the Left. Learning the media has become part of our daily lives. The media are not only now part of the educational curriculum; they are also part of the social and political curriculum.

2 Institutions

'There is no such thing as unmanipulated writing, filming or broadcasting. The question is therefore not whether the media are manipulated, but who manipulates them. A revolutionary plan should not require the manipulators to disappear; on the contrary, it must make everyone a manipulator' – Hans Magnus Enzensberger

'If there had been broadcasting at the time of the French revolution, there would have been no French revolution' – Lord Reith

What's in a picture?

1   John Sturrock/Network

The above picture (Photograph 1) is an example of a media artefact. Before teaching about it we need to pose some questions about it. What is it? Fundamentally the picture is the material composite product of a number of technological processes, specifically a photo-chemical process (photography) and lithographic repro- duction and multiple copying (printing) which reaches its audience in the material form of this book. Yet simultaneously it is a *sign*: its audience will produce meaning from it.

We are going to use this image for teaching. What could we do with it in a classroom? We might be using it as part of a course on photography, in which case we would be discussing it with students as a material composite product of a number of technological processes such as photo-chemistry, lithographic reproduction and multiple printing. However, the image is also a *text* containing a number of *signs* from which students will produce meanings. So the photograph is a specific material and technological product which has meanings, and so we could also discuss with students the ways in which we produce meaning from it.

When examining images with students it is accepted practice that the class should begin by describing as exhaustively as possible what they think is in the image before proceeding to analyse what they think it might mean. Our stock of cultural knowledge enables us to recognise immediately an image of a violent clash between the police and another group. The lack of demonstration cards, their clothes, and the proximity of an industrial building suggests a mass picket in confrontation with the police. Analysis of the photographic codes – its composition, lack of lighting, black and white fast filmstock – designate it as a news photograph. We know this because these codes are conventional within a specific photographic practice called news photography which is related to the wider practice of news journalism. This form of photograph depicts 'real' events of social importance (it is not an advertising picture or a family snapshot) and 'violent' industrial disputes are 'newsworthy' in our culture. Only when we have assigned the image within the discourse of news journalism can we produce meanings from it. Given that it is not a particularly ambiguous photograph, the class is likely to agree that it is a news photograph of a violent industrial dispute.

We can then proceed to discuss what we think the photograph

signifies through analysis of the connotations or associations which the different elements in the picture might have. The immediate connotations might be that the forces of law and order are defending property against an illegitimate attack by an undifferentiated mob. However, it is difficult to discern who is attacking whom, and the camera's position is also ambivalent. Although it is conventionally placed behind the police lines, thus positioning us as spectators in the same space as the police, its height is at ground level, making the horses tower over the frame and us. Do the photograph's formal codings place the readers with the police or with the pickets? Might readers' own political and social positions motivate their readings more forcefully? What meanings would be produced if the camera had been behind the line of pickets? Does the photograph depict violence in the abstract or document a particular incident during a dispute of momentous political and historical import?

The meanings we have produced from the text are so far rather indeterminate. Roland Barthes argues that photographs are intrinsically *polysemous*, i.e. have the capacity to produce a whole variety of meanings, and that nearly all photographs are accompanied by words which serve to 'anchor' and close down the number of potential meanings in order to 'counter the terror of uncertain signs' (Roland Barthes, 1964). We could now tell the students that the photograph was taken at Orgreave during the 1984 miners' strike and ask them to write captions for it. To make the assignment more interesting, some might write headlines for the popular press, some an 'objective neutral' caption, and others headlines for papers explicitly supporting the miners. From these we choose three:
1. SCARGILL'S MOB RUNS RIOT
2. MORE VIOLENCE AT THE ORGREAVE PICKET LINE
3. MINERS TRIUMPH OVER BRUTAL POLICE TACTICS
(None of these is a real headline, but they are deliberate caricatures of the numerous possible commentaries within whose terms this photograph might be circulated.) The meaning of the photograph, previously indefinite and ambiguous, is now specifically assigned to it by any one of the captions. The range of potential meanings are severely curtailed. The picture now performs distinct ideological work by inviting us to take up a specific position *vis-à-vis* the miners' strike. Again simplistically,

we could identify (1) as positioning us explicitly with the forces of law and order, (2) as the concerned liberal observer uninvolved in the conflict, and (3) as an unambiguous identification with the miners against the repressive use of the police.

Students could now be asked to write down whether they imagine the following people would agree or disagree with the different captions (or disagree with them all). A random selection might include a trade union official, a middle manager in insurance, a housewife, a farmer, a working miner, a striking miner's wife, an unemployed and middle-aged man, a black small businessman, an unemployed white teenager, a woman working a factory night shift, a black student, and a pensioner. There will obviously be considerable disagreement over various interpretations during discussion, but students will have been introduced to the crucial concept that meaning is not frozen and fixed by the text but is actively produced and contested by its audiences.

2   John Sturrock/Network

Discussion might be developed by introducing a second image (such as Photograph 2). Students can divide into editorial groups with the task of deciding which of the two pictures to use as their front page picture, bearing in mind the editorial position they want to take about the strike. When each group reports its decision to the teacher (the proprietor?) the processes of editorial selection should become readily apparent and can lead into discussion of how the priorities of news coverage and news values inform the setting of the ideological agenda for the way in which the miners' strike will be discussed in society at large. Consequently the exercise is beginning to raise the question of media institutions. The class could proceed to draw up a list of all the possible places or contexts in which they might encounter the photographs. These might include books, newspapers or magazines, TV or the cinema, an advertising poster, conceivably a court of law, or an educational or photographic exhibition. The photographs can only function through the operation of one or more of the institutions or apparatuses that organise and control the production and circulation of discourses in our society – the law, church, education system, the media. Their meaning will be partially determined by the nature of the specific institution into which they are inserted, and indeed students can discuss how the photographs might be used in an advert as opposed to a court of law or art exhibition. We can also draw their attention to the fact that anyone seeing the photographs will have paid for the privilege by buying a newspaper, paying a TV licence fee or the price of admission into a cinema or exhibition. They have an exchange value in the information or cultural market-places, and primarily in the market for news information which extends from the freelance photographer in the street to the transnational flow of news via satellite. These photographs are *commodities* produced, distributed and consumed in the same way as dishwashers or cars – with one crucial difference. Unlike dishwashers or cars, photographs have symbolic value. They are not valued as technological products but for their 'newsworthiness', as documents depicting events that are deemed 'news'. They circulate primarily in a discursive form but remain commodities. The essence of a media artefact is its *dual* form as *commodity and text*. Media institutions are both industrial production centres producing commodities whose value can only be realised on the market and

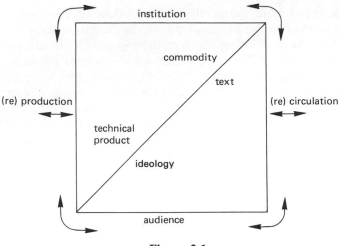

Figure 2.1

also ideological apparatuses engaged in a continual process of ideological reproduction similar to the education system or the family. Accordingly, each media artefact is produced, distributed and consumed within a specific set of institutional practices and codes which articulate a further set of social, political and economic relationships which are embodied, inscribed and embedded within the artefact. We can no more separate a media artefact from its institutional existence than we can the classes we teach from the education system as a whole. We would (crudely) represent this complex process in the diagrammatic form shown in Figure 2.1. While the audience are producing their meanings from a media text, all the institutional processes indicated come into play simultaneously.

Anyone believing in the 'free market' of information might well feel that the above account is immaterial. Everyone, it is claimed, in our society is free to produce and distribute ideas and opinions which everyone can choose to receive or reject. The mechanism for securing this remarkable equilibrium is the 'free market' in which the wishes of the consumer reign supreme. But if we were to ask our students which one of our two pictures, and accompanied with which of our captions, we are most likely to encounter, they would have no difficulty in deciding that the picture of Orgreave, with variations of the first two captions, typifies the most widely disseminated media artefacts. Both pictures were in fact taken by Network, a radical photographic agency, and were distributed in *City Limits* and the *New Statesman* respectively,[1] so they were historically circulated within some form of oppositional framework. The crucial point is that they could have equally well been circulated with anchorages drawn from the dominant ideologies if inserted into the major media institutions, in which case their material and ideological circulation would have been amplified on a scale inconceivable for the few examples of oppositional media that we have in this country.

Like other commodities, media artefacts are produced (in both private and public sectors) in an industrial system based upon mass production, the means of which are owned and controlled by a relatively small group of people. This material power over media production and distribution necessarily entails considerable ideological power as well. Media institutions are not monolithic; they have their own imperatives such as profitability and cultural prestige which may conflict with demands for ideological coherence. Ultimately audiences produce meaning at the moment of consumption and may not read the media texts in the same way as the institutions have produced them. But overall the case remains that overt challenges to the dominant discourses and representations are rarely produced and circulated within the mass media, and remain confined to the margins of media production.

Media artefacts cannot tell us their story. They cannot grass on their institutional determinants. Our two photographs cannot tell us why and how they (rather than other images, other texts) were produced and distributed and nor can our own experience. So when teaching media institutions our central concern must be to lay bare the processes of struggle that have informed the production and circulation of any media artefact, and in so doing reopen media texts to enable other meanings to emerge from them which the institutions have attempted to extinguish or marginalise.[2]

Why teach media institutions?

Pragmatically, teaching a narrative analysis of *The Sweeney* is always going to be a more tempting proposition than teaching the BBC Charter or ownership structures. But the inter-penetration of media artefact and institution suggests that whenever we teach a text we teach about an institution. The pedagogic decision lies between consciously teaching media institutions as an intrinsic component of studying the media or unconsciously as nebulous shadowy presences lurking in the background of the text, the ghosts in the media machine.

However, it would be glibly foolish to pretend that the decision to teach media institutions does not entail considerable problems for the teacher. Not surprisingly, resistance to teaching the institutions in the secondary school is felt more by teachers approaching the media from the liberal progressive tradition of English than those based in the social sciences. In his first book, *Teaching About Television*, Len Masterman argued that institutions were an inappropriately abstract area of knowledge for secondary level students:

> The major problem lies in the distinct differences which are likely to exist between what is considered important and interesting by the teacher, and what is of interest to his pupils. Like most articulate people who don't possess much of it, teachers and lecturers tend to be fascinated and even preoccupied with questions of power and control. It is not, by and large, a preoccupation which is likely to be shared by many of their pupils. And even assuming that pupils are able to see its significance there is a genuine difficulty in relating questions of organisational structures or patterns of control to the direct experience of the pupil. (Len Masterman, 1980, p.5)

Masterman has now modified his views considerably, and his later study, *Teaching the Media* (1985), includes a chapter with many useful teaching suggestions. Indeed, there is now a consensus among media teachers on the necessity to teach about media institutions. Students' experience is a potentially valuable resource for questioning the media's relationship with their audiences. But the media, among other institutions, have played a role in representing our own experience for us. Therefore our experience alone cannot satisfactorily answer those key questions which media teaching needs to ask of media texts.

Who produces the text? For what audience? In whose interests? What is excluded? The consequences of an exclusively text-centred approach are that these questions are marginalised in our teaching unless there is a direct engagement with the institutions themselves. For, as Masterman allows, a text-centred approach cannot 'reveal mediating frameworks which exist outside of the medium itself; it cannot directly disclose those images which have been excluded from the screen, and it cannot inform us directly of the many constraints and influences operating upon the form of a particular communication' (Masterman, 1980, p.11). And the reason that such questions are central is precisely *because* they cannot be satisfactorily answered from direct experience which has been re-presented for us by the media themselves alongside other institutions. It is important to remember, however, that students' experience of the media is a vital resource for teaching and learning about the media's assumptions about their audiences.

The media institutions on which we shall concentrate our attention here will be those of broadcast television. Theoretical orthodoxy has deliberated upon cinema as institution. Those deliberations are still pertinent, but most students watch the television rather than the cinema screen.

Media organisations are, of course, essentially cultural institutions and therefore need to be analysed and taught about in such terms. This, in turn, entails a need to introduce the concept of the state and the nature of a state's relationship to a culture and its cultural workers. As Stuart Hall points out:

Of course, the British state has assumed wide responsibilities for the *conditions of culture* in a broader sense. Especially through its education systems, it assumes responsibility for the definition and transmission of cultural traditions and values, for the organisation of knowledge, for the distribution of what the French sociologist, Pierre Bourdieu, calls 'cultural capital', throughout the different classes; and for the formation and qualification of intellectual strata – the guardians of cultural tradition. The state has become an active force in *cultural reproduction*. (Stuart Hall, 1981)

The introduction of the concept of the state forces an interesting – and for the media teacher, very important – distinction between film and television. We would suggest that the state views films (and cinema) as being essentially cultural institutions, while it views the television institutions as being essentially political. What is meant by this latter assertion is not only that television is not viewed as being cultural (because, to a large extent, it is not concerned with the dominant culture of high art) but also that it is its political significance that is the major concern of the state.

Thus, in Britain, the state plays a very clear role in relation to television and broadcasting in general, but relatively little when it comes to the cinema. For example, the British state plays a far less extensive role in cultural matters than is the case in other European cultures. Britain has no ministries of culture and keeps no cultural statistics like other UNESCO member states to indicate 'cultural development'. All Britain formally possesses is the Department of Education and Science and the Arts Council, which, though financed by the state, has its policies defined by 'independent' committees. Thus the role of the state – outside the relatively small-scale funding of the British Film Institute – in relation to film has been ambiguous and shifting.

On the other hand, the role of the state in relation to television has always been clear and powerful. Thus a cultural history of television (or, more usefully, of broadcasting) instead of privileging the usual technologically defined dates, would instead examine the cultural partnership between the state and the BBC and the political control of independent television.

However, even broadcasting institutions represent an almost infinite field of study which has to be delimited and defined. *What* should be taught about media institutions and how?

Mapping courses

Fundamentally, media institutions are both objective material forms and subjective ideological processes (as are the artefacts they produce), an ambiguity that can be traced in the term 'institution' itself:

> *Institution* is one of several examples of a noun of action or process which became, at a certain stage, a general and abstract noun describing something apparently objective and systematic;

in fact, in the modern sense, an *institution*. (Raymond Williams, 1983, p.163)

The teaching and study of institutions needs to engage with this duality. Therefore, rather than advocate a 'core curriculum' of information, we suggest that study of media institutions, whether in relation to a specific medium or a range of media, should engage with three key determinations:

1. the relationship between the artefact and the institutions through which it is produced, circulated and consumed;
2. the relations between media institutions and private and public capital – teaching about television as an industry involving a number of institutions;
3. the relations between media institutions and the state – teaching about television as an institution, a duopoly of the BBC and the IBA, regulated and increasingly controlled by central government.

To teach about media institutions is to teach about the relations involved in the productions of meanings: no *text* without *production* and without *audience* is possible, and to teach about institutions is to teach about the relations, determining or otherwise, between those three. Inevitably, such work will necessitate a considerable amount of direct teaching, where students will need to be presented with specific information about the institutions and their mode of operation. However, this needs to be integrated with as much simulation work as possible if students are to grasp the complex subjective dimension of institutional determinations, neatly encapsulated by Raymond Williams in a discussion of the range of uses of the word *determination*: 'Perhaps nobody has yet said "I am determined not to be determined", but this illustrates the actual range' (Williams, 1983, p.102). Students need to understand institutions as actively determining processes, embodying struggle and contestation over meaning, rather than as merely inert oppressive monoliths.[3] It is the tension between Williams's 'noun of action or process' and the 'general and abstract' noun denoting the objective, systematic or organised that we wish to rely upon for our purposes here.

In many Media Studies courses, 'institution' is a term that has been used to mean the patterns of ownership and control in the

film industry, broadcasting, the press or the music business. Because these are difficult areas to teach about, institutions on these courses have been either hazy 'background' material or heavy dollops along the way. Recently, 'institution' has come to be understood as a much more embracing term, one which indicates, however a text, or set of texts, can be contextualised, whether that is
(a) how it generates, or partially composes an ideological currency;
(b) how it comes to construct an audience;
(c) how it operates its own terms of address, its own terms of reference.
We shall use 'institution as industry' to describe the more conventional understanding of the term and 'institution as holdall' to express the more comprehensive notion which we have described above.

There are pedagogic and conceptual difficulties implied in both the descriptive terms we have coined. 'Institution as industry' assumes both a 'boring' kind of knowledge and a 'boring' kind of pedagogy. Teachers accustomed to using discovery-based, child-centred pedagogies fear instructional modes. Access to such knowledge is often difficult for teachers to gain. There is, however, another, more significant difficulty with the notion of 'institution as industry'. Having enabled students to realise their own power in bringing meaning and interpretations to any group of texts (through image analysis or investigations of narrative or representation), teachers are reluctant to risk making students feel powerless in their recognition of the determining power media institutions have. 'Institutions as holdall' may be more promising in this regard, but since it can literally include everything – everything is in the end institutionally determined and determining – then the danger is that 'institution' becomes too vague and unwieldy for the purposes of analysis. Institutions will be understood as 'givens' which can be acknowledged but not properly examined because they become too protean and elude our conceptual grasp.

The grid shown in Figure 2.2 is provided to assist teachers in delimiting their choices to particular case studies of their own making which will nevertheless enable the institutional relations we describe earlier to be taught about. However, before explaining how the grid may be used to plan a course on media institutions,

Media institutions	Production practices	Finance	Technology	Legislative / social	Circulation	Audience construction	Audience use	Ideological articulation
Television								
Cinema								
Video								
Press								
Radio								
Music								
Books								
Magazines								
Photography								

Figure 2.2

we need to discuss the different notions of power which our two definitions, 'institution as industry' and 'institution as holdall', bring into contention.

The former definition emphasises an understanding of (and teaching about) allocative and operational power. By these we mean the levels of policy-making, appointments of personnel and the allocation and distribution of resources (see p.75 and Pahl and Winkler, 1974). The latter definition emphasises an understanding (and teaching about) the formative power of discourses. By this we mean how words, sounds and images are deployed to include (and thereby exclude) audiences in the construction of an understanding, of a consensus of acceptance as to the very terms used in the discourse, so that its authority is unquestioned. 'And that's all the news for tonight' – or rather, that's all we're allowed. Clearly, we assume that isn't all that happened in the world, or even Britain, on that day.

These kinds of power are mutually maintaining rather than independent of each other, but in order to sophisticate our understanding of the term 'institution', while we try to make it teachable, it is useful to be able to distinguish between them. This is not to imply a hierarchy – to say that one kind of power is more important to teach about than another – but to insist that both kinds of power should be taught about when 'institutions' appears on the syllabus.

The grid on p.51 might enable teachers to formulate a finer taxonomy of media institutions to meet their particular course requirements. On the grid's vertical axis are listed various media forms. This list could obviously be extended. On the horizontal axis are listed what we consider to be institutional determinants. The grid is not an ideal model because there are often links between each of the media forms and there are determining relationships between, for instance, the financial and the technological, between the technological and circulation. The grid is only intended to be a guide to planning a course, and its limitations need to be recognised!

Under the headings on the horizontal axis the following examples might be considered:

Finance: patterns of shareholdings; grants; profits reaped and reploughed.

Production practices: studio systems; video workshops; home taping; pirate radio.
Technological: wide lens; sound; colour; ENG; DBS; cable systems; the Sony Walkman.
Legislative: Broadcasting Acts; Video Recordings Act; censorship.
Circulation: magazine and newspaper distribution; international video markets; news agencies.
Audience construction: the aesthetic conventions of realism; the use of pronouns; publicity material.
Audience use: video timeshifting; going to the cinema; home taping; scratch video.

How all or any of these interrelate in the formation of an ideological conjuncture will in turn determine changes in future media texts and in institutional determinants. The recent anxieties about the circumstances of childhood can be seen, through news on television and in the press about child abuse, through films about 'youth' and abducted children, to be forming an ideological conjuncture. Adultery has been mediated through Ken and Deirdre's near break-up in *Coronation Street*, through the problem pages in women's magazines, through the narratives of Cecil Parkinson and Sara Keays, and through Alan Horrox's series on Channel 4. In 1985 Madonna sang a few hit singles, became a movie star, connoted a fashion style.

There can be endless pleasure in discovering infinite relations, but that cannot alter the fact that there are some kinds of institutional determinations and interpellations which are easier to teach about than others. Film posters, book covers, TV title and continuity sequences are relatively easy to obtain and use to teach about media institutions. Information about allocative power in the media is now more accessible,[4] but that does not mean to say it is any easier to mediate in the classroom. However, there is no reason why discovery-based methods cannot take place alongside more instructional pedagogies. What we propose here is that teachers consider the interests of their students and the requirements of their courses, see which parts of the grid offer the most illuminating prospects, and then prepare accordingly!

The question 'How does the text/genre/audience come to be as it is?' is the question which has conventionally introduced the concept of 'institutions' to Media Studies courses. We think that the advantage of our planning grid broadens that question. As well as enabling us to trace the means of a text's production, it also enables questions about a text's reception: audience construction and audience use are as much a part of media institutions as their financial structures, technologies or production practices. Using the grid, we can begin to ask the question 'Into what kinds of institutionalisation does the text/genre/audience feed?'

This is an important question because in addition to teaching about how the mechanisms of power are maintained (be they allocative, operational or discursive), we also need to teach about how our own positions (and those of our students) are implicated in that maintenance and change. We have to guard against merely reinforcing a sense of the existing structures as being the only ones possible. Just as teaching representations has to involve the teaching of absent representations as well as those present, so must our teaching of institutions continually pose the existence of alternative institutions, alternative possibilities. We might, therefore, as well as teaching about how a text or an audience is produced, also bring students to a knowledge of how they can be active or resistant in that production process. In other words, by teaching about media institutions in this way we can participate either in maintenance or in change. This power to participate may seem a relatively minimal one, but it is certainly better than none.

Television as institution

Teaching television as a set of institutions instead of a collection of individual television programmes initially has to engage with the medium's unique form of institutional schizophrenia. Paradoxically, television continually denies its own institutional status, asserting its cultural role as our window on the world, and yet the rival television companies, in order to ensure their own institutional survival, are in a constant process of constructing an identity for themselves and their audiences – building channel loyalty.

Continuity material is the one aspect of broadcasting output to challenge the audience's conception of the screen as a transparency, an unproblematic mediator of real events and fiction. During continuity sequences the screen retains the metaphor of the window, but of a somewhat different window . . . the audience [is encouraged] to observe the window itself, to look *at* it rather than through it. The continuity window is a stained glass window, studied for itself rather than being disregarded as transparent. (John Morey, 1981, p.5)

TV as institution and as a set of institutions manifests itself in two different but interdependent ways:

1. The omnipresent *visibility* of television in its modes of circulation and consumption. Not only is the TV set just part of the domestic furniture, but the rival companies are also devoting more and more resources to build up their corporate image in on- and off-screen promotional material.
2. Its '*invisible*' mode of production – its construction of meanings, which remains largely invisible to its audience.

Circulation and consumption

Students inevitably experience television as an institution at the moment of reception, so circulation and consumption represent the best starting point for teaching. Paradoxically, we tend to teach the media through analysis of discrete texts, yet as Raymond Williams suggests, our actual experience of watching TV is best theorised as one of *flow*:

What is being offered is not, in older terms, a programme of discrete units with particular insertions, but a planned flow, in which the true series is not the published sequence of programme items but this sequence transformed by the inclusion of another kind of sequence (commercials), so that these sequences together compose the real flow, the real 'broadcasting'. Increasingly, in both commercial and public-service television a further sequence was added: trailers of programmes to be shown at some later time or on some later day, or more itemised programme news . . . with the eventual unification of these two or three sequences a new kind of communication phenomenon has to be recognised. (Raymond Williams, 1974, p.90)

Our primary teaching task must be the interruption of this flow, fragmenting its homogenising trajectory back into its discrete units. The viewing experience of 'flow' is composed for the viewer by presentation departments which 'knit' together individual programmes, trailers and continuity and advertising into a seamless whole. Textual analysis of presentation output is an accessible introduction to television as institution.

Channel logos can be subjected to ordinary image analysis. The logos or symbols for each channel are their primary form of identification, so analysis should reveal how they would prefer their audience to perceive them.

The revolving globe is the BBC1 logo. What are the connotations of a globe for a national TV network? What does its revolution add to that? How are we meant to regard the BBC as a result?

Channel 4's logo is a multicoloured '4' which fragments before each programme. What does this abstract figure suggest about the channel (compare BBC2's '2' symbol)? Why is the 4 multicoloured? Why does it dissolve? How does this relate to the channel's status as a publisher and not a programme producer?

Continuity announcements vary according to the different channels. While the BBC always use voice-over announcements, the ITV companies usually have in-vision presenters. These different styles can be analysed and compared by students as a way of beginning to outline the institutional differences between television channels. They can also write or devise their own continuity material for a channel's schedule, perhaps paying attention to producing continuity which addresses a specific audience – teenage, female, male, unemployed, and can be compared to the institutional continuity which is directed at an abstract viewer, a mass audience of individuals. Analysis should also be directed at the absent voices from continuity. What effect would a Caribbean accent have on a BBC announcement?[5]

Promotional material such as programme trailers are also a fertile source for analysis. Particularly useful are the more extravagant promotions of special events such as the Olympics, or yet another 'new season' with its promise of novelty – 'Autumn Drama', 'A Summer of Sport', 'Spring Entertainment'. Trailers compactly signify how the institutions wish to represent both themselves and the forthcoming attraction. The BBC's extravagant trailer for the 1984 Olympics, using the theme music of *Chariots of Fire*, presented BBC1 as the 'Olympic Channel' in order to identify the BBC itself with the Olympic connotations of excellence and patriotism.[6]

This can be supplemented by analysis of off-screen promotional material. Comparative analysis of *Radio Times* and *TV Times* often reveals different institutional priorities in terms of presentation and their selection of output to be given the hard sell. Students can also design their own programme pages, write publicity material for particular programmes, or devise their own trailer for a selected programme.

Title sequences are another accessible form of teaching how the institutions define different types of material and how they then offer them to particular audiences. Image and sound analysis can reveal some of these assumptions: what level of cultural knowledge does the *South Bank Show* assume about its audience? What kind of pleasures are promised by *That's Life*'s opening montage of programme highlights? What kind of information is signified by news title music? What would happen if the image track was juxtaposed with reggae, classical, jazz or heavy metal music? Students can devise alternative titles for existing programmes which would change the interpretation of the programme.[7]

Genre identification exercises provide the teacher with the means of introducing students to the restrictive and institutionalised nature of television's dominant formats which underlie its surface diversity. As John Ellis suggests, the limited range of television genres is related to the economic base of TV institutions: television companies

can broadly predict what [their] income will be from whatever source (advertising, licenses, central government), and can therefore budget each programme or series as a fraction of that production total. This element of planning enables TV production to become far more industrialised than film production . . . TV programmes are therefore budgeted with reference to an overall financial policy and predicted income for the broadcasting institution . . . each programme or series is thus a matter of balancing the channel's income against the different kinds of programmes. (John Ellis, 1982, pp.213–15)

Small extracts from different genres – documentary, drama, light entertainment, soap opera, current affairs, sit-com, etc. – can be assembled on one tape so that students can question the processes whereby programmes' generic identifications are made sometimes clear, sometimes confusing.

Scheduling exercises introduce students to the unseen aspect of TV flow which is its planning, its scheduling, by the channel controllers. Masterman (1980, p.126) provides a useful simulation game where students are provided with a selection of programmes for one channel which have to be placed in an evening's schedule against the other channels in order to maximise the audience. Students have to pay particular attention to scheduling ploys of *inheritance*, in which an audience is 'inherited' from a previous popular programme, and *pre-echo*, where an audience will watch part of any programme which precedes one they definitely want to watch.

The arrival of Channel 4 allows this form of exercise to be developed. The channel had considerable teething problems in its scheduling due to its dependence on the other channels' established practices and its own statutory commitment to 'minority' and 'innovative' programming. It therefore represents a particularly useful scheduling exercise as it introduces students to the difficulties of alternative programming within the present system of TV institutions. Students can be provided with an evening's schedule for both BBC channels and ITV, and with a selection of programmes from Channel 4's weekly schedule (including the one-hour news slot). Their results can then be analysed: Why were certain programmes given peak time? How would that affect the audience ratings? Such work will begin to introduce scheduling as a political practice rather than a professional 'art'.

Production

Teaching about the production process is rendered difficult by its institutional invisibility and inaccessibility. With perseverance it is sometimes possible to arrange visits to television companies, but this can easily end up reinforcing the sense of being overawed by the 'technological marvels of telly'. Consequently, a critical understanding of the essence of the TV production process can be achieved through simulation exercises in producing TV or radio news magazine programmes (or a newspaper front page). Teachers can either provide their own source material of newspapers stories, press releases, newsagency copy, etc., or take advantage of the material that has been produced already.[8] However, any simulation which is to achieve an understanding of TV news production as institutional process must involve three key stages:

1. Editorial selection: students, either collectively or individually, have to select the items for the programme from a range of available material, decide on its form of presentation, place in the running order, the editorial 'angle', etc. This should take place within a deadline, and have a number of institutional directives such as running to time, and having at least one 'soft' story.

2. Production: students are given specific production roles, which will vary according to the resources available. If there is access to a small studio, there would be camera operators, sound and vision mixers, a floor manager, director and producer, reporters and presenters, and interviewees.

3. Assessment: it is easy to get so engrossed in the production of the artefact that the most important part of the exercise is squeezed out. The class assessment should not be on 'how we did in comparison to the pros', but on what editorial criteria were used and why. Why was that story dropped? Why did we interview X and not Y?

As the production process is gradually demystified, the teacher can introduce institutional variables. Different groups in the class can produce programmes from the same available material according to different editorial criteria (audience maximisation, attracting younger/older/more female or black viewers, deliberate bias towards employers, unionists, the unemployed) and different conventions (interviewees with direct audience eyeline, presenters in big close-up, no interviewers so that interviewees become their own 'presenters'). The different results can then be compared and the relative merits of the different criteria and conventions discussed, raising on the way the question of why the TV institutions use the editorial criteria and conventions they do and not others.[9]

The purpose of this kind of learning is to enable students to begin to engage with television as an institution which defines the world according to a series of institutional needs, procedures and imperatives as it produces and circulates its images and sounds. However, the more complex task for analysis and teaching remains: to discover the relations between internal institutional determinants and their external historical and political determinations. What follows is our analysis of some of the institutional relations that are currently pertinent.

Institutional structures

The key structural determinations on the operation of the media are the economic imperative for capital accumulation (profit) and regulation by the state through such forms as laws, charters, and the appointment of personnel in regulatory bodies. Both media workers and audiences have their own levels of autonomy and influence through trade unions and pressure groups, but nevertheless have to operate within the parameters laid down by capital and state. The role of the state is particularly complex in so far as it is normally represented as preserving the interests of the general public – the audience or consumer – against the crude directives of the market. The state has preserved broadcasting from being controlled totally by the profit motive. But, in our view, its role must be also understood as the intervention of a political structure which, far from transcending class, gender and race, ultimately protects the interests of a particular class, gender and race. Capital and state are therefore represented here as mutually reinforcing structural determinants on the operation of the media in its daily ideological work, although historically they have contended for control of each new communications technology as it appears.

The free market: newspapers

Although we are concentrating on television, newspapers deserve a brief mention, as they represent the medium which beyond the odd ineffectual probe by the Monopolies Commission, receive least overt state intervention. The libel laws and the Official Secrets Act are a legal curb, but generally Fleet Street is given a free rein. Historically newspapers were a crucial instrument in the mercantile challenge to aristocratic dominance in the eighteenth century. The provincial commercial press provided the middle-class voice of opposition to the metropolitan political newspapers, whose allegiance was to the aristocratic landowning state. 'The freedom of the press' has been articulated as 'freedom from state intervention' ever since, rather than as opposition to capital: 'The coincidence between the "free" individual, the "free" market, the "free" press and the "freedom" to accumulate private property is forged in this moment, and provides the basis of the real relations in which the press stood *vis-à-vis* the struggle of the classes' (Stuart Hall, 1978, p.43).

Because newspapers are most subject to market forces, they exhibit the largest concentration of ownership of any medium. Since the mid-nineteenth century technological advances have made the cost of entering the newspaper market prohibitive (even Eddie Shah, with all the latest information technology, needed £22 million to start *Today* in 1986). The growing dependence on advertising for revenue meant that the radical, working-class press was killed off as its audience held few attractions for advertisers and so could not compete with the advertising that subsidised circulation prices of capitalist corporations. Since the war, competition has intensified further with the emergence of multinationals buying up newspapers such as the Thomson organisation, Pergamon Press, and Rupert Murdoch's infamous News International. Over 95 per cent of national newspapers are now produced by the leading five firms (see Table 2.1).

Table 2.1   *Newspaper ownership*

Paper (national dailies/Sundays)	Owner
Star *Daily Express* *Sunday Express*	United Newspapers
Daily Mail *Mail on Sunday* (50% London *Evening Standard*)	Lord Rothermere's Associated Newspaper Group
Daily Mirror *Sunday Mirror* *Sunday People* (in Scotland *Daily Record* and *Sunday Mail*)	Robert Maxwell's Pergamon Press
News of the World *Sun* *Times* *Sunday Times*	Rupert Murdoch's News International
Daily Telegraph *Sunday Telegraph*	Conrad Black's Argus Corporation (Canada) 51%
Guardian	Guardian and Manchester Evening News Group
Observer	Lonhro

Whenever this astonishingly restricted pattern of ownership is questioned, the same answer is always given – of how the freedom of the press must remain sacrosanct, to which one might reply with Marx's comment that 'it is not individuals who are set free by free competition; it is rather capital which is set free' (Karl Marx, 1973, p.649).

Public capital: the BBC

Whereas the modern newspaper emerged in opposition to the state, broadcasting has always been subject to strict state regulation due to the relative scarcity of broadcasting frequencies. Radical advances in wireless technology in the early 1920s, stimulated by its use in the First World War, forced the state to devise some form of apparatus to organise and develop the new communications technology. Its preferred solution, the product of accident as much as design, was the BBC.

The crucial factors in the setting up of the BBC were its financing from the sale of licences for wireless receivers and monopoly. In 1922 a consortium of wireless manufacturers combined to form the British Broadcasting Company, who were to provide programmes for broadcasting within the strict terms (such as not dealing with matters of controversy) laid down by the Post Office and the State. In 1926 the company received a Royal Charter to form as a public broadcasting corporation. This was a typically British compromise between the demands of commerce and the fear of state control. The BBC owes its existence to an ideological division within the British ruling class. British aristocratic distaste for both the deregulated wireless anarchy breaking out in America and the populism of the *nouveau riche* press barons enabled Reith to gain a monopoly of broadcasting. Yet the traditional bourgeois fear of 'state intervention' ensured that the BBC did not become a Department of State. The licence fee was represented as the guarantor of the BBC's independence from the government, while the grace of monopoly saved it from the vulgarity of the market-place. Raymond Williams has qualified the orthodox view of the BBC's independence. He states that the BBC was established as

> a state-regulated and state-sponsored public corporation which was yet not subject to detailed state control. The flexibility which was latent in this kind of solution, though continually a matter of dispute, permitted the emergence of an independent corporate broadcasting policy, in which the independence was at once real, especially in relation to political parties and temporary administrations, and qualified, by its definition in terms of a pre-existing cultural hegemony. (Raymond Williams, 1974, p.33)

This state of 'licensed independence' has continued ever since 1926, and the BBC has lurched from crisis to crisis in its relations with the state whenever there has been an extensive breakdown in the social democratic consensus over a political issue.

The General Strike, Suez, Northern Ireland, and the Falklands/Malvinas war are just the most dramatic crises in a protracted series of negotiations and compromises between the state and the BBC over its programming policy. The root of this problem lies in the fact that the BBC is economically dependent on the state.

Politically the BBC is constitutionally separate from the state. The Royal Charter (next to be renewed in 1996) sets out its constitution. Twelve Governors are appointed by the Privy Council for a five-year period. They in turn appoint the Director-General, who heads the Board of Management. This executive is accountable to the Governors, who are meant to be the custodians of the public interest, although in practice, judging by the remark of a past Chairman Lord Hill, this does not prove too onerous for the BBC: 'I think the Governors should remain what they are, amateurs, who assume a responsibility for what is broadcast, who gain an understanding of how the BBC works, but whose task is to defend the Corporation, resist the pressures on it and to defend those who work in it'. Yet the essential weakness of this diluted accountability is that the Governors are appointed by the state from the predictable narrow and unrepresentative range of people ('the great and the good') who compose every public body in Britain and who are therefore unlikely to perceive the interests of the public as anything other than the interests of the state.

This latent form of control was made explicitly manifest in the summer of 1985 when the BBC Governors complied with a request from Home Secretary Leon Brittan to ban a *Real Lives* documentary featuring Martin McGuinness, a Sinn Fein leader. Only after alteration to the film and an unprecedented campaign by BBC and other television workers was the film re-instated.

The BBC's claims to independence were further damaged when the *Observer* revealed in 1985 that MI5 were vetting BBC production staff, even to the levels of researcher and assistant film editor level in some cases.

This political figleaf is more thoroughly exposed by consideration of the BBC's economic base. Contrary to BBC mythology, the BBC is funded from the Treasury out of general tax revenue (the licence fee being paid to the Treasury via the Post Office) which is voted upon by Parliament. Therefore it is economically a state institution, as its resources are essentially state capital. It cannot dispose of its income as it pleases – the BBC cannot diversify into motorway cafes like Granada. The state licenses its transmitters, collects its income through the Post Office, and then gives it its grant which has been voted upon by Parliament. (The BBC only received 100 per cent of its licence fee after 1950.) The licence fee arrangement is a weak financial base because, while it will rise satisfactorily during the expansion of a market field (radio sets, TV sets, colour, satellite dishes), once the market is saturated, the income reaches a plateau. When in 1984 the BBC wished to raise the licence fee, the government responded by instituting a committee chaired by Professor Peacock to investigate the financing of public service television in Britain with a view to devising alternative sources of revenue. At present, within an inflationary economy, the BBC is forced to negotiate a licence fee increase from the state to maintain the same operation and accordingly deems it wise to have considerable ideological credit in the state bank. In other words, the BBC is a public corporation which is only accountable to the state and not to Parliament; paradoxically this very lack of accountability is cited as proof of its independence from the state.

State-mediated private capital

During the economic growth of the 1950s, British capital was searching for potential growth sectors which might repay investment. A general dissatisfaction with the BBC amongst its traditional friends (Churchill thought it a nest of reds) enabled the commercial television lobby to succeed in breaking the BBC's monopoly. 'Independent' television was set up in 1955, but the state ensured that it would retain a considerable measure of control by setting up a regulatory body called the Independent Television Authority (renamed after the advent of commercial radio in 1972 as the Independent Broadcasting Authority or IBA). Just as with the BBC, the state, this time through the Home Office, appoints twelve members who act as a benevolent state authority overseeing the new television service on behalf of the public interest. However, the IBA's role is considerably broader than the role of the BBC Governors, and has a staff of 1500 people. It has several functions:

Figure 2.3   *The BARB map of ITV areas*

Transmission of programmes. Commercial television's licence to broadcast operates through the IBA, which owns and operates the transmitters which it then leases to the companies for a set period to use for broadcasting. In 1984–5 the IBA received £62.6m. in rent from TV and Radio.

Selection and appointment of companies. When commercial television was first set up, there was a strong attempt to ensure both competition and regional diversity by establishing a federal system of individual companies who would thus avoid what was felt to be the excessive over-centralisation of the BBC. Consequently the ITA (as it was then known) invited potential programme companies to submit for franchises for given areas for an eight-year period. In 1967 and 1981 companies were invited to re-submit for franchises (and new companies to apply). The IBA's ultimate sanction is the power to withdraw or extend the licence to produce programmes; this also applies to commercial radio franchises. There are fifteen regional companies (see Figure 2.3) and the IBA also licenses a breakfast franchise to TV-AM and a network news franchise to ITN. Channel 4 is a wholly owned subsidiary of the IBA.

Regulation of advertising. In order to avoid programme sponsorship (which was seen as being responsible for the worst excesses of the American television system) it was decided that the new TV channel would carry 'spot advertising' (short periods of advertising which interrupt programmes at set intervals or at junctions) and which would not be made by the programme companies. The programme companies would sell 'time and space' to advertisers, a system which, it was hoped, would avoid blurring the responsibilities of editorial independence. The IBA polices the use of advertising, ensuring that it is limited to six minutes an hour and accords with the usual codes of 'taste and decency'; this enables it, for example, to ban an advert for *Gay News*.

Supervision of programme planning. The IBA has to monitor the companies' output, not only to check they are within the statutory requirements of 'balance', 'good taste', etc., but also to ensure that companies are fulfilling their various obligations such as serving their franchise area and providing sufficient current affairs, religious arts, and children's programming.

Administration of the Levy. The excessive profits made by commercial television in its early years (after a disastrous beginning), which prompted Lord Thomson of Scottish TV to remark that a franchise was a 'licence to print money', led the government to introduce a levy on advertising revenue. Each company is allowed, free of levy, a slice of profit amounting to 2.8 per cent. The remainder is subject to the 66.7 per cent levy. The remaining balance of profit is then subject to the normal 52 per cent corporation tax.

While it is fair to say that the IBA has so far managed to preserve the independent television system from the worst excesses of the far less regulated American system, its overall record is of increasing failure to go beyond its statutory minimum duties.

Crucial to this failure is the IBA's condonation of the practice of *networking*, which started after the disastrous first year of broadcasting. The 'big five' companies – Thames, LWT, Central, Granada and Yorkshire – constitute the Major Programme Controllers Group of the ITV Network Programme Committee, which decides which programmes will be networked. Due to an initial inequitable distribution of capital and the disproportionate amount of advertising revenue afforded by different franchises the large companies have built up almost total control of the ITV network. All the companies need the network to fill their screens, as none of them could afford to on its own. Control of the network committee means that the 'Five' can guarantee their own products networked slots (thus ensuring a return on their investment), a guarantee denied the smaller companies, which are therefore reluctant to commit themselves to major programme investment. Unlike American commercial television, which is based on the principle of television companies competing with each other, the British commercial television companies act in consort and are thus able to determine, for example, high advertising rates. As Nicholas Garnham writes, 'In other words ITV is run not on the basis of competition in either price or quality, but is a carve-up based on proportion of total advertising revenue' (Nicholas Garnham, 1978, p.24).

This situation indicates one reason why the commercial television companies in Britain are as keen to preserve the licence fee system as is the BBC itself! Since 1981, the situation has become rather more complex, with some of the mini-majors such as TV South becoming increasingly bullish.

However, the fundamental flaw with the IBA's control is that its power, although absolute, is only negative and retrospective, as it cannot itself initiate programme production. The power to withdraw franchises seems potent, but is in fact ineffective, for while the companies go into a flurry of creative activity whenever the franchises are due for renewal and occasionally one is axed *pour encourager les autres*, the main effect is that the companies diversify into other areas or are themselves consortiums of the shareholdings of large corporations with no allegiance to television. A company's own market survival is inevitably its main priority, and as competition intensifies the IBA's role is increasingly becoming the spokesperson of commercial television rather than its watchdog. The decline of TV-AM from its initial franchise-winning 'mission to inform' has been totally unchecked by the IBA because it is only too aware that the commercial viability of the breakfast franchise is at stake. When it does withdraw a franchise all that happens is that one section of private capital replaces another. In 1981 Southern TV had its franchise withdrawn. One of the main shareholders was D. C. Thomson (a right-wing publisher based in Scotland) who transferred its 25 per cent stake to a new company, Central. Trident TV was forced to divest its controlling interest in Yorkshire and Tyne Tees, so 25 per cent of Yorkshire was bought up by the multinational S. C. Pearson. The names change, but structually the formation of power – large, private capital – in commercial television remains the same.

In 1982 Channel 4 (and S4C) began broadcasting. A wholly owned subsidiary of the IBA, the company is financed from subscriptions by the ITV companies. They are meant to recoup this through the selling of advertising on Channel 4 within their region. Channel 4 does not make programmes itself but instead commissions or buys them from independent production companies (many of whom formed to supply the channel) and from the ITV companies themselves. The channel has had a fraught history in trying to satisfy the irreconcilable demands of the two dominant forces in its setting-up – the desire of the ITV companies for further profits and the need of disenfranchised voices (women, youth, blacks, etc.) for access to the means of television production. Although it has significantly extended the broadcasting agenda (betraying many hopes along the way) Channel 4 has been subject to an unequal power struggle between those determined it should stick to its statutory obligation to innovative and minority programming and those footing the bill, the ITV companies. Pressure from the companies for the Channel to improve its ratings almost from its first transmission, has meant that many early hopes have been dashed as recycled mainstream product from ITV has steadily shunted other programming to the margins of its schedule and more mainstream programmes commissioned than at first.[10]

Conglomeration and technology

The relationship between state and capital in the communications sector is now entering a new phase. Both recognise that communications are a key strategic area in western industrial capitalism's massive microchip technology-based restructuring. The state's anxiety that Britain should not be left behind in this process means that it is encouraging the growth in concentration of control by a few large corporations or conglomerates of the whole communications sector.[11]

Concentration of control in the major sectors of the UK economy has been in a spiral of acceleration for many years. It has been estimated that by the 1990s the largest 100 firms will produce 80 per cent of UK net manufacturing output (compared to 21 per cent in 1949). This concentration has been complemented by the dominant structural movement in contemporary capitalism – *conglomeration*. Mergers between different companies, both nationally and internationally, are becoming increasingly diversified as companies assimilate other firms from either different or related economic sectors. In 1955 only 12 per cent of mergers were of this type; by 1972 the figure was 51 per cent. Communication is very typical of this general trend. Many of the ITV companies have diversified out of TV production in order to insure against a possible adverse IBA franchise ruling. The most adventurous is Granada TV, as Table 2.2 illustrates. In a different league are the multinational media conglomerates such as Robert Maxwell's Pergamon Press, Rupert Murdoch's press empire News

Table 2.2   *Granada*

Media interests	General interests

Granada Television
Publishing – Panther, Granada, Paladin,
  Triad, Mayflower, Dragon imprints
Television and video rental (in 1984 also
  acquired Rediffusion from British
  Electric Traction, now world's largest
  TV rental company)
	Motorway service stations,
	  cinemas, music publishing,
	  property, bingo halls

Table 2.3   *Pergamon, News Corporation, Thorn-EMI*

Media interests	General interests
Pergamon Press	

Mirror Group Newspapers
Central TV (12% approx)
Selec-TV (cable programme supplier,
  17.5%)
Caxton Publishing
	Printing – British Printing
	  and Communications
	  Corporation.
	Educational publishing, data
	  systems

News Corporation	

*Times/Sunday Times/Sun/News of the
  World*
LWT (9%)
William Collins (40% Scottish publishers)
News Ltd (Australian newspaper chain)
American newspapers (*New York Post,
  Star, Sun-Times Chicago, Boston
  Herald,* etc.)
Sydney and Melbourne TV stations
Satellite TV (runs Sky Channel)
News Satellite TV (trying to start up news
  satellite service)
	Oil and minerals, airlines

Thorn-EMI	

Thames TV (controlling share)
Cable TV (shares in Swindon, Ulster and
  Coventry pilot franchises)
Radio Rentals
Cinema chain
Records
Video distribution
	Film production
	Electronics (defence contracts
	  especially)
	Information technology
	Engineering,
	  telecommunications,
	  hardware, electrical goods

International, and the giant Thorn-EMI which resulted from the 1979 merger between Thorn Electrical Industries and ailing entertainment firm EMI (see Table 2.3).

Thorn-EMI is the main communications conglomerate operating in the UK due its command in both hardware communications products and the 'software' which are the attraction for people to buy their hardware in the first place. However, there are also more generalised conglomerates whose major stake in the media is just one of many interests.[12] Tiny Rowland's Lonhro owns the *Observer*, a Scottish newspaper chain and Outram publishers, although the firm's main spheres are minerals, oil, property, hotels and transport, especially in the Third World. Another typical general conglomerate is S. C. Pearson (see Table 2.4).

Table 2.4   *S. C. Pearson*

Media interests	General interests
Financial Times, 12 regional newspapers Magazines (56 weeklies, including *The Economist*, *Investor's Chronicle*) Goldcrest Films (who own 25% of Yorkshire TV, produce feature films, and have a stake in Premier and Music Box cable channels) Publishing (Longman, Penguin)	Leisure (Madame Tussauds, Warwick Castle, Wookey Hole) Land (vast estates in Scotland and Sussex) Oil Information technology (Fintel dataservice) Banking (Lazards)

The increasing involvement in communications generally by the conglomerates who have an international capital base, and especially their involvement in every type of media, suggests that capital conglomeration is initating a 'process of convergence and integration of once disparate technologies . . . into what may be seen as an overarching communications industry' (Kevin Robins and Frank Webster, 1979, p.285). The most immediate developments are the arrival of satellite and cable television, although they constitute only the vanguard of the formation of a new world information order embracing electronic mail, teletext, databanks, computers, word processors and automated labour.[13]

Cable and satellite are essentially based upon extending the means of distribution and circulation, finding new markets for the media products which are increasingly expensive for the companies to produce. However, the prohibitive cost of entering the cable and satellite markets will ensure that only the established leaders will be in a position to exploit the new technologies. In 1985, plans for a Direct Broadcast Satellite, in which the BBC, ITV and 'independent' companies such as Thorn-EMI would be involved, collapsed, as the companies were unconvinced that the profits would ever recoup the enormous starting-up costs, particularly given the British government's insistence that British satellite technology be used. This decision was suddenly revoked towards the end of the year. In the meantime Rupert Murdoch is already broadcasting on the European satellite channel Sky and is trying to establish a satellite news channel in the USA which would build on his press empire. Even the largest companies are finding the scale of investment required difficult. Originally there were going to be three music channels for cable in the UK; now the companies offering them – Thorn-EMI, Yorkshire TV, and Virgin records – have combined to provide one channel, Music Box. As competition intensifies for the increasingly diversified communications market, all but the largest corporations will be driven to the wall.

SKY CHANNEL

4.00 Music Box. 6.00 Cartoon Time. 6.05 Wayne & Shuster. 6.30 Green Acres. 6.55 Charlie's Angels. 7.40 Vegas. 8.30 Starsky & Hutch. 9.15 Plants That Climb. 9.30 Nature Of Things. 9.55 12.00 Music Box.

Schedule of the future? Thorn-EMI's Music Box, together with American imports, are transmitted to Europe on Rupert Murdoch's Sky Channel, and advertised in the Murdoch-owned Sun.

At the time of writing there is considerable uncertainty over the future of satellite and cable. Both companies and financiers are being distinctly lukewarm about such high-risk investment, and the state has been pressurised into making several major concessions to capital to maintain any momentum at all. The ITV companies have had their franchises extended to compensate them for the level of investment needed in the new satellite project, while the eleven pilot cable franchise holders and any further licencees given a franchise by the new Cable Authority will not be faced with any statutory requirement to provide access to the communities of their area. They will also have an almost infinite duration on their franchises. Even with the aid of a crystal ball, any prediction on the shape of media institutions would be foolish and beyond the scope of this book. However, there can be no doubt that we are entering a new era of intensifying corporate control of communications in the UK, with a parallel dilution of even the limited accountability that exists at present.

Teaching the structures of media institutions inevitably has to be in a fairly direct mode. The absence of any form of reader means that the teacher has to rely on redeploying existing material, some of which has already been indicated. Extracts from Stuart Hood's *On Television* (1980) are accessible for fifth-form and upwards, as is Comedia's useful guide to the media for unionists, *The Press, Radio and Television* (Morley and Whitaker, 1983). A useful supplement in teaching historical detail is television's now continual recycling of its own past as a cheap source of programme material; these self-congratulatory exercises can be educationally appropriated. Teaching can focus on the programmes being produced by a particular company such as Granada (there is a useful BFI dossier on the company) allowing concentration on a range of determinations. *Viewpoint* no. 8 'Showbusiness' was an entertaining look at the implications of conglomerate control in the media. The series, produced by Thames TV, was refused re-transmission following a complaint by Southern TV over 'bias'. It remains, to date, the only educational TV series to be banned.[14] The BFI's education pack, *Selling Pictures*, includes a students' book, *The Companies You Keep*, which provides an accessible and detailed account of Thorn-EMI and other conglomerates and analyses how this affects representation. However, questions about institutions are best raised through teaching about forms of institutional control, which is the concern of the next section.

Institutional controls

Progression from the presentation of empirically verifiable 'facts' about media institutions to the analysis and teaching of how such a system affects the production and circulation of particular texts (and the absences of other texts) is fraught with difficulties. Any media text embodies a complex set of determinations. The teacher's choice of which determinations to concentrate on will depend upon his or her theorisation of power and control.

Whereas a liberal theory of power stresses power as being diffused throughout the social formation between different groups who balance each other into some form of social equilibrium (and this model is the dominant one used in schools), we would stress power as being the preserve of those who own or control the means of production. However, it is too easy to construct for students an ogre of a monolithic system of iron control strangling free expression; in order to avoid such a caricature of the process of control it is useful to follow Graham Murdock's distinction following Pahl and Winkler, between *allocatory* and *operational* control (Murdock, 1982).

Ownership gives allocatory control, which is the control over long-term policy and the strategic use of resources. Allocatory control determines the limits of operational control, which is day-to-day management. In practice they operate simultaneously at different levels; a head teacher has more allocatory control than a departmental head, but the eventual control of her or his budget lies with the LEA and the DES. Allocative control of media institutions is shared between private capital and the state, while operational control is the preserve of media personnel. The media in Britain enjoy a considerable degree of working autonomy from state and capital, unlike many more centralised or commercial systems, which accounts for the degree of ideological credibility afforded them by their audiences. However, operational control in practice internalises the structural requirements of allocative control so that media texts are produced within the constraints of reaching a particular size or type of audience or of editorial 'impartiality' as interpreted by the state's custodians. Disputes between 'allocators' and 'operators' only tend to arise when the latter feel their professional autonomy is being infringed, as in the dispute with the Ministry of Defence in 1982 which, broadcasters felt, was hindering the professional duty of reporting the war in the South Atlantic. The debate about control of the media takes place over the ambiguous terrain where one form of control converges into another; it rarely trespasses into the fundamental issue of whose interests are served by the present distribution of allocative control.

Allocative control: capital

Even if the media's role in ideological production and reproduction cannot be explained in terms of their individual personalities, entrepreneurial figures such as Victor Matthews and Rupert Murdoch wield a vast amount of power over huge systems of communications and do not hesitate to use it. Individual allocatory control by capitalists tends to attract more headlines than structural control but is actually less important, although it would be mistaken to theorise away the significance of 'proprietorial control' altogether. The definitive, and oft-quoted, statement on allocatory control belongs to Victor Matthews (Chairman of Fleet Holdings): 'By and large the editors will have complete freedom as long as they agree with the policy I have laid down'. The usually reactionary views of proprietors contribute to Fleet Street's rabid opinions. Lord Rothermere supported headlines supporting Mosley's Blackshirts, and the latest arrival, Robert Maxwell, despite avowed Labour sympathies, said that no paper of his would have run a story on the Thatchers' involvement in the Oman deal. Tiny Rowland of Lonhro has frequently threatened to sell the *Observer* because of its reports from Zimbabwe, where Lonhro has vital business interests. Occasionally such direct intervention happens in television as well, for example when Tyne Tees cancelled at the last moment a programme on gambling because the parent company Trident was engaged in a controversial bid for the Playboy casinos.

However, the capitalist market system itself remains the main source of control for, as Marx commented, most actions by capitalists are in fact reactions to market forces. The dynamics of profit or capital accumulation are more powerful than the intentions of an individual capitalist who must make a profit or go bankrupt. Despite their assurances to the contrary, Reed International sold Mirror Newspapers to Robert Maxwell in 1984 because Maxwell offered them £30m more than the favoured public flotation could possibly raise.

As already noted, media artefacts are commodities in the market-place and therefore exist to make a profit. To be profitable they have to be either consumed by a large mass audience or a smaller one with significant economic resources. Television companies, and newspapers to a lesser extent, make their profit by selling audiences to advertisers. Increasingly, the sale of artefacts for international distribution on cable or satellite is a crucial component of costing the production process. Overall, this policy entails the erosion of the contentious or 'alien' text in favour of the text which can be easily assimilated. Alternatively, it can appeal to an affluent audience who provide an attractive target for potential advertisers. Consequently, there is a polarisation between texts designed for a mass audience and those for an economic elite. Fleet Street has been polarised on such lines for many years, and television, as competition for audiences intensifies, will undoubtedly follow the same path. The BBC, although supposedly above such vulgar matters, is as subject to the market as anyone else because its production costs are fixed by the general communications market, and because if the BBC's share of the audience drops much below 50 per cent then it becomes difficult to justify the licence fee. The role of BBC Enterprises in selling programmes on the international market is becoming an important supplement to overall BBC income, and if the satellite BBC channel is by subscription, then the Corporation will be even less immune to the market system than it is now. It will therefore be increasingly subject to the general process in which 'market forces exclude all [material] except the most commercially successful' and which is not 'random but systematically excludes those voices lacking economic power or resources' (Graham Murdock and Peter Golding, 1977). Sadly the statutory defences against such a dynamic are progressively weakening, as witnessed by the retreat of Channel 4 discussed earlier.

Teaching the processes of capital control can concentrate on this selling of audiences as a means to raising the wider phenomenon.

Audience research. Scheduling exercises will have introduced students to a consideration of broadcasters' attempts to maximise the audience. This needs to be extended into a consideration of how the schedules complement the needs of advertisers to reach certain audiences. Audience research is conducted for the institutions by the Broadcasting Audience Research Board (BARB).[15]

Students can produce their own audience research on an

evening's or week's viewing in their own family or through street interviews. The results can be compared to the findings of BARB for that evening, perhaps focusing on differences in viewing habits according to age or gender.

Family scheduling. Such discussion will probably lead into discussion of how the schedule is constructed around the family – or rather the institutions' conception of the family audience. Schedulers take it as axiomatic that the audience is

> maximised by constructing particular family viewing patterns in the 'domestic situation' – this is how to aggregate the 'popular' audience for offer to advertisers. At the heart of this strategy is a particular analysis of the domestic – the ideology of the home as haven, the notion of family as site and agent of socialisation . . . the schedule singles out the dominant 'voice' of the family at specific times in order to ensure the maximum audience. Whether or not this is a conscious policy, it nonetheless underlies the conventional practices of both the BBC and the commercial companies. (Richard Paterson, 1980)

Schedules can be analysed to see what their assumptions are (including the daytime schedules directed at 'women and children') and tested by devising alternative schedules for a 'working mother' or 'unemployed father'.[16]

Advertising. Advertising practices can be analysed by the selective recording of adverts on breakfast television, in the afternoon and early evening, and Channel 4 and ITV mainstream programming (C4's adverts are generally considerably more upmarket). Worksheets can also be devised with students being 'time and space' buyers where they are given a series of adverts with different target audiences and asked to place them in a schedule. This can be elaborated by the introduction of spending allocations and prices for different viewing times.

Stereotyping. The imperative for audience maximisation is centrally implicated in the representations produced and circulated by the media. Texts have to be sufficiently new or different for us to want to consume them, yet they also have to be sufficiently familiar to the audiences' expectations for the producers to guarantee a sufficient audience size for the artefact's commodity value to be realised. This means that the supply of representations is extremely limiting and repetitive, with frequent stereotyping and reliance on narrative. Invaluable here is the BFI pack, *Selling Pictures*, which links stereotyping as 'an ideological process which obscures fundamental arrangements in society' to the economic needs of the media companies which produce such representations.

Stars. Another media strategy for maximising the audience is the reliance on media celebrities or 'stars'. A considerable body of work has developed in Film Studies around teaching the functioning of the star system in Hollywood cinema.[17] TV and radio have also produced their miniature version of the stars, with fan clubs, elite status and the other accoutrements of stardom. The difference is that unlike cinema stars, TV personalities usually play 'themselves' rather than appearing in fictional roles. Yet the functioning of 'Bruce Forsyth', 'Cilla Black', or 'Terry Wogan' is analogous to the functioning of 'Paul Newman' or 'Meryl Streep' in the cinema. Both have a commodity value in terms of giving media producers a 'banker' in guaranteeing a large audience, and also have an ideological role in embodying and containing certain ideological tensions. Selina Scott and Anna Ford embody social tension about female roles as both 'independent career women' and yet also 'feminine women' who are attractive to men. (Anna Ford's status is especially problematic, as shown in hostile press coverage when she has attacked sexism in television.) By teaching such 'stars', links can be made by the students between the media institutions and the representation of women. Alternatively, perhaps, the career of Terry Wogan might be analysed as an example of how a star image is constructed, moving from a radio star because of being a 'sexy' male voice in the (female) home, then used for advertising directed at women (Flora), then as 'Uncle Terry' for the BBC appeal 'Children in Need', and presently developing the show-biz profile in his own chatshow *Wogan*.

Allocative control: the state

The state's allocatory control over media institutions is

3   Christine Fitzmaurice

conventionally represented as being the operation of public accountability. While the state is clearly subject to public pressures, it has always used its allocatory control of media institutions more to defend the interests of the ruling-class formation it represents than those of the public. While it has cheerfully allowed the concentration of ownership in Fleet Street to kill off even a facade of diversity in opinion (Mrs Thatcher personally intervened to stop Rupert Murdoch's takeover of Times Newspapers being referred to the Monopolies Commission), by choosing not to use its powers to intervene to prevent such a process, it has not hesitated to use its power to prevent the dissemination of information and opinion hostile to ruling-class interests.

This is partially performed through the maintenance and use of laws and official practices which are inimical to the production of material the state would rather keep to itself, such as the Official Secrets Act and the D-Notice system (which is an *ad hoc* restriction on the reporting of security matters agreed between editors and the Ministry of Defence). Other laws such as the Obscene Publications Act (1959) and the Video Recordings Act (1984), by which every video has to be submitted for viewing and possible censorship by an officially appointed censor before being distributed (acts which are legitimated as being concerned with pornographic or 'violent' material), can be used to justify the harassment of anyone producing and distributing material deemed to be culturally 'deviant', as in the repeated use of the powers of the Obscene Publications Act to raid gay bookshops and confiscate material.

These negative and repressive forms of power, however, are less significant than the state's ideological power as the 'official voice' of society. The media use the state as a primary source of information and, more often than not, an issue is defined with the state's interpretation, while its spokespersons have privileged access to the media as of right, unlike other sections of society. In the words of a BBC executive, 'I certainly feel that the Army, as the lawful and useful arm of the state, must be given a right to speak its voice and version of things to the people of the state through the public broadcasting system' (quoted in Philip Schlesinger, 1978, p.225).

It should also be noted that the state is not above using its status to disseminate what can only be described as state propaganda or misinformation. Liz Curtis describes how Army public relations officers have planted fake stories in the press about [Irish] Republican violence and activities – all in the cause of 'psyops', the psychological operation needed by a modern army in a war situation (Liz Curtis, 1984a).

During the Falklands/Malvinas War the Ministry of Defence regularly misinformed journalists about military operations. Indeed, the media were subject to 'psyops' when one paper ran a fictitious story about the exploits of the Special Boat Service in the invasion of South Georgia following an official 'planted' story. However, as one journalist put it,

> the episodes which caused the most disquiet . . . were not necessarily unique to the Falklands crisis. The instinctive secrecy of the military and the Civil service; the prostitution and hysteria of sections of the press; the lies, the misinformation, the manipulation of public opinion by the authorities; the political intimidation of broadcasters; the ready connivance of the media at their own distortion . . . all these occur as much in normal peace time in Britain as in war. (Robert Harris, 1983, p.151)

The state's relationship with the media cannot be reduced to such practices, since its control of the broadcasting system is far more extensive than the above outline indicates. The state's allocatory role in broadcasting is legitimised through the valid argument that those bodies designated to use scarce frequencies should be publicly accountable. But, as Garnham points out, 'the state has from the start used its powers in a non-technical and restrictive manner to reinforce central control' (Nicholas Garnham, 1973, p.17). These state controls are constitutionalised in the form of the BBC's Royal Charter and its licence, and the Acts which give the IBA its statutory powers. These allow the use of the frequencies for broadcasting; in return they have to guarantee editorial impartiality and balance and the maintenance of standards of good taste and decency. Theoretically these rights can be withdrawn, but a more effective sanction is the state's power to use the licence fee and the levy as a form of economic control. In effect this system amounts to what Garnham calls 'an unwritten contract' between broadcaster and state:

> The state says to the institution, 'You may use these frequencies to broadcast what you like, so long as you maintain standards of which we approve. These standards are to be those of the Establishment and are defined as impartiality and objectivity in factual coverage of political and social affairs and as good taste in less contentious areas.' The institution then says to its employees, 'You are responsible creative broadcasters. Feel free to broadcast as you see fit so long as you maintain the highest standards of impartiality, objectivity and good taste.'
> (Nicholas Garnham, 1973, p.31)

The allocatory terms of this unwritten contract are formally and informally mediated down the hierarchy into the operational level. The top executives of the BBC and ITV companies are accountable to the Governors and the IBA, who, beneath the rhetoric of the separation of powers, are drawn from the same ruling-class formation as the rest of society's elite. The pyramid of power extends down to the production staff through the practice of referring up, in which producers refer any controversial decision to their superior, who may then refer on upwards. For instance, any BBC programme on Northern Ireland has to be cleared *before* production commences by the Northern Ireland Controller. In practice, producers gradually internalise the parameters laid down by the state so that self-censorship begins to operate at an early level in the production process.

This contract normally works to the mutual satisfaction of media and state. Its evident weakness is that terms such as 'objectivity' can only function within a consensus about what constitutes the boundary of legitimate debate. When the legitimacy of the State's own actions are challenged in times of acute crisis that consensus breaks down, there is a collapse of hegemony which can only be retrieved by the state attempting to withdraw the relative autonomy normally allowed. The General Strike, foreign adventures such as the Falklands/Malvinas War and Suez, the nuclear issue, Northern Ireland, industrial violence, extra-Parliamentary political activities: these are the areas in which the consensus supposed to underlie British social democracy breaks down.

The Glasgow University Media Group, in their book *War and Peace News* (1985), reveal the minutes of the BBC Editorial meetings during the Falklands/Malvinas War. These include directives to ban interviews (including phone-ins) with bereaved relatives unless of men given posthumous awards. The minutes show how the BBC progressively institutionally internalised the Government's representation of the Falklands as a just war. One executive reminds colleagues that the BBC is the '*British* Broadcasting Corporation'. In 1985 the Glasgow Group wanted to reproduce extracts from the minutes on a BBC2 *Open Space* programme. The BBC refused and also cut the two minutes of 'blank screen' which the Group intended to leave on instead of the missing material. This response indicates broadcasters' sensitivity to criticism of their coverage of acute social conflict.

When the consensus breaks down the broadcasting institutions are left in an exposed position which they have always retrieved by adopting the State's definition of why the breakdown occurred. Or, as Lord Reith famously defined such a policy at the time of the General Strike:

> . . . since the BBC was a national institution . . . and since the Government in the crisis was acting for the people . . . the BBC was for the Government in the crisis too.

Northern Ireland has been particularly problematic because as the Army became integrated into the Protestant structure of the Northern Irish state in repressing the Catholics, so the state's policy became the 'criminalisation' of the IRA which meant that the media should represent them as 'alien' to the Catholic community.

The broadcasters' policy was defined by a government Minister, Christopher Chataway, in 1971; he argued that the BBC should not be balanced between the Army and the 'terrorists' because while 'nobody wants propaganda substituted for truthful reporting . . . it would be just as obnoxious to have the soldier and the murderer treated like the employer and the trade unionist – as if they were moral equals'. Lord Hill, the BBC Governor of the time, elaborated on this state directive: 'between the British army and the gunmen the BBC is not and cannot be impartial' (Philip Schlesinger, 1978, pp.212–13).

Northern Ireland is the paradigm of the relationship between broadcasting and the state, as their normally covert links are exposed whenever the broadcasters look like showing a programme which challenges the state even in a very limited way. The archives of the broadcasting institutions are full of banned programmes from the 1970s; others were re-edited or postponed, while many never got further than the 'offer' stage. Following the 1979 outcry at the BBC for interviewing an INLA representative after the death of Airey Neave, there are now rigid rules effectively banning any interviews with 'terrorist' groups (which have posed problems since the electoral advances of Sinn Fein), and the state has let it be known it would consider proceedings under the Prevention of Terrorism Act against any offending broadcasters who might contact the 'enemy'.

State anxiety is not exclusively focused on Northern Ireland. The BBC's celebrated banning of *The War Game* in 1965 was the first in a series of incidents where the state has expressed concern about an unhealthy public interest in mass destruction. In 1983, Michael Heseltine, as Minister of Defence, successfully bullied Yorkshire TV into allowing him a right of reply to a screening of the American film *The Day After* (ABC TV, 20 November 1983). The IBA insisted that John Pilger's *The Truth Game* (Central TV, 1983) about the propaganda of the pro-nuclear lobby be 'balanced by a documentary putting the other case' to be done by Max Hastings. Other cases of IBA interference have been the cutting of a sequence advocating violent direct action against vivisection in *The Animals Film* (1982), the withdrawal of Ken Loach's four films entitled *A Question Of Leadership* because of imbalance in presenting rank-and-file criticisms of union leaders (1983–4), and ordering Granada to cut a sequence from a *World in Action* on Oman which dealt with the Thatchers' involvement in business deals there, despite clearance from Granada's lawyers (1984).[18]

Disturbingly, such instances of overt intervention by the state or its appointed delegates seem to be increasing, along with a general shift towards a new authoritarianism. However, it would be a misrepresentation to leave a picture of the state's allocatory control being primarily the corporate ego restraining the tempestuous desires of individual broadcasters for expressive freedom. What needs to be analysed is how that control is mediated into operational control.

Operational control

Media workers have a considerable degree of autonomy in their work. Only the crassest form of reductionism would reduce the production of media artefacts into a mere ideological assembly line. Professional and technical practices such as the conventions of news journalism, the reliance on the codes of realism and narrative, or the technological defence of technical 'standards' of the video image, are all significant determinations on the meanings an audience will produce from any given text. However, it is important to recognise how these operational practices are related to the allocatory requirements of capital and state.

Division of labour. The existence of media texts as commodities means that they are produced within an industrialised system of a highly specialised division of labour. This applies particularly to newspapers and television:

> Broadcast TV is geared to producing a series commodity consisting of a number . . . of individual programmes which have a high degree of similarity. The production of these commodities is organised on industrial lines. The tasks involved are specified and personnel are organised into various grades responsible for a particular task or tasks. The tasks involved are standardised as much as possible to provide the maximum interchangeability of labour. (John Ellis, 1982, p.222)

Media production is not just divided into management and labour; there is a further division of the production process, primarily based on class and gender lines, between 'creative' production staff and 'technical' staff. Producers and directors are responsible for the content and overall style of the programmes and are 'serviced' by technical personnel who implement their 'creative' ideas – there is an analogous distinction between journalists and printers. The technicians cope with a considerable degree of alienation through an allegiance to 'technicism' which judges the final product purely in terms of technical criteria such as colour balance, lighting or electronic effects, with no regard for editorial criteria.

This division of labour has the pernicious effect of dividing media workers into a bewildering variety of unions, thus reducing their overall strategic power in negotiation with employers. Moreover, technicism has had the particularly unfortunate effect of setting very limited 'economistic' aims for the unions:

> the concentration on matters of grading and of wages by the television unions had led to an attitude which maintains that what is sometimes called the 'nitty-gritty' of industrial life is the only aspect of trade union activity that matters . . . and that therefore there is no question of their using their power politically by blacking screens, for instance, when programmes are attacking the workers, supporting racism and sexism, or slandering the trade union movement. (Stuart Hood, 1983, p.34)

This 'divide and rule' policy has been increasingly challenged recently, especially by the Fleet Street print unions, who have refused to print or distribute particularly blatant reactionary coverage (an intervention attacked as an infringement of 'editorial freedom'). The emergence of the Campaign for Press and Broadcasting Freedom in 1979 as a broad Left alliance of unionists, Labour politicians and media workers has widened the agenda of the media unions considerably. However, even in the unlikely event of its demands for industrial democracy in the media being implemented, a fundamental political problem would remain:

> Might there not be a profound contradiction between 'worker participation with elections to departmental head level, with union representatives on the boards of each organisation' and broader notions of social accountability and control? Can one assume a simple correspondence of interest between highly-paid workers in the industry . . . and the wider viewing public, or constituent groups pushing for greater representation within TV? (Carl Gardner and Julie Sheppard, 1984)

Professionalism. The working ideology, embracing technicism, of 'professionalism', is the primary means of mediating the state's allocatory control of broadcasting into the operational level. 'Professionalism' is a new ideology which emerged, especially within the BBC, at the end of the 1950s as its previous cultural hegemony was eroded with the coming of commercial television and a general dissolution of post-war cultural consensus. This represented a fundamental shift in the perceived purpose of broadcasting from Reith's aim of 'lifting the British nation to new moral and cultural heights' (professionalism being a means to an end) to where professionalism is 'the prime virtue of the communicator' (Krishan Kumar, 1977, p.232). This process is interrelated with the state's requirement for balance and impartiality, as professionalism designates the function of the broadcaster to be the empty vessel for the spirit of society to pass through, the pluralistic means of disseminating every strand of opinion. David Attenborough, in his earlier incarnation as BBC Director of Television Programmes, likened broadcasting to a 'theatre'; the task of the theatre staff is to 'find from society . . . a whole selection of voices – the most prophetic, the most significant, the most amusing, the most dramatic, the most typical – and to enable those voices to be heard in that theatre' (quoted by Kumar, 1977, p.246).

Consequently, broadcasting necessarily adopts particular codes and conventions such as realism (a window on the world) and narrative (just telling it how it happened) in order to render its own practices as transparent. Only 'amateurs' have microphones in shot, or jumpcuts, or other signs of the production process. Professionalism represents its own practices as the mere construction of a neutral arena in which they just take 'professional' decisions about making 'good television': aesthetic conventions of film and studio practice; assessments of the personalities involved; the presenter's delivery or handling of an interview; or running to time and not 'boring' the audience. These criteria are seen, and *believed*, to be ideologically neutral, a mere channelling of reality into the home. So professionalism is always marshalled as a defence from the state or other interested parties. The professional must not be seen to identify with any social group or ideological position in society, and accordingly is ' "taking the role" of "us" as the "unrepresented", the "consumers", the "suffering public", the victims of planners and public servants of all kinds, as well as of large industrialists, selfish trade unions, property speculators and the like' (Kumar, 1977, p.247). But, paradoxically, this public persona of representing 'us' reproduces the state's own representation of itself as a neutral structure which transcends political differences between sections of society. Just as the state is above capital and labour, differences of race, gender and age, so is the professional broadcaster – whereas in fact, just like the state, broadcasting is a deeply engaged partisan:

> Television journalism does not accomplish [its] work of reproduction by being 'biased', as this has been defined by the conspiracy thesis. It is not accomplished *despite* the basic editorial criteria, but rather precisely in and through their practical implementation. It is because this policy is put into practice that a complex unity is forged between the accounts produced by television and these primary accounts which are constituted in the social formation as the dominant, sometimes hegemonic, definitions of political-economic antagonisms. (Ian Connell, 1980)

Teaching some of the processes of institutional control through work on news is well established in media studies.[19] Teaching about censorship obviously presents problems for many teachers because what the media institutions have deemed to be too offensive for circulation to audiences will arouse a similar reaction from educational institutions. Northern Ireland especially may be a problematic area for many teachers, but, should the institutional space exist, no other area of censorship raises so many questions about the essence of media control. *The British Media and Ireland*, produced by the Campaign for Free Speech on Ireland, although now quite dated, contains a wealth of material on the subject. Contextualised screenings of banned programmes concerned with other issues, such as *The War Game*, where considerable documentation exists of the institutional arguments which preceded the banning,[20] can provide students with ideas about how institutions function. Peter Watkins's film is especially useful as it raises other questions about how television as an institution worries when the boundaries which demarcate 'fact' and 'fiction' are blurred. (Other 'dramadocs' such as *The Death of a Princess* (9 April 1980) would stimulate similar discussion.) There are also a number of films and television programmes available which discuss or dramatise the processes of control in ways that can be used to stimulate discussion. A particularly valuable example, but unfortunately now difficult to obtain, was Channel 4's *Acceptable Levels* (30 April 1984), which shows how professionalism's definition of 'good television' acts as an insidious form of self-censorship. Finally, it should be stressed perhaps that the issue of censorship, although it has obvious 'sensational' appeal, should only be taught within a programme of work directed at analysis of how the routine processes of television production and distribution are in themselves inevitably a form of censorship.[21]

Alternatives

As a class's knowledge of institutional determinations increases, so the teacher can introduce them more to both textual analysis and practical work. However, the fundamental problem in teaching media institutions, beyond obvious practical difficulties, is that one merely ends up reinforcing a sense of existing institutions being the only ones possible and that they now form an overwhelming and irremovable mass in the minds of students. Consequently we would reiterate that in all our teaching about institutions, the possibilities of alternatives must be continually raised, which involves providing some sense of institutional history and consideration of existing alternative media practices.

While the use of archive material can be deployed as a defamiliarisation exercise to remind students that media institutions have a history, it is also possible to devise simulations for older students where they can 'act out' some of the historically determining moments in the formation of our present institutions. The class divides into 'committees', who are charged with the task of devising an institutional structure for, say, broadcasting when it first started (formation of the BBC) or the formation of commercial television. The discussions thus stimulated will raise most of the political issues involved with the concomitant recognition that institutional forms are determined by wider social forces.

If there is time and space within the course it is also crucially important to 'problematise' the structures of British broadcasting by introducing accounts of the broadcasting structures of other countries. A useful introduction here is the fifth and final programme in Thames TV's *Understanding TV* series, 'A Different System: Dutch TV', which offers an account of broadcasting in the country which, with some justification, claims to possess the most democratically accountable system of broadcasting in the world.[22]

The independent sector

All the dominant media institutions have spawned rival alternative media systems which are concerned with challenging their cultural and political hegemony. Radical newspapers and magazines (such as *City Limits, Spare Rib, Outwrite, Hackney People's Press, Leeds Other Paper, West Highland Free Press*), with a tradition derived from the radical working-class press of the nineteenth century, continue to struggle against the press monopolies. The Hollywood-dominated cinema is challenged by independent cinema; television and radio by independent video and radio workshops. A few independent record labels survive from the heady days of 1976 and the 'punk explosion'.

'Independent' is, of course, a misnomer, as no media can function independently of some social formation. 'Independence' refers more to an independence from the profit imperative of the large corporations and companies. The independent sector is heavily dependent upon subsidisation, either from state bodies such as the Arts Council, the BFI, Channel 4 and local government, or from the committed financial and ideological support of a specific audience (as well as considerable unpaid labour). While it is simplistic to try and embrace all the media production and distribution outside the dominant institutions as being either 'independent' or 'alternative', it is possible to outline a set of common concerns centring on the evolution of a radically different set of production and distribution practices and a concern for formal innovation and experiment.

Whereas the dominant media work through a hierarchical division of labour, the independent sector tries to work in a more collective and democratic manner in which the 'production group tends to replace the production crew' (Sylvia Harvey, 1981). The corollary of this is attempting to break down the dominant pattern of a centralised and unaccountable production centre producing for an undifferentiated mass audience and instead to involve the audience in the production and distribution phases as well as consumption. Most independent products are intended for a specific audience, defined by locality or common social or political concerns, thus allowing the dissolution of the usual communicative hierarchy between producer and audience in favour of a two-way communication process. For instance, film-makers would involve the participants in a film in decisions about the production and might well exhibit the film where there was space made available for audience discussion and feedback.

The other independent concern has been with formal innovation. This is particularly pronounced in the independent film sector, which was heavily influenced by the cultural politics of 1968 in France and the experiments set up by the Dziga-Vertov film group which centred around Jean-Luc Godard. This influence is embodied in a concentration on the formal means of -representation, which are conceived as having a politics of their own – the idea that conservative 'form' is inimical to a radical text no matter how radical the 'content'. Consequently this type of film eschews realism and narrative and other dominant media conventions in favour of a Brechtian distancing of the spectator from the film, where 'ideas and arguments [are presented] in such a way that the spectator is invited and encouraged to take part in the work of assessing and analysing these ideas'. However, Sylvia Harvey goes on to warn that 'the problem with some of these films has been that they have been issued more as a challenge than as an invitation to their audience [causing] the spectator either mentally or physically to leave the field, to refuse engagement (Harvey, 1981).

We are certainly not advocating the use of such a body of work as a form of magical palliative to dominant media practice, as an ideological injection. Such texts should be subjected to the same process of critical interrogation as any other media text.[23] However, independent texts do provide a potentially valuable resource for teachers who can use them comparatively with dominant ones, perhaps with a similar theme, to stimulate discussion on the ways in which different modes of production result in radically different texts.

Ultimately the independent sector has one immense advantage as a teaching resource, providing evidence of an alternative form of media practice. It is unlikely that many students will express a preference for its productions over those of the dominant media, but that should not be its purpose. Its purpose is the same as all teaching of media institutions: to enable students to understand that the present institutions are the product of history and represent a particular way of ordering a social formation, and as such are subject to change.

3   Realism

'Cinema is not the reflection of reality, but the reality of that reflection' – Jean-Luc Godard

If we aim to enable students to assess critically the workings of the real world by our teaching about the media, then the concept of realism needs to be addressed. In a sense it is inaccurate to write or think about *the* concept of realism, for there are and have been many different ways of conceptualising how the 'real' might be constituted. Media artefacts can be analysed in terms of two kinds of relationships. The first is a mimetic one which any media artefact purports to have with the world it represents. Was London really the way Dickens depicted it in *Bleak House*, or was the BBC serialised adaptation more faithful to an historical 'reality'? How far do schools match their portrayal in David Leland's television drama *Birth of a Nation* (Central, 19 June 1983)? Do the media really tell it how it is? Mimesis between artefact and world has provided not only the central problem for art and literary criticism since the sixteenth century, but has also been what most artists have striven for and the yardstick by which audiences have measured artistic achievement.

The second relationship is the one we might construct between one media artefact and another. Do the westerns directed by John Ford share similar features which might be attributable to his 'authorship'? What kinds of cultural references are being called upon when we see Peter Davidson (an erstwhile *Dr Who* Doctor) in a commercial for Prestige saucepans? What relationships can we construct between the *Bleak House* of Dickens' novel and the television adaptation?

Most discussion and writing about the media has revolved around the question of realism. To describe a film as being 'realistic' is also to pass affirmative judgement. The film is good because it appears to be 'true to life'. We might describe such

94

evaluations as offering 'common sense criteria' because such criteria are rarely questioned – they seem to be self-evident. However, the realism that is the 'fidelity to life' has various criteria based on aesthetics which are determined by historical and technological contexts. Within those contexts artefacts have been produced by those who work within traditional conventions and styles, preserving their art against attack by those who have adopted new strategies and practices, claiming that they are creating works more realistic than the old. The Cubists, for instance, insisted that the multi-faceted representations of the planes of an object on a two-dimensional surface were more 'realistic' than the use of the conventional monocular perspective. In the word 'realism' multifarious meanings and connotations are impacted.

Having come to this recognition, we are going to try and distinguish various meanings more clearly so that we can be more precise about our use of the word 'realism'. A more precise understanding on our part as teachers should in turn help us define our aims in teaching about realism and the media more clearly.

One group of students might consider a fast-moving, action-packed series, sprinkled with just the right amount of violence, to be more 'realistic' than another. *Miami Vice* could be considered 'realistic' in these terms. Another group of students might consider Ken Loach's *Looks and Smiles* (1981) to be 'realistic' because of its black and white grainy look at the more gritty aspects of life. In both cases aesthetic criteria are being used alongside criteria based on pre-existing knowledge of the media and of their codes and conventions of representation. Different codes and conventions have been acceptable at particular historical times. Impressionism and surrealism both strove, although in radically different ways, to articulate relations with the 'real' more clearly than had been done before. In addition to these aesthetic codings, however, there are also technological ones. In the case of film and television, technological codings of the 'real' have developed in two ways.

In the feature film industry and in television drama technological developments have aimed to increase versimilitude by heightening and accentuating the 'real' to the extent of making it more of a spectacle. The introduction of sound, then stereo and Dolby sound, deep focus, colour, wide screen, 3D, multi-camera operation – all have been considered to reveal more of the real. Paradoxically, the more special effects a film has, the more 'realistic' it is sometimes held to be! Technological developments in documentary film and television programme-making, on the other hand, have been rather different. The introduction of increasingly lighter equipment, faster film stock (reducing the need for lights), better sound recording equipment, and ENG (electronic news gathering) cameras have all encouraged many documentarists to believe that they could be more 'true to life'. Needing fewer crew and possessing lighter equipment, they might intrude less on people and situations they observe and record.

Implicit in all these strivings towards and arguments for a greater realism, is the notion that it is somehow both aesthetically and technologically possible to open a window on to the world. Implicit is the idea that the real can be perceived through the transparency of the medium which readily presents it. At the time of their invention, both photography and moving film images did mark pinnacles in the mimetic endeavour. 'From today painting is dead' was the slogan which indicated for painters from the 1830s onwards that they had been freed from the responsibility of portraying the world as faithfully as their skill allowed. They could simply hand over their enterprise to the mechanical modes of reproduction. It was recognised that however 'realistic', a painting must still of necessity be a form of hieroglyph if only because a three-dimensional world is being represented on a two-dimensional canvas, but this recognition did not enter film debates. Instead it was assumed that because the camera offered a mechanical means of recording the world within a time continuum, the 'subjective' viewpoint of the film-maker was no longer a considerable factor in this apparently straightforward recording of reality. However, it is now clear that the age of mechanical and electronic reproduction has done no more than complicate what is essentially the same problem. In the same way that the painter's perceptions, knowledge, techniques and materials are all brought into play in the production of a new work, so too the film and television-makers choose camera positions, angles, exposures and lenses and, more importantly, they are responsible for editing and dubbing the footage after it has been shot.

These aesthetic and technological codings and conventions, various in cultural and historical contexts, re-present what is conceptualised as 'the real'. They do not simply give or present the real world to us, the audience. Media are material. What we mean by realist aesthetics are those sets of codings and conventions which deny the materiality of their medium and the perceptions which disregard it. Realist practices apparently reveal the real to us while making invisible the processes whereby that revelation is made possible. In teaching about the media, we have to understand the implications and presumptions of such practices and perceptions.

To begin, we have to understand why the obvious appears to be so, perhaps in some cases by making it seem strange, unfamiliar. Photographic (and even pictorial) images have generally been considered to correspond more closely to the 'real' than either the written or the spoken word. A photograph of a dog, for instance, is taken to signify a real dog more immediately than the sight or sound of the word 'dog'. And whereas different languages signify dog differently, an image will supposedly signify across themselves and what they represent. They are, to use Barthes' terms, more 'motivated' signifiers than the 'arbitrary' signification of language. The image appears to be more realistic and therefore more accessible. The success of early silent cinema in New York has been partly attributed to the fact that it had a ready-made audience in the large number of immigrants, many of whom were illiterate and most of whom knew no English. The apparent transparency of the image, its more direct relation with what it represents, offers a 'promise' of the real which language does not. Images are not the same as the 'real', but they can appear so much like it that they are almost as good. Surely some of the pleasures of looking at photographs, of watching television or cinema screens, is based on our recognition of the promise of the 'real' which images beam out to us. The pleasure experienced is one of constant anticipation, because alongside it lies the knowledge that the promise can never be fulfilled.

We have already argued here that 'reality' is re-presented; it cannot be simply presented or revealed. No 'reality' is ever independent of any signifying process – we can only make sense of the real by means of the language we use to describe and explain it and by the examples and images we use to illustrate it.

The image appears more 'realistic' because it seems to have a more direct relation with what it represents than language does; its realism allows us to believe in it almost as the thing itself.

The philosopher C. S. Pierce elaborated the distinctions between signifiers into what he termed the iconic, the indexical and the symbolic. Language is symbolic in that words only stand for what they represent. There is no reason, other than that it is conventionally agreed by English-speaking people, that a table should be so named. An index has a more direct connection with what it represents: an item of clothing may point to a particular lifestyle or belief, a sneeze might indicate a cold or hayfever. The iconic sign actually bears a resemblance to what it represents – a map, a photograph, a road sign indicating a roundabout. It is the iconic nature of the photographic image which, partly because it can be compared with more symbolic systems of signification, allows us to think of it as being somehow more 'real'.

In contrast to photographs in newspapers and magazines or images on the cinema screen, images on television promise to deliver a 'real' more immediately and even, on occasion, 'live'. Television seems to be able to guarantee the 'truth' of its images and sounds because they are moving and because they claim an actuality. The moving images on a television screen offer a promise of the 'real' different to that offered by moving images in the cinema. Their movement is not restricted to a particular narrative entity, but flows in Britain almost throughout the day on four different channels. In this sense the movement of television images is far less limited than that of cinema images. Television is part of our daily lives and its images pass us on the screen in living rooms, bedrooms and kitchens. Television images are literally part of the furniture, whereas going to the cinema for most people means a night out, a special treat. The familiarity of the TV set, the habit of watching television, or at least having it switched on, offers not so much a promise of the 'real' as an affirmation of its presence. The images are here with us now, as they usually are. The immediate and constant presence of television images makes them seem more 'real' than those in a magazine or on the cinema screen, whose presence proclaims their absence as soon as the page is turned, as soon as the film is over. Television is not only 'actual' in the sense that it is part of the very fabric of our daily routines and conversations, but also because to guarantee the 'truth' it has to pronounce itself continually anew. Television relies on its dependability, its familiarity *and* on its ability to give us the latest, to relay what is actually happening out there, to our domestic spaces, here and now.

The here-and-nowness of television enables it to become 'natural', almost too obvious to be questioned. Even horrific or outlandish images and sounds become part of a day's and then a week's viewing routine. In order for televisual representations of the real to appear as 'real', to correspond apparently exactly, then they must be able to deny their own status as products. They must be able to deny that they are re-presenting a part in a particular way. It is this denial of a production process, posing as the 'obvious' and natural, which is a realist mode of production.

If, in our teaching of the media, we aim to acknowledge those modes of production as material, then we must also recognise that the realism television professes is not a singular kind. There are various televisual realisms, and audiences easily recognise the distinctions between them. The decision to watch and/or tape a boxing match, a pop concert, a drama documentary or an episode of a favourite soap opera recognises a range of distinct realisms which television offers. The recognition is as familiar as television is ordinary. In the course of this chapter we shall examine only three television realisms: the realism of documentary, of drama and of actuality. We shall also suggest possible ways of teaching about them. We shall also discuss ways of teaching about the still image which might begin to raise questions among students as to how 'real' realist representations are.

The image

René Magritte's painting *Ceci n'est pas une pipe* proclaims the painting as material, not the object it represents. Beneath a scrupulously authentic rendering of a pipe is written 'ceci n'est pas une pipe' (this is not a pipe). And, of course, it's not; it's merely a representation of a pipe, a painting using codes of realist painting to depict a solid item of three dimensions on canvas in two dimensions. Any photograph which could generally be considered to be 'of something' could be captioned in the same

4

way – we offer an example of commercial advertisement which 'plays' with this idea. Students could be asked about the ways in which lighting, camera position, focus, etc. represent the object in a 'realist' way and then be asked to explain what they think the caption 'this is not a . . .' means. The idea that representations are in fact the realities with which we deal when studying the media can in this way be introduced. Different representations of the same object can elucidate this point: a photograph of a house, a painting of it, a written description, a ceramic or plasticine model, a cartoon, all these could be produced by students themselves. On display they can be returned to the point of different representations, as different realities can be constantly reiterated.

The limitations of the camera as an all-seeing eye which can simply reproduce reality must be taught if the iconic is not to be accepted as equivalent to the real. The same, still object, photographed under different lighting conditions, from different angles, distances and focal lengths, framed differently and using different film stock, can show how a single reality can be represented photographically in so many different ways. No one photograph is necessarily more real than any other.

Most single-lens reflex still cameras are sold with a 50 or 55mm lens, which is commonly held to be the lens giving a field of vision closest to that of normal human sight. It is important to note, however, that this is the case for landscape-type pictures. For portraitures such a lens is considered to make the nose appear too big, and therefore a lens in the 80–120mm range is preferred. Taking photographs using interchangeable lenses (e.g. 28mm and 135mm) can point to the ways in which familiar modes of representation have been naturalised.

Here it can be taught that realism is based on particular conventions of signifying practices, that it is itself a particular ideological and historical construction. The conventions of pictorial perspective 'developed during the Renaissance' proportion objects to a size similar to how they would appear if seen by a spectator with normal binocular vision: large objects look small if they are distant from the point of vision; items actually smaller may be represented as apparently larger if closer to the point of observation. These conventions of perspective forge particular relations between the observer and the observed. The observer has the field of vision, the eye sees and the brain has knowledge of the whole painting. The observer is in a position of mastery, all the more controlling if one actually owns the painting. Of course, we can now all own photographic reproductions of paintings! We can accept these conventions as 'natural', but visual artists of the Middle Ages would have been outraged: they painted a world in which relative size indicated relative importance. Surrealist artists like Magritte refused to make their modes of representation problematic ones. Magritte's train emerging from a fireplace (*Time Transfixed*) not only disturbs the conventions of perspective (the train is a good deal smaller than the fireplace) but also disturbs the observer, preventing him or her from having knowledge or mastery of the picture in the way that realist conventions allow.

5   René Magritte, *Time Transfixed* (1932)

So in teaching about the ways in which images construct meanings for us we should not simply focus all our attention on images themselves. They also have to be understood in terms of the relationships they construct with their spectators and in terms of the contexts of their production, exhibition and circulation. By way of introducing the idea that images carry extra textual meanings, it might be useful to consider the various significations of a single image (a) in a newspaper, (b) on television, and (c) in a film at the cinema. News photographs are often circulated in this way: media variables of the Iranian Embassy siege in 1980 provide good examples for teaching.[1] The factors which determine the selection of particular photographs for newspapers – picture size, ideological emphases on the event, the personalities, the moment, etc. – all these need to be explored first. The layout of a newspaper page, the captions, headlines, adjacent articles, will also have some bearing on the meanings a newspaper photograph might carry. Comparing photographs from a selection of dailies treating the same news 'story' can often be revealing. Students can also cover a local event themselves with cameras, each selecting a single photograph (or part of a photograph) from the set of contact sheets the class has produced. The teaching pack, *Choosing the News*, offers materials that can be used to stimulate (and thereby investigate) the processes whereby copy, captions, headlines and photographs are chosen for particular ideological reasons and because of particular economic constraints.

Newspapers rely on television for news stories more than vice versa. (The extent to which they do so is in itself an area worth studying.) Television stories are often themselves defined as news: the most notable examples recently have been the *Coronation Street* 'scandals' and a child's liver transplant engineered by the *'That's Life'* team. The single moment newspaper photographs capture often serve to recall the moving pictures repeatedly shown on television from the evening before. Again, the immediacy of television guarantees the realism of its pictures. News photographs of WPC Yvonne Fletcher, shot outside the Libyan Embassy, are a case in point. Centre-page spread photographs showed they had been taken from video pictures on freeze-frame. A split second can literally be defined as a news event in this way. On occasion, television will use newspaper photographs to recall history. When television needs to document a time pre-television, the newspaper photograph assumes a realism which it now lacks in comparison. But certain photographs have come to stand for events, and more recently the captured moment which newspapers can offer in the still image, having been taken from film footage, are re-circulated by television to mobilise memories. The South Vietnamese police chief about to shoot a suspect, the Royal Wedding kiss on Buckingham Palace balcony, Neil Armstrong's first steps on the moon, these need no explanation. They are reference points known well enough to be able to trigger memories which television and newspapers constructed for us in the first place. Feature films often depend on the ways in which newspapers and television have mobilised visual memories so they can appear, in comparison, to offer a bigger and better account, at once claiming accuracy, but explaining away 'distortion' as part of fictional licence. *Apocalypse Now* (1979), *Raid on Entebbe* (1976) and

Who Dares Wins (1982) are possible examples for classroom use. A very useful set of teaching materials can be found in *Talking Pictures*, where the ways in which images signify and the uses to which they are put are introduced.[2] The images on the film strip in the pack not only offer intriguing examples for image analysis but also trace links between the changes particular images undergo depending on the medium which employs them. Students could be asked to imagine various media contexts for the images provided on the film strip. Could the photograph of the Twickenham Streaker, for instance, be reconstructed as part of a comedy feature film?

If teaching about the varying signification of images in different media contexts discovers some of the ways in which we are called on to assess the 'realism' of images in different ways and at different times, then we can begin to address questions as to what meanings viewers bring to images. Asking students to describe what an image denotes (what is in the image, what the picture is of) often produces quite different results from asking students what the connotations (associated ideas) of the same image might be. Take two images – one a photograph of a flag, the Union Jack for instance, the other of a sunset. The flag would carry different connotations for different people: a patriotic emblem or a sign of imperialist aggression. It would make a difference, too, if the flag was furled or unfurled, on top of the pole or at half-mast! The sunset might connote a happy Hollywood ending, a 'good' photograph, or a single spectacular moment on someone's summer holiday. Unanchored, the meanings range freely, the images connote variously, according to the ideas people bring to them. Captions provide a context, they 'fix' single preferred meanings which can, of course, be altered by changing the captions. Were the flag and sunset to be juxtaposed, even photo-montaged, the connotations would be anchored more specifically, but they still might depend on the wider context of where the image appeared and of who produced it: the sun sets on the British Empire, or Britain grows ruddy, at the end of the day all's well with the world. *Talking Pictures* offers useful images to exercise denotative/connotative analysis and ideas to be developed further by using the notes and slides in Guy Gauthier's *Semiology of the Image* (1975) pack.

So the media do not simply reflect a one and only 'real', but represent and reflect segments of a plurality of reals through various realisms. We contend in Chapter 5 that the privileged repetitions of some representations above all the possible others are determined ideologically.

Here we have discussed, albeit briefly, the ways in which iconic correspondences to 'reality' are mediated according to available or selected materials and techniques, the contexts in which they appear, and the range of meanings available to the people who view them. Study of the still image in the ways we have outlined here could possibly complement or introduce studies of the three realisms of television which we now consider.

Documentary

Looking through old family albums reveals how most people have used photographs and why they have kept them – to document significant events in their histories, new babies, weddings, trips out, the family together with the old patriarch in the middle. Old photographs now appear 'unrealistic'. The people in them pose stiffly for the occasion in the dress of yesteryear, the sepia tones look paled, washed out. Yet the novelty of photographic representation was acclaimed on two counts: the photograph documented reality more accurately than sketches, and it could be mechanically reproduced and therefore made accessible to much wider audiences. Although it is more familiar on television, documentary film began (and still may be found) in the cinema. Many writers about the earliest films made by the accredited inventors, the Lumière brothers, even suggest that the earliest cinema was in some senses a documentary cinema. Their films of a train entering a station, of workers leaving a factory, were extremely popular examples of the new ability to duplicate the appearance of reality. That those particular events in the lives of city dwellers were selected must have contributed to the feeling of how 'real' this novelty was. Once the novelty of this realism wore off, however, we embark on a technological history of the cinema, of photography, of television which tells us that as time progressed, every new development refined representations of the real. We are on the trail of improvements in the attempts to get 'closer' to the 'real' world, which was described on pp.95–6.

However, using extracts from early documentaries can point to the material with which representations, realist or otherwise, are produced. The technological history is more an economic one than the story of men having even better ideas and being able to put them into practice. Cinema and television both evidence numerous technological achievements which seem to have enabled a smoother purveyance of the 'real'. But this illusion of the 'real' without intervention, of its own accord, depends as much on 'artificial' means whereby the verisimilitude is made possible, is made so readily visible.

In most cases the inevitable activity of mediation, the material process of documenting this reality, remains an uncomfortable fact to be disguised, as the BBC handbook *Principles and Practice in Documentary Progress* makes clear: 'the equipment is a constant obstruction between the producer and his subject, and a great deal of his skill is devoted to presenting his subject matter as if the equipment and the technical processes were not there'.[3]

Realism depends on this effacement. To admit the 'artificial' would be to deny the 'real' which the 'artificial' enables to appear so naturally. To declare the material and institutional means whereby the realist representation was made possible would also lay bare the reasons why it was produced, the presumptions upon which the production was based. Such explanations would prevent any assumptions about the production being 'natural'. It would cease to be a realist representation because it would no longer be able to claim, implicitly, any simple correspondence with the 'real'. Using older documentaries for their 'difference' can enable students to recognise that any kind of representation, however close to the 'real' it might seem, depends on material (tape, celluloid, cameras, studio crews, props, costumes, time, money) for its production. Exactly how the materiality of representation has been apparently effaced needs to be taught. To teach why they have been effaced is to delve more deeply into questions as to why some conditions appear to be natural while others do not.

Even without being able to compare old cinema documentaries with more recent television ones, students possess sufficient competence in reading television documentary to be able to discover differences of visual and aural style in terms of framing, editing, pace, mode of address, the presence of voice-over, the use of music – to be able to distinguish Roger Graef's *Police* series, for example, from items of filmed reportage on *Breakfast Time* or *TV Eye*. The existence of a variety of documentary styles suggests at least a variety of realities, a repertoire of documentary modes. Even in documentaries, then, which explicitly purport to relate and document the 'real', the 'reality' cannot be a fixed or constant one, simply open to either the right or wrong interpretation. Rather, it is constantly changing, contingent, open to reformulation.

One way of investigating the particular ways in which a single documentary programme represents the 'real' is to ask how else that 'real' could have been represented. Looking at the ways in which various newspaper television pages signal a programme, immediately shows how that programme has been introduced to a heterogeneous audience in a number of different ways. What other blurbs could have been written? To whom would they have been plausible? If interpretation of the documentary is directed by the authority of a voice-over, what meanings were excluded? What other voices (or tones of voice) could have been heard to interpret the information in other ways? To what ends were music and sound effects used? Could others have achieved different effects? Were 'leading' questions asked in interviews? What questions and which people were not asked? What images could have appeared on the screen but did not? Where production accounts are available,[4] answers to such questions might be easier to come by, but we should not be too eager to discuss the hypothetical. After all, a set of answers to the kinds of questions above would provide only another version of representing the 'real', not necessarily less valid than that privileged by the broadcasting networks. What should become clearer is that realism is not simply a matter of corresponding closely to 'the real', but of how sounds and images organise a reality for us.

Having distanced students from the programme in this way it might be easier to analyse its modes of representation rather more critically. In addition, students might produce their own documentaries in order to appreciate how selection processes and limited resources determine how a particular 'reality' is constructed. The class could be divided into groups, each group briefed to document the school, college or community in different ways – as a tourist resort or as a local eyesore, for instance. The teaching pack, *Teachers Protest*, provides slides of a demonstration which students can arrange according to their different accounts of the demonstration which they tape as a voice-over commentary. In the same way as captions 'anchor' the meaning of a photograph, sound – be it voice-over, dialogue or music – tends to 'anchor' the meanings of moving images. In fact, it is often the 'realism' of a regional or class dialect which allows a documentary to claim if not a truthfulness, then at least a lyricism which tends to stand in for 'the truth'. Students could dub alternative soundtracks on to broadcast documentaries, thereby reconstructing that particular representation of 'reality' which hitherto might have been seen simply as 'given', naturally part of the way things are.

Drama

Most people could assert a knowledge of the difference between television's fact and its fiction. Documentaries are more 'real' in that they present us with the 'truth' about things that are happening or have happened in the real world. Drama, on the other hand, declares itself as fictional; it is not about what happened but about what could have happened if. The 'truths' of television drama are symbolic or moral. Yet, paradoxically, to praise a television play for its realism is to pay high tribute. *EastEnders* is generally supposed to be so popular because it is 'realistic', down to earth, true to life. When a series or a *Play for Today* is praised for being 'realistic', this usually means that it has been more explicit about the underside of life than television usually is – we get to hear more swearing, perhaps see more sex and violence. The epithet 'realistic' is, of course, used in different senses. A play's daring often lies in being as apparently close to the 'real' as possible without losing its status as fiction. A documentary must appear to be as 'neutral' or 'unmediated' as possible if it is to effect an illusory immersion into the 'real' which is its subject-matter. These different uses of the word 'realistic' indicate how television's realisms can invoke expectations of different kinds of verisimilitude.

If we have established some of the differences so commonly recognised between television and drama and television documentary, where are the similarities? There are similarities of narrative structures (see Chapter 4), but in terms of aesthetic codings and conventions the realism of drama resembles that of documentary in its arrangement of a particular version of events, its particular combinations of sounds and images. Like documentary, television drama seeks to deny itself as material. The credibility of its realism depends on the effacement of the processes by which it was produced.

This effacement is brought about by combining a wide range of effects and devices, many of which are not considered to be devised simply because they have been for so long just a 'normal' part of the way we read television. Sets and locations fix us solidly in a 'real' world which the drama constructs. They help to establish both characters and audience in a setting which has to be credible as a 'real' one if the drama is to convince. The characters are supposed to move, speak and dress as befits their time and place. Accounts of drama productions in the daily press and television weeklies usually stress the trouble the production team have taken to get everything down to the last lace cap and watch chain absolutely 'right'. British television's hallmark of excellence is the 'authentic' stamp of its period drama serials. In the same way as the theatre's 'fourth wall' helped to feign ignorance of the audience (to deny that the drama was a product being constructed), characters in television drama rarely face camera and address the audience directly. To do so would be to acknowledge that audience as somehow separate, as somehow not implied in the world that is 'real' if only for the drama's duration. However, the moving television camera allows the audience to inhabit the dramatic world in ways which even the 'fourth wall' convention could not. Editing is fluid, so that we do not stop to notice how we shift from long shot to close up. We are literally moved around the characters and the set. We watch, apparently not from a single fixed position (which of course we do, ensconced with a TV dinner in the armchair) but from a variety of angles and distances. We are also moved to hear in particular ways. Conventions of auditory realism are quite often contradictory. On the one hand, corresponding to the 'real' as closely as possible means having to alter volume and reverberation levels according to changes of shot. But quite often dramatic intelligibility depends on close-up sound, even when it might not 'naturally' fit with a long shot. In cases like this the realism of the image, which depends on a convincing correspondence with the real, is overlayed by the realism of sound which is motivated by narrative coherence.[5] The convergence of these different conventions of realism occurs not just in television drama but also in forms of documentary and actuality. What needs to be made clear, however, is that there are often various conventions working at once to make an illusory 'real' quite plausible. And the realist devices which construct such an illusion serve to involve us at every level possible: the more involved we have been, the more 'real' is our experience of the drama.

Once these devices have been pointed to and the particular illusions they construct have been explored, the premises upon which realist television drama is based can be revealed more clearly. So conventional are the kinds of technique mentioned above that in the course of our regular viewing they almost invariably escape our attention. By pointing them out we are also teaching about how they function.

Another means of accentuating realist devices is to examine those forms of television which break the conventions which television's codes of realism developed in the first place. Where access to equipment is possible, experiments with video deliberately breaking realist conventions illustrate the extent to which conventions do exist and the strength of their naturalisation. Examples of some forms of television drama which most readily exploit such conventions are cartoons, some comedy shows (notably *The Young Ones*) and old Hollywood musicals. Strictly speaking, musicals belong(ed) to the domain of cinema, but most students' experience of musicals is of ones they have watched on television.

Animation celebrates its very difference from the 'real'. Real cats squashed flat as boards cannot in fact raise themselves up, inflate themselves out and rip towards the horizon in a whirlwind of dust after a mouse that can never be caught. The 'realistic' setting of a squalid student household is so exaggerated in the *Young Ones* as to verge on the implausible, and therein lies some of the pleasure. Rik and Vivian's speech and behaviour are completely over the top. They often face the camera and address (or abuse) the audience. It is not usual for people to burst out into song with or without full orchestral backing just at the drop of a hat. But it happens in musicals. It has to be stated, however, that although these are examples of realist codes being broken, they themselves belong to a separate set of conventions which are organised in specific ways to mobilise credence in them as coherent television programmes. There are a number of alternative representational practices of television in which the use of special effects and distortions of the image seem to be legitimised. The most obvious examples are *Top of the Pops* and other pop video programmes, where the music's beat, its rhythm and the outré world that 'pop' connotes mark a televisual world that is far out of the 'real'. But because the construction of such special effects is effaced, because they are presented as occurring quite naturally, we would want to argue that even these programmes are produced in a realist mode.

As there are various kinds of documentary realism on television, so too are there various kinds of dramatic realism. In fact, there is a vast range of drama on television, from *Edge of Darkness* (1985) and *A Country Practice* to *Minder* and *Hill Street Blues*. There are single plays, soap operas and classic serials. The variety of dramatic styles and forms produce numerous realities. The main forms of television drama in Britain may be characterised as follows: single plays, series and serials.[6]

Single plays are usually attributed to an author – Ian McEwan's *The Imitation Game* (1980), for example. They often last longer than an hour and are self-contained narratives. They tend to connote serious 'art' rather than 'entertainment'.

Series can be defined as exhibiting a continuity of characters and, generally, location, over a number of episodes, but with a self-contained story per episode – for example *Bergerac*, *Minder*, *Fame*.

Serials have continuity of action, characters and location with various story lines running from episode to episode. Often episodes end with a 'cliff hanger' ending to encourage viewing next week. *Brookside*, *Dallas* and *Dynasty* are examples.

There are of course variations in and between these categories. Some serials are of a finite number of episodes; these are often 'classic serials' which have been adapted from novels – *Brideshead Revisited* (1981), *Jewel in the Crown* (1984), for instance. Other serials are seemingly infinite. *Coronation Street* has now been running for well over twenty-five years.

Two other categories ought to be mentioned, since both employ some of the techniques of realist drama. Drama documentary, although not a homogeneous category, employs the visual rhetoric of television drama to dramatise 'real'/historical events. Situation comedies often use some of the elements of a series – a single location (*To The Manor Born*) and a continual set of characters (*Are You Being Served?*), and there is a new story line in each episode. However, since situation comedy is produced by Light Entertainment, not Drama, departments, the separation may well be more institutionally than aesthetically determined.

Soap operas are the kind of serials which are particularly useful in teaching how realism operates in television drama. Popularly held to be 'realistic', soap operas are also discussed in terms of how far from the 'real' some of the characters and situations seem to be. Sue Ellen Ewing and Alexis Carrington are hardly recognisable as women most of us know but as 'types'. *Coronation Street* is set in the present but is a construction of the 'real' world as it might have been thirty or forty years ago. These matches and mismatches often stimulate debates among students as to what actually constitutes a 'realist' representation. In British soap operas, illusions of reality are very carefully produced. The life of the street or motel exists, apparently in parallel with the national life of the audience, sometimes outside transmission times. Christmas and New Year come and go, prices and rates of unemployment go up. Soap operas like these display a concern with the common details of daily life. In Channel 4's *Brookside*, fidelity to the real is the absolute aim. The set *is* thirteen houses on an estate in Croxteth, Liverpool, and some of the actors are local people.

The popularity of these dramas does not merely arise from the ways in which they appear to reflect real situations, but also in the ways characters are organised to negotiate plots and subplots – what they think, say and do. Fidelity to the way things are, however, means that representing how things could be is beyond the bounds of the format. Realist drama on television invites us to recognise and thereby confirm existing social relations rather than question them or see them anew. It could be that by inviting us to explore possibilities, television drama might enable us to imagine and construct realities which would be more popular than the ones at present.

Actuality

The term 'actuality' has been coined from the French *les actualités*. By it we mean a whole area of television representations which are transmitted as being 'the latest' if they are not transmitted live. Unlike film, television reproduces sounds and images electronically rather than photo-chemically. Television has no time-consuming and costly developing process. It can relay immediately. This does not mean, however, that television events are not edited or pre-arranged, as any apparently live programme from the studio (such as *Question Time*) will show. The most dramatic pictures often provoke the question, 'how did a camera get there?'. The answer, of course, is that because a camera was there the picture is news. Furthermore, 'live' transmissions are not always uncensored. What the audience does not see are the activities which take place behind the cameras, the rules and regulations, the briefs and directives laid down before production teams are sent out to 'cover' an event. Live transmissions do not simply happen. The Live Aid concert or the FA Cup Final are media events and are primarily experienced as such. Programme journals such as the *Radio Times* often emphasise the pre-planning and care taken in the siting of cameras at such events, and accounts like these construct live coverage as a feat of television's technology to be wondered at. Watching a cricket match live from Australia or the Open Golf Championship beamed via satellite from the United States enhances the idea of television institutions as munificent. They bring us pictures. Emphasis on live coverage tends to disguise implications. Who is being paid for these images and sounds? Are these the only ones available? Is the commentary part of the package? How many people around the world are watching and listening to the same transmission?

Live pictures are spectacles unique to television, and the commentators and pre-publicity materials celebrate them as such. As viewers we are inscribed as witnesses, asked only to see for ourselves. Thus the re-presentation, or rather the construction of spectacle in television news and outside broadcasts, tends to be underpinned by the guarantee of authenticity to which documentary lays claim. Had we the time and money we too might possibly experience these events first hand. Nevertheless, it is the immediate relay of the pictures which gives actuality television its particular potency.

The conclusion of the Iranian Embassy siege in 1980 was, at least in its later stages, carried live by all three channels in Britain and also by American and other broadcasting institutions. Normal programming was interrupted to present 'live' pictures of the 'spectacular' event. Restrictions on the angle of vision and proximity to the Embassy itself meant that the reality mediated was a rather tenuous and remote version of the central events inside the Embassy building. In fact, such restrictions probably served to connote 'reality' or 'truthfulness' to the audience, no doubt familiar with the visual and aural codes of *verité* documentary or abrupt camera movements. Millions around the world participated as witnesses. The empirical truth of 'seeing is believing' reasserted the power of television to 'tell us the truth'.

Contrast the Iranian Embassy siege with the conflict in the South Atlantic two years later. Government restrictions on the rapid transmission of actuality news film and videotape from the battle sites, ostensibly for reasons of 'operational security', led to a sustained conflict between broadcasting institutions and the MOD. Although a supply of images from the war was not completely denied, it was the absence of topicality, of immediacy, that was most distressing to the broadcasters, who felt that news from the South Atlantic had to be in the world's headlines. They had to be content with voice reports over artists' impressions. Live transmission from the South Atlantic would undoubtedly have been technically feasible, since at least one ENG unit was sent with the British forces. American broadcasting units transmitted live footage to the United States. But the absence of recent news film or video meant that such recordings that were made could only be broadcast as items of historical interest and not as part of the spectacle of television news.

Like documentaries, the ostensible purpose of news broadcasts is to inform us. Information is regarded as a fairly unproblematic commodity which can simply be transmitted so long as 'both sides' of a 'complex' issue can be given representation. However, as the Glasgow Media Group have painstakingly testified, the odds are quite heavily weighted against powerless groups of people at the sharp end of 'complex' issues.[7] Analyses by students and teachers of how 'news' is constructed, of how selection procedures are determined, are worth undertaking. What programmes are scheduled before and after the news on each of the four channels to try and make sure people don't switch over or off? How is the news made dramatic in order to compete with the evening's 'entertainment' quota? Are one channel's 'main stories' the same as those of the others? How do the commentaries and selected bits of footage compare? How much is explained? To what extent does footage determine the commentary? News is delivered to us by a newscaster so familiar that he or she is a well-known 'personality' in their own right. What effects does this have? What codes of camera work enable them to appear as the authoritative source of news? Students could be given a list of news items from a broadcast to select and arrange as they see fit and then compare their versions with the 'original' one.[8] They might then be in a better position to consider how television news could, or indeed, should, be.

Local and national newspapers, radio and television channels all cover sports events. Sport is no less contentious or political than news, nor is it any less mediated. A simple exercise students could undertake would be to attend a local match or competition and produce their own written and photographic report. Comparison with the pre-publicity material and the ways in which the event is re-presented by the media afterwards will indicate just how selective such representations are. But what ideas inform the ways in which these selections are organised and presented?

It would seem that players' personalities are more inquired about than their skills and strategies. Emphasis is often placed on the individual (the same often applies to the construction of news), especially on winners. Losers are invisible at the end of a race. The 'fans' who go to enormous trouble to follow their team are constructed as 'hooligans' by those who watch matches from the press box or on a monitor in the studio. Men's sport is given a great deal more coverage than women's. The BBC and ITV define the year's sporting calendar: the Boat Race, the FA Cup Final, Wimbledon, the Test Matches, the Grand National, the Derby, etc. In athletics, and still to an extent tennis, the amateur was assumed to be rather more decent (because a gentleman of leisure?) than the professional. The economics and politics of sport are kept well and truly in the background. To admit them on to the field would just not be 'fair play'. There is no reason why students should not try to map these discourses, and others, for there is no limit to them. Again, 'alternatives' help to highlight assumptions which seem so natural. Comparing coverage of the US Open Championship with Wimbledon reveals a range of different conventions in camera work, vision mixing and commentary. Football matches 'live' from overseas also make useful examples for comparison.

It might also be interesting for students to learn about the ways in which television (and therefore sponsorship money from advertisers) has necessitated for vast audience sports like snooker and darts. What makes a game televisual? Students could devise ways of televising other sports which do not often appear on our screens – volleyball, backgammon, anything! Conclusions to be drawn from doubtlessly animated discussions are not that any one coverage of a sport is more realistic than another, but that a game with its own set of rules and regulations can be represented in many different ways. But more significantly, far from merely 'giving' us the sport by way of 'reflection', the intrusion of media coverage affects the reality that is 'sport' and hence our knowledge of it.[9]

It might be argued that in teaching about the media we are and should be doing no more than that. The internal operations of media institutions, the merits of particular media texts, warrant special attention as the manifest ephemera of everyday life. On the other hand it might be argued that the media should be taught so that their relations with the real world can be exposed and made clear. When study of the media was first introduced in schools, one of the main political concerns of those who taught it was to make explicit what was considered to be a false relationship between the media and the real world. Bias detection would enable students to see how the real was mis-represented by the media which should not, as a result, be trusted. However simply these two arguments have been characterised here, they are both still pertinent to our current project.

The media do manifest issues and concerns which are latent in our society. As pervasive sources of information, education and entertainment they *are*, to a large extent, our experience of 'everyday life'. But they do not merely reflect 'reality'. They are neither transparencies which allow us to perceive things 'as they are', the real world 'as it is', nor do they simply trick us. The media construct and re-present the world for us, and so our understanding of the real world is almost equivalent to our understanding of how it has been and is re-presented to us, whether by the languages of our schooling, of our everyday experience, or of the media. In studying the media, then, we are learning about the ways in which the real world has been mediated, about how our understanding and knowledge have been constructed. The purpose of this pedagogic enterprise ought to be stated as clearly as possible at the beginning of any media studies course.

The different kinds of understanding and knowledge that such a study of the media might construct could enable us to presume anew when we speak of 'the real'. We might not only be able to perceive different realities but also re-present them using the different conventions of another 'realism'. We might begin to presume differently. Brecht understood this hope well and he understood it urgently: 'Now we come to the concept of *realism*. This concept, too, must first be cleansed before use, for it is an old concept, much used by many people and for many ends. This is necessary because the people can only take over their cultural heritage by an act of expropriation.' For Brecht, conventions of realist re-presentation must become 'realistic'. In Brecht's terms 'realistic' means:

> discovering the causal complexes of society/unmasking the prevailing view of things as the view of those who are in power/writing from the standpoint of the class which offers the broadest solutions for the pressing difficulties in which human society is caught up/emphasising the element of development/making possible the concrete, and making possible abstraction from it. (Brecht, 1977, p.82)

Dominant media realism does not often allow the 'causal complexes of society' to be discovered. Abstraction from the concrete is presented to us so immediately as evidence of, as equivalent to, the 'real'. This evidence of the 'real', what Brecht called the 'concrete', is supplied by the media in their profusion of images.

In this chapter we have examined the concept of 'realism' and have distinguished between three kinds of realism which television employs. We have tried to offer ways of teaching about these and to suggest why they need to be taught. Realism ostensibly presents us with texts of which we, as spectators, auditors or readers, are offered complete knowledge. The sense of completion which this knowledge offers, suggests that since 'this is how things are' there are no other things to know. But as teachers and as learners we know this cannot always be the case. We have argued here that if we can investigate how realist modes of representation claim to present us with the 'real' as 'given', we are then in a better position to ask what other kinds of representations, what other 'reals', are possible.

The crux of our concern has not been with the correspondence between representations with a 'real' somewhere out there, waiting only to be as accurately 'reflected' as possible, but with the ways in which representations organise and constitute the 'real' and, thereby, our knowledge. To be able to teach how knowledge is come by is to do more than merely impart it.

4 Narrative

'The narratives of the world are numberless . . . narrative is international, transhistorical, transcultural: it is simply there, like life itself. Must we conclude from this universality that narrative is insignificant?' – Roland Barthes

'What moves in film, finally, is the spectator, immobile in front of the screen' – Stephen Heath

In Chapter 3 we argued that to teach about how we come to understand the world through representation is as important as teaching about the world itself. The problems we addressed were those of reference, of the relations between subject and object, between perceiver and perceived. We tried to show that there are real people, real events in a real world, but that they are never simply and naturally 'given'. They are, on the contrary, always perceived and understood within a set of discursive practices (journalism, television, literature, talk in the launderette) which are themselves constantly producing both the objects spoken about and those who speak about them, the knowers and the known. We argued that there can be no simple or direct analogy between any 'real' object and any representation of it, even though what we defined as 'realist' modes of representation presume, in their mimesis, a belief that such analogies exist.

Realist modes of representation are able to presume analogies between the real and the re-presented precisely because they are never declared *as* modes of representation. Readers or spectators have their attention drawn to the content of the representation – what the picture shows, what the story is about – rather than how it is represented, how the story is told. In most arts or humanities courses, the pedagogical endeavour is to enable students to name what might be considered the essential meaning at the heart of a text. Full marks go to those students who can extract a text's kernelled meanings and then express them in their 'own' descriptive nutshell. What we propose in this chapter is a different kind of endeavour, one which does not seek a tautological description of meanings but instead one which enables analyses of the processes whereby those meanings are produced and whereby our understanding of those meanings is made possible. The use of the term *narrative* is crucial to any definition of these processes.

Everything is narrated – the match, the birth, the funeral, the meal, what so and so said about such and such, yesterday, today and possibilities for tomorrow. We tell, we listen, we watch. Narration marks processes of selection and organisation which structure and order the material narrated so that it can be invested with significance and meaning. All subject disciplines possess narratives, too, and we can therefore talk about the narratives of history, physics, home economics, etc. Narration can never be isolated. It is dependent on narrators and narratees. Implicit in all narratives are their receptions. To continue our references to Barthes: 'Narration can only receive its meaning from the world which makes use of it' (Barthes, 1966). We are the points at which narratives make sense. However, just as a narration implies its reception, so it constructs positions for receivers to take up and from which they can understand. Narratives position their audiences in particular ways, and audiences, in turn, in their infinite readings, reconstitute and re-position those narratives. The processes of narrativity involve endless series of interactions which bind and separate narratives and narratees. The pleasure is being 'completely caught up' in the story. In Conrad's *Heart of Darkness*, men huddle, solitary in the gloom, bound by and to the yarn that Marlowe spins:

> For a long time already he, sitting apart, had been no more to us than a voice. There was not a word from anybody. The others might have been asleep, but I was awake. I listened, I listened, on the watch for the sentence, for the word, that would give me the clue to the faint uneasiness inspired by this narrative that seemed to shape itself without human lips in the heavy night-air of the river.

At the end of his tale, 'Marlow ceased, and sat apart indistinct and silent, in the pose of a meditating Buddha. Nobody moved for a time'.[1]

But one of the listeners does move eventually, or so it seems, to retell Marlowe's tale, to re-order it through his own use of inverted commas, to invest it with another significance which he makes his own. Extraneous to the narratives within the text there are, however, others. We become involved in the history of Conrad as author, of our own histories as readers, and then of the histories of Conrad and Coppola – *Heart of Darkness* is transformed by *Apocalypse Now*. And so on. There are narratives and narratives. We are positioned by them and can re-position them again.

Our concern here is not so much with the possible infinity of narratives (we too must select and organise) but with those narratives that are *motivated*, that have been willed into artefacts. More specifically we are concerned with the narrative discourses within which, and which, the media operate – newspaper copy, photographs, TV programmes, films and advertisements. We wish to stress, however, that such products never exist independently and that as textual products they are enmeshed, intertextual. We, as spectators and readers, are no more independent of narratives than narratives are of each other. We come to watch each programme or film, to look at each photograph with a knowledge of other programmes, films and photographs. Knowledge of other narratives and our own particular blends of knowledge can determine what we expect and what we understand of narratives, which constantly situates us anew.

Students might be alerted to narrativised accounts of the world by being asked simply to make a note over a specified period of time of all the narratives they heard, read, see, tell. Not only would they be surprised to see that, over a day for example, they have been engaged in numerous narratives, but they could then be asked to assess the different functions of those narratives and their own degrees of interest or investment in them. Making an excuse about 'forgotten' homework, telling your friends about last weekend, the lyrics of a pop song, wondering what will happen next in a favourite TV programme – these are all narratives which will be interpreted differently, and some will be awarded greater prestige than others. An assignment to follow this activity might be to take one of the narratives that a student has brought into the classroom and to re-write or re-present it in various ways. It could be related from different points of view, in different tenses, it could be presented for a variety of different contexts – a letter to a friend, as a newspaper article, as a comic strip, as a radio play. The underlying purpose of such an exercise would be to draw attention to *narration* itself, as material as all the other discourses within its folds.

It is our assertion that narrative is material which links the arguments posed here with those we defined in the previous chapter. When a tale is told it often seems that although its details can be disputed, the narration itself poses no questions. It is as though narration is a kind of corral into which various characters, places and events can be herded. The old division of form from content. The tale might be dubious, but the fact of its narration is not. Narrative, in its ubiquity, seems quite natural, 'given'. Just as realism implies an equation between the representation and the represented, so narrativity implies a denial of itself as a process which selects and shapes accounts of the real in particular ways. Narrative orders and constructs our knowledge of the world while at the same time suppressing the possible knowledge of how that knowledge is produced. 'Whereas other discourses within the text are considered as material which are open to re-interpretation, the narrative discourse simply allows reality to appear and denies its own status as articulation'. Narrativity is part of the realist enterprise in so far as its operations appear so obvious as to be transparent, simply allowing the 'identity of things to shine through' (Colin MacCabe, 1974), equating the perception with the perceived.

By discovering narrative as material we attempt to challenge the 'transparency' that is presumed and thus show how the principles which organise a text significantly explicate how that text constructs positions for its readers or spectators so that they come to understand its meanings in particular ways. The importance of this challenge in educational terms should not be underestimated. To see, critically, how particular meanings are constructed by the narrative processes in which we all engage, to understand how we are positioned by and within those narrative structures, is to bring those processes and structures under our control. No longer 'given' as part of an apparently natural order of things, we can begin to demonstrate as teachers that narratives could select and order our understanding differently.[2]

Students are traditionally asked to make a distinction between 'fiction' and 'non-fiction'. In making this distinction the yardstick is often a notion of the 'realistic'. If it documents the real in an apparently unstylised way then the text is 'non-fiction'. There is clearly something contradictory about such a distinction, especially when something entirely fabulous – say a horror film – has to be 'realistic' in order to convince and entertain. Cardboard sharks just won't do. The distinction between that designated as 'fiction' and that designated as 'non-fiction' is little more than useless. Both 'fiction' and 'non-fiction' generally share a realist discourse and are both narrated. TV news and TV fictions, whether the 'high' drama of the classic serial or the 'low' drama of a popular soap opera, have narration in common. Their narrative structures, the ways in which their stories are told, bind (even grip) audiences in specific ways and offer those audiences within their grasp particular modes of understanding.

How do narratives bind and position us so that they determine our understanding of them? The principal answer lies in the notion of narrative as a *selective and shaping process*. Bordwell and Thompson, in *Film Art* (1979, p.52), delineate this process by usefully distinguishing 'story' from 'plot'. By 'story' they mean the chronological order of events, their duration and their frequency. 'Plot' denotes the order in which those events are related. In films and television programmes events are rarely presented in their chronological order: parallel editing and flashbacks, for instance, construct those events into a 'plot' order. Even more rarely do films allow events to take place in 'real' time. Not only does a film have approximately ninety minutes to present a complete narrative, but each constituent scene will rarely occupy 'real' time and will instead only focus on the most pertinent elements of the story. Thus time is foreshortened, and the most cliched example of this condensation are the shots of the hands on a clock, of leaves blowing off a desk calendar, of whirling newspapers and their crescendoing headlines. Bound by the 'plot' while watching, we are able, once the curtains close or the set is switched off, to reconstruct it as 'story'. We are able to reconstitute the narrative which the film or programme gave us as 'plot' into our own as 'story'.

To enable students to make this distinction for themselves is to teach the power narrative has in its selection and organisation. Students might be already aware of this if they carried out the first set of assignments in this chapter. By way of complementing or reinforcing that learning, having been given a basic story line (itself already a narrative), students could take a set number of photographs and arrange them so that the features of the story appear in chronological order. The photographs would then have to be rearranged into different 'plot' orders and the difference between 'story' and 'plot' arrangements could be discussed. There are various photoplay packs already available if time and expense will not allow the practical activity suggested; *The Visit* (1973) and the sections on documentary in Andrew Bethell's *Eyeopeners Two* (1981) are good examples.

What should be learnt from these activities is that in its selection and organisation narrative re-presents time. In the exercise above, we suggested using a series of photographs to teach the concepts of 'story' and 'plot'. However, there is no reason to suppose that narrative analysis could not be taught using a single photograph. A common supposition is that far from constructing representations of time, photographs represent moments snatched from time. A good photograph seems more chanced than a painting or a film partly because even professional photographers often talk in terms of being in the right place at the right time. Assumptions like these foreclose possibilities of considering photographs in terms of narrativity. But single photographs do represent time's flow. Precisely because they are, apparently, extracted from that flow and then frozen, they testify to it. Photographs order events in so far as they raise questions as to what might have occurred before they were taken and what might have occurred afterwards. Photographs depicting some kind of action would provide obvious examples, but simple portraits or holiday snaps from family albums also narrate in that they are evidence of a time that once was, a person who once looked like that but has now changed. Family albums, if they include photographs taken up to thirty years ago, tell tales not just about the family represented but also about photography and its techniques. The sepia tints and decorated frames represent the past as much as enlarged colour prints represent the present. There is a useful set of such photographs reproduced in Andrew Bethell's *Eyeopeners One* (1981).

Single photographs do not only contain their own narratives but they indicate others beyond their frames. Photographs are quite commonly used to start conversations which are, more often than not, concerned with something that isn't actually in the photograph itself. Often people will show their holiday snaps and remark, 'Well, it didn't really look like that', or 'It was just after that was taken that a terrible storm broke out'. On school trips students take endless photographs of their group getting on or off the coach. What these photographs signify – the narrative of the day's journey and these people as part of a group – is more significant than the narrative within the photograph – this group of people about to get onto this coach. Questions about why a photograph was taken, how it was taken, who it was for, where it would be seen, indicate the different narratives of production and circulation. These questions are especially significant ones to raise when news or documentary photographs are discussed. Why this photograph? For whom? What narratives, in its immediate presence, does it omit? The importance of such questions has been explained elsewhere: 'In terms of analysis and study, these questions make it possible to challenge the authority of the photograph, its status as the record of *how it was. How it could have been* is politically a more interesting question' (Manuel Alvarado, 1979, p.8, original emphasis).

Exercise three in the BFI teaching pack on image study, *Reading Pictures*, is a good case in point. Students are given part of an image (a brightly lit figure of a doll lying diagonally across some wooden slats) to analyse according to a set of questions which aim to tease out various narrative possibilities. These possibilities are developed when more of the image is revealed, and until the complete photograph is given to the students the specific objects in the photograph clearly limit the range of narratives possible. Once the whole photograph has been revealed to students they can begin to construct different narratives by contextualising the photograph with different captions. It tells different tales about itself and its production and circulation when captioned as a publicity still from a film, as a charity appeal photograph, or as a newspaper photograph.

The slide pack and notes which accompany Guy Gauthier's *The Semiology of the Image* (also available from the BFI) show how captions determine the narratives of photographs, but they also show how a single image can be recuperated to produce narratives other than the one originally intended. The photograph of a blind soldier has its meanings altered when it appears on the front cover of *L'Express* in 1968. Here the narratives which tell of an imperialist America are used to proclaim on the narratives of an imperialist France.

The single still image then refers to other narratives outside its framed space. This is what needs to be taught on any course in which single photographs are used to teach about narrative. The regime of the photograph, its presence and its apparent plenitude should not remain absolute, standing in for a completeness which its own partiality contradicts, but instead must be subjected to an analytic look, seeking to discover the absences, the narratives without – not simply what *is*, but why and what could have been. The sense of narratives taking place elsewhere is a difficult but crucial one to grasp if we are to enable our students to understand how we can at once identify with a narrative and its characters and yet remain apart from them.

A film, a series of photographs moving consecutively at twenty-four frames a second (the movies), structures its narrative through formal codes of lighting, acting, *mise-en-scène* and camera movement and through its codes of editing which arrange sequence. The two sets of codes together, supplemented by the soundtrack, construct positions for us, the narratees. In this respect useful work can be done in the classroom using photo-stories from romance magazines. With their captions blanked out, a set could be duplicated with the question 'what happens here?' inserted between gaps at several points in the sequence. The aim here is to sharpen critical focus on what seems so obvious and 'natural', namely that as our reading normally bridges those gaps, we make assumptions and predictions as to the narrative's outcome. Such assumptions are, of course, dependent on our knowledge of other photo-love stories. Having answered the 'between frame' questions, students can proceed to 'anchor' the narrative possibilities in the story by filling in the speech and third person captions within each frame. The exercise is all the more interesting if the object is to make the narrative ending defy the expectations which the students have themselves perceived between the gaps. In this way students can explore how knowledge of a particular genre (here the photo-love story) does not necessarily exhaust the narrative possibilities of that genre. Indeed, the girl who does not fall in love with the boy in the final frame might well push that particular narrative outside the boundaries of a love story to raise more fundamental questions about the power relations assumed under 'romance'.

Questioning the gaps in a photo or comic strip story enables us to discover exactly what the visual clues are that allow us to anticipate and to predict events which are likely to follow in the narrative. But more than this, such questioning also helps to reveal the power of editing. Paradoxically it is the fragmentation (the cut) which ensures the narrative's continuity. Fragments of film or tape (footage) are assembled so that not only is a sequence obtained but consequences are organised into coherence. As Stephen Heath (1976) writes, 'fragmentation is the condition of a fundamental continuity').

It is this sense of narrative producing a completion, a coherence, that underlies Todorov's assertion that a narrative marks the progression between 'two equilibriums which are similar but not identical' (Tzvetan Todorov, 1975, p.163). Most narratives are motivated by a problem, a disturbance of the status quo. The movement from the original stasis is punctuated by a series of disturbances and enigmas, 'events' in the plot. Events selected and arranged in the plot are motivated in that they have functions, serve purposes. There are no superfluities. Everything the plot churns in its wake is part of the narrative momentum, either regulating or thrusting its onward pull towards narrative closure. Barthes (1976) categorises the functions which constitute narrative as either 'cardinal' or as 'catalysers'. Cardinal functions are those which cause disturbance, pose enigmas compelling the narratee to continue reading or watching in order to discover enough to solve the mystery. Catalysers lay out breathing spaces in order to prolong the pleasures of suspense and to forbear the abruptness of closure.

Aesthetic and editing codes combine to determine which elements in a narrative serve cardinal and catalysing functions. For example, in *Coma* (1977), Mark Bellows serves both functions at different points in the film. At one point there is a crucial edit which can only leave an audience in doubt as to whether Mark wants to help Susan or whether he is in fact conspiring against her. After an agonisingly long chase, Susan has heroically imprisoned her pursuer under a pile of dead and frozen bodies in the hospital freezer. As she slams the door shut, the films cuts and she sinks into Mark's arms. Mark is in his flat. The cut forces us to make a stronger association between Mark and the coma conspiracy than we have been persuaded to make before. Mark lulls Susan into a doze on his bed. The film cuts to Susan listening to his making a 'phone call. To whom does he speak? What is he saying? The narrative does not allow us, any more than Susan, to know. The film cuts. Mark returns to find that Susan has left the flat. Her suspicions of him, and ours too, are confirmed so that when, in the end, Mark saves his damsel in distress, the memory of our mistrust may yet persist.[3]

Slides from a television programme or film can be analysed as separate images, preferably in the sequence in which those images appear. Students should be asked to search the visual clues offered and to discern which objects or characters might serve (in the image under scrutiny or in one to follow) as cardinal functions (pose enigmas, create disturbance) and which serve as catalysers (offer distraction). If the film (or extract) from which the stills have been taken is then shown in its entirety, it is possible to consider how narrative action organises the image, particularly since many of the suggestions students made in the initial analyses will now be made redundant. The principles which organise narratives vary from text to text, as the media could not sustain themselves as profitable industries if all their products were the same. Narrative action may be determined by the visual which, because of the iconic nature of photographic representation, is usually the ultimate guarantor. On the other hand the soundtrack may well undermine the visual guarantee. It has been contended that this is what happens at the end of *Klute* (1971), when Bree Daniels's voice telling her psychiatrist 'it won't work' is superimposed over footage of her packing and leaving with the detective played by Donald Sutherland (Colin MacCabe, 1974).

So while the 'clues' can define our anticipations, they do not do so discretely. Together with camera movement, editing and sound, these clues imbricate and weld positions for our understanding in the text. We are caught in this architectural process that is narrative, but we are never completely trapped in it. An evening's schedule comes to an end, the cinema finally closes, and however long it may take 'to get over' a particularly 'moving' text, the spectator can eventually relocate her or his understanding of the narrative not merely by re-constituting the 'plot' into 'story' but by reading that narrative in terms of others. The arrival at a new equilibrium, the detectives' restoration of the status quo at the end of *The Bill*, marks the text as closed, complete. But other narratives, tales of rather less heroic police brutality, serve to rupture that textual coherence. At once we are involved by textual narratives and satisfied by their closures, yet we also straddle the gap between them and the world's incoherence.

This is not to say that we can simply compare television or film texts with accounts of everyday experience in the 'real' world. Narratives from endless sources are multifariously enmeshed in our various intellectual and ideological formations. This intertextuality prevents any easy drawing of boundaries between the media on the one hand and society on the other. But what we can at least try to teach is an examination of how coherence and completion can be forged out of incoherence and contradiction. The logic of what has been termed the 'classic realist text' compels us towards a closure which marks coherence, an equilibrium (Colin MacCabe, 1974). Precisely as a selecting and organising process, narrative strains to make and bring us to a sense, an understanding, of what would otherwise be, without narrative, formless and senseless. In forming positions for our understanding, narrative is nevertheless partial. Because it is selective, no single narrative, nor any set of narratives, can present the whole truth. And yet, because realist narrative denies the signs of its own production, because it equates the represented with the representation, its movement towards coherence binds us into a representation of partial truths standing for whole truths. Brecht complained that realist narrative, ostensibly offering a complete and balanced account, was in fact limited and limiting because:

> it tended to be local rather than global . . . it favoured the actual rather than the possible and the observable rather than the unobservable. It was descriptive rather than explanatory. It effaced contradiction. (quoted in Peter Wollen, 1980, p.23)

Assembling fragments, the edit joins difference into an apparently seamless unity. The viewer is effortlessly transported from one scene to another, the present can dissolve into a remembered past or a speculated future. This construction of a unity is what Metz refers to as 'the power of cinema', and he conceives of that power as 'a kind of generalised "trick effect"', catching out the 'victim' spectator in the belief in the film narrative as 'reality' (Christian Metz, 1975). As spectators we are bound into this unifying process because we are involved with the camera, with its positions and its movements. Metz declares, quite unequivocally: 'the spectator can do no other than identify with the camera'. We can only see what the camera allows us to see. Not only does the sealing edit prevent our look from venturing between the cuts, but our conference of vision with the camera ensures our blindness as to possible narratives taking place off screen, beyond the frame. The camera lens controls and organises what we see of the screen space, the space in which narrative takes place. As spectators, then, we are subjects of the camera's authoritative gaze. To teach students this basic premise is to reinforce the idea of film and television narratives as constructed by their own specific codings of images and sounds rather than as transparent 'windows on the world'. Most of these codings (although predominantly the visual ones) and the ways in which they construct our understanding of images have been discussed in Chapter 3. However, in the context of this chapter, the particular codes of camera position and movement need further discussion.

During a film or a programme's narrative progression we will be placed in a variety of positions from which to view. The camera can either make us identify with a particular character's viewpoint or, in more complex narratives, with more than one character. We can also be placed as observers, maintaining a 'distance' and yet travelling with the camera in impossible spaces – inside a sea anenome, along the span of a bat's wing in nature programmes, or revolving on several axes of fast zooms, high and low angles which the many cameras used in constructing a rock concert make us get with it. Cameras often place us in positions as impossible as these. The question of how narration could possibly originate from a position which moves above a landscape at one moment and then from a ground shot the next, is one that is repressed while we view, for it is precisely at such points that either careful editing or complex tracking and craning will carry us through. Thus are we woven across the various narrative threads.

Using slides, or more conveniently freeze-frame on a video recorder, it is quite easy to devise 'eyeline' exercises to deduce both the look between characters within the narrative and the look the camera positions invite us to take up. A freeze-frame facility allows study of still images and can also allow students to trace camera movement, especially when the speed can be slowed down. Such analysis is painstaking but rewarding. Classic teaching examples have been the famous opening sequence in Orson Welles's film *Touch of Evil* (1957). The tracking and craning camera both disturbs and involves us across a number of divisions and insecurities. In *Citizen Kane* (1941) the camera movement and editing, feats of amazing technical complexity, connect disparate parts of the narrative which is to follow. Students' own production work, even if it cannot get beyond the storyboard stages for want of technical facilities(!) can demonstrate how camera positions, movements and edits construct relations within the narrative and our viewing relation to it. Such activities, we would argue, enable students to 'map' our narrative involvement as these formal codes might construct it and who will therefore be in a more authoritative position when assessing that involvement.[4]

To analyse how narrative organises our understanding, expectation and suspense, students might work on the photo exercise entitled *The Visit*. The pack consists of a class set of thirty-two photographic images which have to be arranged to create a narrative sequence which maximises suspense – the combination of anticipation and delay which drive the narrative forward. Part of the pack's value is that it can encourage students to recognise and explore how the 'meaning' of a single image is neither its inherent nor fixed property but rather how it exists as a form of narrative potential. That potential is only realised once the single image has become part of a series of others juxtaposed. Individually the meaning of each image is radically indeterminate; it is only in its relations with different images that particular meanings are produced and coherence ultimately established.

We have reproduced here two images from *The Visit* (Photographs 6 and 7). The positioning of the camera in each places the viewer in very different relationships with the potential

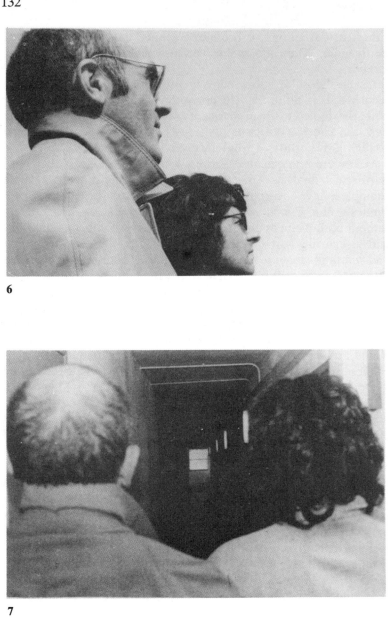

6

7

narrative action. In Photograph 6, the camera's point of view is distinct from that of the 'visitors'. As viewers, we *observe* the two characters gazing at something out of frame. We are distanced from both of the characters and from the object of their gaze. At the same time, though, this object, located somewhere in the imaginary out-of-frame space, becomes a source of narrative enigma which attracts our interest, creating a desire for the narrative to move forward, for this frame to yield to another which may reveal the absent object. In Photograph 7 the point of view is very different. The camera is positioned at eye level in the space immediately behind the two characters. As we look at the image we are forced into a close proximity, even perhaps into a kind of unwilling complicity with characters whose faces we cannot see.

What these two images can be made to show in the classroom are the ways in which point of view contributes to the processes of identification and of more disengaged observation which shape our experience of film and television narrative. Once the two images reproduced here are edited into a sequence which includes the other images in the pack, then those shifts of position are linked into a continuity that is narrative.

Having completed this exercise it would be useful to look at the opening of Don Siegel's version of *The Killers* (1964). Unlike the Welles' film, this offers a very simple and direct narrative flow – the plot line is identical to *The Visit*'s, i.e. two men visiting one man in a room – but, like the Welles' movie, one of great power.

Film and television narratives pertain to another, namely the history of cinema and television as institutions. The degrees of spectator involvement in narratives have been qualitatively different since the days of early cinema. Work on the narrative cohesion of early films can usefully point out the different ways in which spectators have become involved in, and have enjoyed, the cinema and television. A useful preliminary teaching film is Noël Burch's *Correction Please*,[5] which traces the history of cinema in terms of the development and consolidation of particular uses of the camera. These have fundamentally shifted the relationship between the spectator and the images on the screen. In very early films the camera was fixed directly in front of the scene filmed, generally at eye level and at sufficient distance to register the entire scene. Its place was very similar to that of someone in an ideal seat in a theatre audience. Indeed, many early films were in fact photographic motion recordings of staged vaudeville acts. Only gradually (and in conjunction with technological development and changes in the cultural and economic space occupied by the cinema) did film-makers begin to experiment with camera angle and movement, focal length, cutting and editing. Now, in defiance of the sequential order of shots, we have learned to read certain shifts, signalled by particular kinds of cutting (the dissolve to flashback) as designating the simultaneous occurrence of a series of actions or events (the alternating shots of pursuer and pursued in a chase scene). These techniques, however, were only gradually developed, and the use of explanatory intertitles in many early films ('Meanwhile, back at the ranch') is evidence of a stage at which these techniques had been neither fully developed by film-makers nor learnt by film audiences. The narrative of *Correction Please* traces the developments of the ways in which the camera movement and the addition and synchronisation of sound affected the identification and observation of cinema audiences. Noël Burch's *Theory of Film Practice* (1973) might provide useful material for teaching to complement classroom investigations and discussions of *Correction Please*.

Camera movement and editing largely constitute a film text's narrative apparatus. Television texts also rely on these to involve audiences in their narratives, but, generally speaking, television programmes are so much more diverse than films that we have to consider other ways, apart from camera movement and editing, in which television compels our viewing. On television, as at the cinema, we can only see what the frame contains, but instead of paying to watch a single narrative unfold we may watch a series of narratives during an evening, which will itself provide other narratives as interruptions to the ones on television – a meal, telephone conversations, the various accounts of a day's domestic and waged labour. Television's 'flow' (see p.55) through an evening's viewing binds very different sets of narratives. There might be the early news followed by an episode from a soap opera, or a magazine programme followed by sport or a film and then a documentary and then the news again. We can switch off or on in the middle of these programmes, thus structuring different narratives. We are not, as at the cinema, necessarily compelled to closure (though you can, of course, walk out of the cinema, but the fact that you have paid good money and have to risk stumbling over other people's knees and feet makes you think twice about it), nor are we positioned anonymously in the darkness. Television addresses us altogether differently, and indeed its awareness of, perhaps even a deliberate construction of, a 'mass' audience makes our involvement in television narratives a much more public experience, one which we have in common with millions of others. All the individual narratives indicated above are themselves constituent elements of the overarching narrative which is our 'evening'.[6]

The sense of being part of a networked audience is still strong despite the advent of Channel 4 and its (token) provision for 'minority' audiences, and despite the increasing use of home video. Nevertheless, our social experience of television is a domestic one, and a cabled nation may well mean an increasingly atomised audience. So although we have many experiences of television narratives in common with others (and after all, our knowledge of certain television programmes is a mark of our national identity), those experiences are shared for us. They are signalled and mediated by a range of ways so that we come to watch television with determined expectations, and discussion of our television experience is not always our 'own'. The *Radio Times* and *TV Times* (the best selling weeklies in Britain) begin to lay hermeneutic trails before audiences reach for their on-off switches. Newspapers' dependence on television for copy is enormous. Not only are the evenings' schedules listed, but the centre pages are crammed with stories about television personalities, comments and reviews on the previous night's programmes. To cap them all, in Britain a new daily national newspaper, the *Star*, was created and designed to concentrate on the 'world of television' rather than on the world itself! Interesting teaching points might be made about how audience expectations are constructed in terms of the different social classes which different newspapers address. Compare, for instance, these 'blurbs' about *Carry On Doctor*, broadcast on BBC1 at 7.25 p.m. on 31 July 1984:

These seaside postcards of the British movie industry have become a kind of institution, and here regulars Sidney James,

Kenneth Williams, Charles Hawtrey, Barbara Windsor, Hatti Jacques, Joan Sims, are joined by Frankie Howard. If you're quick you can spot Penelope Keith as a hospital worker. (*The Guardian*)

Kenneth Williams is Dr Tinkle and Jim Dale is Dr Kilmore in this hearty British frolic among the bedpans. Some of the puns could seriously damage your funnybone. (*Daily Mirror*)

Cinema proclaims its offer of a discrete text by way of publicity posters (although more and more cinema chains are advertising their films on television and on radio) and display advertisments in local newspapers. These posters are 'narrative images' of the films on offer, whetting appetites but never revealing the whole story, because that ultimately depends on the narrative itself unfolding (John Ellis, 1982). Competition for ratings means that regional networks are beginning to advertise single television programmes in much the same way, so that spending the evening at home will seem comparable to the treat of going out to the cinema if only because viewers will be able to talk about having seen a programme others will also have seen. However, television programmes are usually announced as part of continuity sequences between programmes. Thus, having read *Radio Times* and *TV Times*, the day's paper, heard an advertisement on the radio, and seen yesterday's continuity sequences, the television viewer approaches a set of programmes already hailed by a variety of discourses. So, before coming to the texts, audiences have already been subjected to different forms of institutional address. Comparison between the ways in which a film and a television series are packaged, exhibited and reviewed makes for interesting individual or group projects, and makes it possible to relate texts to their contexts of production and distribution. Moreover, and pertinent to our concerns here, such projects can be used to examine the links between publicity, text and consumption in terms of a *narrativity* extraneous to the text but nonetheless determinant.

The form of television's narrations are altogether different from those of cinema. Television narratives involve and move their audiences but not always in the same way as cinema narratives do. At home or in the classroom the television set is part of the furniture, the screen on 'the box' is small. Viewers can usually see one another easily and may be engaged in other activities or conversations while the television is on. From the cinema screen, as broad and tall as a wall, light emanates into the darkness of the auditorium where spectators are literally dominated by the spectacle. Dolby and quadrophonic sound systems help to enclose the audience within the experience of the film narrative. Television cannot indulge in the spectacular or auditory to such a heightened degree as cinema, hence television tends to be less sound affecting and is organised in closer spaces. Many television programmes are recorded within a studio, where at least three cameras negotiate a relatively small space. Close-ups and mid-shots are far more common than long shots, and so instead of dramatic scopes (even *Panorama* is presented in a studio) television demands a concentration on to the small space that is its screen. Television narratives tend, as a result, to be concerned with interpersonal relationships. These relationships are structured by the shot/reverse/shot that is so frequent in soap operas, or by the fist-to-face confrontation in 'action-packed' dramas. The face-to-camera address and the voice-over commentary on the news, game shows, documentaries and sports programmes, structure relationships between viewers and programmes which are no less narrational than dramatic 'fictions'.

In order to teach the narration which television 'fiction' and 'non-fiction' share, students might be asked to trace the different narratives or narrative strands within a programme or across a set of programmes during an evening's viewing. What should become clear is that television continuously narrates, but whereas cinema's narration is organised around a central problem, the resolution of which signifies the end of that particular narrative, television's narration establishes and negotiates a series of enigmas throughout the day, across a week. Within programmes designated for children there will be several stories told, each item of news constitutes a narrative, advertisements narrate, the evening play or film is a separate narrative, but one made up of many different strands. A football match poses the enigma, 'Which team will win?' and as we watch, the narrative of the game unfolds. A simple listing of such various narratives should help to draw attention away from the 'commonsense' distinctions between 'fiction' and 'non-fiction' and instead focus discussion on the more useful concept of narrative.

The flowing narrative of a television day is itself punctuated by different 'segments' of other narratives. These segments are not quite as causally related as the different strands within a film narrative which together tend to weave a textual whole; rather, each yields to another which deals with a completely different set of characters, problems and locations. Analyses of different title sequences is an extremely useful way of pointing out the 'segmentation' of television's narration. Questions about the graphics, photographs and tunes which combine in a 'title sequence' can enable students to deduce how our expectations are constructed as to the kind of narrative each programme will deliver. Often title sequences themselves constitute miniature narratives, signalling the nature of the one to follow. There are other instances of how viewers are addressed by institutions: the music which signifies the beginning of *Crossroads* or *News at Ten* proclaims Central's and ITN's immediate demand on our attention. The BFI teaching pack *Starters* provides a useful set of material for use in the classroom. Although, as the pack's own title suggests, television title sequences do mark the beginning of every programme, so that differences between narrative segments are marked, they also mark the end of previous segments. Students can also construct expectations of a narrative by producing their own title sequences on storyboards, by video animation or by exploiting the possibilities offered by a television studio, where one is accessible.

These narrative segments, endings and beginnings, are television's habitude and renewal. Cinematic narration renews interest through its play of similarity and difference within and across different genres. No horror film is ever the same as the last, but similarities shared by films within that genre allow us to form reasonable expectations which can then be confirmed or surprised by the next horror film 'with a difference' (Stephen Neale, 1980). While there are genres specific to television (the chat show) and others which it has developed (situation comedy), narration on television extends across segments, unlike film narrative which draws together different strands.

How are television's segmented narratives extended? First, we expect to be able to sit in front of a TV set at a certain time on a particular day of the week. *EastEnders* 'continuously refigures' (Ellis, 1982) three times a week, every week. There are news bulletins at lunchtime, early evening and at night, every day. So the narratives of our lives, from the beginning of one week to another cross television narratives which often form part of our routine ('I must get home in time to watch such and such'). Video recorders mean that we can shift these narratives so that they traverse those of our daily lives at different points, but we still *spend time* watching videos. Students easily recognise this from their own vast experience as television watchers.

Secondly, television narratives generally privilege characters and locations which recur throughout the various episodes of specific series or serials. Students can map these recurrences in a range of programmes for themselves: Sue Ellen and JR; Bob Monkhouse; the rules of *Telly Addicts*. This mapping (elicited by questions along the lines of 'What do *Newsnight* and *Brookside* have in common?) can expose the different kinds of narrative segments which structure television. It can show that although programmes are different and involve different sections of a 'mass' audience in different ways, they at least have narration in common. The trajectory of a documentary usually has arguments to *follow*, and news items are structured within bulletins.

Teaching about the narrative structures in soap operas highlights this 'continuous refiguration' that is peculiar to television; the BFI pack, *Teaching 'Coronation Street'*, provides a possible framework, while the BFI TV Monograph, *Coronation Street*, supports exercises in the pack with cogent theoretical arguments.[7] Because the same characters appear regularly in soap opera, the events that take place, the problems that occur, do not need resolution as urgently as they would do in a film text. 'Real' time is more closely adhered to, or at least is less compressed than in film, and thus audiences have time to ruminate on the characters and events between episodes. New problems, exits and arrivals ensure novelty and renewal against a background which is familiar.

It is this constant play between speculation as to what might happen next and the knowledge of familiar formats and personalities which engages television audiences. There is a balance which both audiences (though their interest) and media institutions (through their production and circulation of programmes) maintain. A practical project that could emerge from classroom analyses based on the preceding arguments is one which shifts the terms of that balance. Having ascertained the recurrence of political characters in narrated news items, students could produce their own dramatised version of similar characters: an extended political soap opera is not so hard to imagine. But speculation makes the novel and different possible, whereas knowledge of the familiar does not. While audiences might want to comment on the sexual politics of *Dallas*, television, radio and newspapers are also harnessing such responses into the only frameworks they declare possible. Here the intertextuality of media forms is limiting rather than liberating.

Earlier in this chapter we suggested that concern with teaching about narrative should acknowledge *both* texts *and* their consumption. To reiterate: implicit in all narratives are their receptions. Familiar formats, dependable characters, predictable news reports – these leave little room for speculation. As part of our domestic furniture, our cultural and political 'baggage', they become easily naturalised, taken for granted. Their repetitions begin to represent normality and to re-present life as acceptable, both on television and off it. Yet many of us, teaching and taught, can draw upon other narratives from our lives' experiences, from our positions within a sexist, racist, ageist and capitalist society, that tell us life is not always quite so acceptable. How can we recognise these apparently 'natural' representations as determined, historically and materially, by an unacceptable society? How can we begin to resist them in order to begin constructing a socialist society that is acceptable? Our next chapter attempts to deal with these questions.

5 Class

'MONDAY: What a varied life it is in Current Affairs . . .
Today, it's setting up a very difficult film – on cocaine and
the young unemployed . . . it's not proving at all easy. For
two solid days a researcher has been punishing phones trying
to find me working-class cocaine users. No luck . . . FRIDAY
. . . Some working-class cocaine users have come out of the
woodwork. The film is getting there . . . MONDAY: Finally we
get to meet and interview some cocaine users anonymously
. . . They're superb on camera . . . so the film is *there* . . . a
good film in the can' – a Current Affairs Producer in the weekly
diary of the BBC staff magazine *Ariel*, 1985.

Class divisions in Britain have become more nakedly transparent
in the last ten years than at any time since the war. And there is
an increasing recognition that the media's role in that development
has not been entirely innocent. For while the 'rich and famous'
pose for the lenses of the press *paparazzi* in Stringfellows, TV
camera crews are attacked on picket lines and inner-city streets.
The media's representations of class are in crisis, and urgently
stake their claim on the educational agenda. The aim of this
chapter is to discuss in more detail what might be involved in an
analysis of the representation of class relations in the media and
how we might begin to teach about them.

Beginning classes

Outside formal sociology lessons, class is rarely an issue that is
directly raised in classrooms in the British education system – a
significant absence, given the proliferation of educational
literature, policy documents and curriculum recommendations

141

more or less overtly concerned with the re-presentation of the curriculum to its captive working-class audience. But while we can safely assume that the presence of class relations is continuously felt during most educational activities, there remains the problem of how they can be sensitively approached within the class-room.

One introductory method might be to approach the existence of class differences in the same way that a corporate magazine publisher such as IPC magazines does. Most magazine publishing is concerned with reaching specifically targeted audiences, who must be either sufficiently large or wealthy to generate the circulation of advertising to render them profitable. A group of students could each be given a magazine with the task of composing a 'reader profile' which could be distributed to potential advertisers (another group of students) who would have to decide whether to use the magazine to advertise their product. Alternatively, worksheets could involve making a content analysis of types of subject-matter, features, advertising, etc. as well as assessing the quality of paper, presentation and price. Suitable magazines might be *The Tatler, Weekend, Woman's Own, Working Woman, Country Life, Homes and Gardens, Cosmopolitan, Spare Rib* (most of these are women's magazines, so possibly some 'male activity' magazine could also be included). Once these 'profiles' are assembled, the information can be pooled and distributed to the whole class. The teacher could then give all students photocopies of ten adverts to be placed in the magazines they think most suitable, or perhaps the most unsuitable. When the results are discussed a range of issues about class relations will be raised:

1. Why does a company such as IPC need to publish magazines as varied as *Country Life, Homes and Gardens* and *Woman's Own*? Why couldn't the latter two magazines be directed at a single 'woman reader' and so cut production costs?
2. What do the different types of advertising tell us about the publishers' and advertisers' assumptions about their readers? What type of society is implied by the appearance of advertising for frozen beefburgers, bacon, tea, and Batchelors rice in *Woman's Own* but not in *Homes and Gardens* (respective cover prices 30p and £1)?
3. What are the differences in the treatment of royalty between

magazines? A magazine such as *Working Woman* totally
ignores royalty, while *Woman's Own* is often openly adoring:
'He was in playful mood, she was full of happy laughter.
They've never been more relaxed together – nor Diana more
stunning' (30 November 1985). *The Tatler* is rather more
irreverent: 'Close friends and observers have noted that Prince
Edward is now the keenest party-goer in the Royal Family. It
is said that if his fists go out and his legs go awry you can tell
he's dancing' (November 1985). One magazine is representing
members of one class to another class, the other is that class in
self-representation.

Alternatively, teacher and students can undertake image
analysis of some of the 'interiors' in a magazine such as *Homes
and Gardens* (see Photograph 8), possibly comparing the images
with students' snapshots of their own home interiors. Some
comments from Rosalind Coward illuminate what might be gained
from such an exercise:

Not much thought is required to realize that we are being
offered the styles and lifestyles of a very precise class fraction.
This self-reflexive and self-congratulatory group has the
hegemony over definitions of design, taste, style and elegance.
The group is not exactly the ruling class; they do not own the
means of production and they are by no means the most
wealthy or financially powerful people in the country. Yet they
control the means of mental production; they are the journalists,
designers, graphic designers, furnishers and publishers who can
tell us what we should think, what we should buy and what we
should like. This grouping clearly has enormous powers within
society because the communications media have enormous
potential to decide our beliefs and tastes. But it isn't even a
matter of this group deciding our views. More nebulous and
perhaps more influential, these are the people who design our
homes, who show us how to decorate these homes, whose
material is on sale in the shops. These are the people whose
tastes dictate the very possibilities for much of our everyday
lives.
And the standards set by this group are remarkably consistent.
The houses are all geared towards a conventional living unit.
And the decors are mere variations on a basic theme. The walls

are plain; there is minimal furniture; an absence of what is seen as clutter; and light, open rooms. . . . Indeed the ideal home is very much directed towards a visual impact, and within this visual impact, towards a display of possessions. Furniture and decorations are chosen with an eye to how they match each other. Walls are painted with an eye to how to display an original painting or a framed print. Shelves and tables are arranged to show off expensive objects to their greatest advantage. Above all, the light colours and plain walls tend to demonstrate constantly how clean these walls are . . . The class basis for this taste is always disguised in the writing, which insists there are such things as absolute good taste and good design. But class isn't the only thing disguised by the vagueness of labels of 'style' and 'elegance' . . .

What is dismissed as bad taste in working-class homes is merely the arrangement of the home according to different criteria. In working-class homes, the pictures and colour are often on the walls as wallpaper, not framed as possessions. Items are often displayed not to demonstrate wealth but because they have pleasurable associations. Here are souvenirs – memories of a good holiday, snapshots – memories of family and friends; and pieces of furniture chosen, not for overall scheme, but because they were liked in someone else's home. This is a different modality of furnishing, not necessarily concerned with the overall visual effect.

The economic investment in home-restoration is also disguised by the language of loving restoration. The idea that home-improvement is merely the expression of individuality through good taste obscures the way in which this kind of restoration is a very real economic activity. People able to buy and restore houses, or build their own houses, are acquiring valuable possessions. These are the possessions which – as this group gets older, dies and leaves the houses to their children – will be creating a new elite – those who have no rent to pay as opposed to those who spend enormous proportions of their income on housing. For the house-owner, even their current property represents the creation of profit out of housing. Doing up one house, moving on to a bigger and more valuable one, with tax incentives on mortgages – home-restoration is certainly also gaining economic advantages over those who can afford only rented accommodation. (Rosalind Coward, 1984, pp.68–9)

8

Another productive exercise might be for students to undertake a 'class shopping list' from a TV programme such as *Brookside*. Much of the narrative in the series (significantly it is often the humorous stories) is generated by the fact that families from different class backgrounds live adjacent to each other in the Close. Accordingly, the programme-makers have to indicate class differences to the audience succinctly and stereotypically. Students can list as many of the signs employed for this function as possible. For instance, the difference between the Collins family (middle-class) and the Grant family (working-class) would include differences in furniture, food and drink, accent and use of language, clothes, expressions of sexuality, use of leisure, relationships with the surrounding community, 'political' sentiments. Other residents of the Close such as the divorced Heather Haversham, or Sandra Maghie and Pat Hancock, who

are the only residents who do not own their house, are more
difficult to 'fit' into a stereotyped paradigm of class relations. Is
Harry Cross less working-class because he owns two of the houses
in the Close? Why do we think of the Collins and Heather
Haversham as middle-class when they still have to sell their
labour in the market-place? Why do we still recognise the Grants
as working-class when they own their own house? *Brookside* is
hardly a microcosm of the British class system (it has had very
few black characters, for instance). But it will open up some of
the complexity involved in discussion of the representation of
class relations.

Work along the lines suggested above begins to get students
asking some pertinent questions about class and its representation.
What, after all, do we mean by class? Do we mean a segregation
of society in terms of income, background, power and behaviour?
How do we recognise differences in class? By characteristics, by
social situation, by what people do at work and leisure? Our
course of work already suggests that the media do recognise the
existence of class at both a *structural* and *textual* level. Structurally,
because, as the magazine exercise illustrates, media economics
determine the production and distribution of media artefacts for
audiences who are at least partially determined by their class
formation textually, because media texts clearly acknowledge and
indeed presume the reality of class divisions – whether in the
form of advertising offering aristocratic status ('Chanel for
Gentlemen'), or soap comedy in *Brookside* (as when Harry Cross
is outraged when Annabel Collins insults him by offering her
'buffet supper' for his wife's funeral wake instead of ham
sandwiches and whisky, which are the traditional marks of
respect) or by offering us the pleasure of identifying with four
working-class women who pull off a spectacular bank robbery in
Euston Films' *Widows* (1983).

Study so far also suggests that the media represent class
relations primarily in terms of differences in 'lifestyle' which we
choose as individuals. Our class position is in fact mainly
determined by our function within the capitalist system of
production, yet in the media this determination is almost
invariably refracted through prisms of culture, dress, dialect,
taste: we are all consumers who just happen to consume
differently. Clearly, the question we have to address as media

teachers is not *whether* the media represent class difference – they clearly do – but *how* the media represent class relations to their audiences and *which* classes gain, which classes lose, in that process.

Class representation of classes

Of course, the media do not represent class relations in isolation from other institutions and discourses. Much ink has been spent, on Left and Right, in attempts to define the nature of class as a social category. Part of the problem in satisfactorily conceptualising class is its intrinsic 'dual nature' (Göran Therborn, 1983). On the one hand our class positions are determined socioeconomically; on the other, our thoughts, activities and lifestyles can straddle any number of cultural gaps and social divisions. This 'dual nature' means that class relations are dynamic, and that changes are possible. How do media representations of class relations enable (or prevent) changes? How do they enable (or prevent) our straddling? (see also Raymond Williams, 1983).

All media representations are enmeshed within this continuous process of class formation and re-formation. Yet the 'dual nature' of class indicates that we cannot either think or teach about representations of class as though it were an independently existing objective phenomenon which the media represent to their audiences. Rather, different classes construct their own ideological representations of both themselves and other classes. These compete within a general ideological class struggle for universal ideological hegemony, a battle in which institutions such as the media and the education system are major participants. Consequently, in a major industrial strike, shareholders, company directors, middle management, supervisors, shop stewards, shopfloor workers, workers' dependants, customers of the company, etc. will all represent the strike and their role within it very differently according to their own class or ideological positions. Should the media report such a dispute, they will produce texts within an ideological framework which will be sympathetic, indifferent or hostile to some of the class ideologies striving to represent the strike in a particular way. The very fact that the media only become interested when 'normal' working (or class) relations have been interrupted is not without ideological significance.

In any complex social formation there are bound to be several competing class ideologies seeking to be the dominant explanation of class inequality. These are intertwined in our everyday awareness of what it means to live in Britain, say, and the world in the late twentieth century. However, in order to teach about representations of class, either in the media or in education, we clearly need some form of theoretical paradigm or map of contemporary discourses which seek to 'explain class'. Crudely and simply we would suggest that there are four broad but distinct class ideologies claiming our attention and allegiance.

'Aristocratic'

Unlike most other capitalist industrial countries, Britain retains a strong aristocratic class formation. The aristocracy still owns approximately 42 per cent of the land in the UK. Moreover, British capitalists such as the Pearson family have always attempted to acquire an aristocratic veneer by pouring their manufacturing profits out of 'trade' into property and prestigious leisure activities (see Tom Nairn, 1981, and James Bellini, 1981).

Accordingly, there remains a vigorous residue of what can only be called a 'feudal' class ideology in many British 'hearts and minds'. This can be seen in the cultural struggles over the school curriculum in the last few decades. Over the last few years the so-called 'New Right' has been attempting to reimpose their feudal vision which 'involves the maintenance of a hierarchy, and the attempt to represent the unpleasant fact of inequality as a form of natural order and legitimate bond' (James Donald and Jim Grealy, 1983, p.89). Roger Scruton's arguments outline how the 'aristocratic' ideology explains a 'rich man in his castle, poor man at his door' society as the product of *innate* differences which are expressed in the differences between 'high' and 'low' culture. It represents social class as rank or caste rather than economically determined category. Scruton states: 'It is not possible to provide universal education. Nor indeed is it desirable'. While the most explicit expressions of this ideology are to be found in the *Telegraph* newspapers and the *Salisbury Review*, the present cult of Royalty should alert us to the continuing appeal of feudalism in Britain.

'Capitalist'

The capitalist Industrial Revolution not only radically transformed feudal society into new forms of class divisions; it also provided a new explanation of inequality as the outcome of fair and equal competition between 'free' individuals in the 'free' market. Society is the aggregate of that competition's 'winners and losers' – the working class is poor because of its lack of thrift, initiative, energy, or mental ability. Capitalist ideology is also hostile or ambivalent towards aristocratic ideology. A thesis in recent years has been that Britain's economic decline is due to the aristocracy's disdain for the industrial and manufacturing process. The demands for relevance in education to the 'world of work', dating from Callaghan's initiation of 'The Great Debate' in 1976 (the *new vocationalism*), is partially due to the aggressive resurgence of this ideology as economic decline accelerates. Students will recognise it as the 'on yer bike' philosophy.

'Social democratic'

While the press is dominated by a mixture of these two ideologies, we would argue that broadcasting (due to the institutional requirement for 'balance' and the disproportionate number of professional middle-class personnel in positions of operational control) is still permeated with the assumptions of 'social democratic ideology'. While social democracy is difficult to ascribe to a specific *class* ideology, it is nonetheless worth differentiating as it has been so dominant in education and in the media as an explanation – indeed as a solution – of class relations. Social democratic ideology acknowledges the unacceptable face of class inequality but represents it as a problem of social distribution rather than one of the economic mode of production. Therefore the solution to class inequality is to distribute resources – income, education, housing, etc. – more equitably rather than to transform the entire system. The excellent *Unpopular Education* (Education

Group CCCS, 1981), a study of post-war education, shows how social democracy was the major organising discourse in education throughout the 1960s and early 1970s. The vision of a meritocratic, more socially mobile society of 'equal opportunities' for all, where the 'prejudices' responsible for class divisions would be swept painlessly away, was the dynamic of Labour Party education policy and the expansion of comprehensive schooling in particular:

> Labour's Fabianism or liberalism has been centrally concerned with the mission of managing or reforming a capitalist society, by removing, especially, the most important inhibitions to capitalism's progressive side – a more 'open' society . . . It has constructed working-class interests as national interests, very largely as the interests of capital. This project of the harmonisation of class interests is what, in the end, warrants the term 'social democracy'. (Education Group CCCS, 1981, p.97)

Oppositional

All class ideologies are oppositional in the sense that they are rivals for hegemony. What we mean by oppositional are those discourses and representations which contest and seek to subvert the dominant ideologies we have already described. In Britain, oppositional discourses on class relations tend to be derived from radical working-class culture (as traced in E. P. Thompson's *The Making of the English Working Class*, 1963) and industrial and political practices such as trade unionism and Marxist intellectual traditions. Classes are perceived as irreconcilably divided because of their different positions – as wage labourers or owners of capital – in the means of economic production. (The managerial and professional middle classes are contradictorily sited in positions of operational control yet without ultimate power.) Outbursts of revolt, such as the 1926 General Strike, are seen as only the most visible expression of a society based upon permanent conflict and alienation. For the subordinated classes 'there is no escape except through the total transformation of the mode of production' (Ralph Miliband, 1977). The formal education system is seen as a process of masking how people are allocated to different positions in the production system so that class divisions are transformed into apparently objective cultural distinctions ratified by the examination system.

However, we would wish to argue that oppositional expressions of disenchantment with capitalist society are more contradictory than Miliband allows. They may articulate a spontaneous resistance to the daily lived experience of exploitation and domination shared by subordinated groups, while, at the same time, they may be situated within the domain of 'common sense' accommodation with 'the way things are and always will be'. While they accord with some aspects of the dominant ideologies, they may also contain elements of a critique of the system (Antonio Gramsci, 1971). Paul Willis (1977) has described how a group of working-class boys recognised their subordinated status within the regime of the formal education system and accordingly rejected its academic culture as being for the 'ear'oles'. Yet this resistance to school is precisely what prepares them for their destiny as manual labourers – or, today, the dole.

Class is a fundamental contradiction within our social formation. Consequently the media (and the education system) are constantly engaged in an institutional *and* textual ideological negotiation and reworking of that contradiction. The four class ideologies discussed above, all represent and construct that contradiction differently – its history, its present manifestations, and its possible future resolution. For instance, 'violence on the picket line' would be represented as disobedience, a criminal act, an extremism by dominant ideologies, whereas an oppositional discourse might report the same incident as the legitimate expression of class struggle. This process is crudely and partially represented in the Table 5.1.

We would argue that it is within the terms and boundaries of this (far from exhaustive) model that the media try to 'make sense of' class relations, to contain class antagonisms, to resolve class contradictions. This involves the media in a set of heterogeneous and contradictory ideologies, discourses and representations which can never finally cohere. Moreover, the differing aesthetic and institutional imperatives of different media ensure that they do not merely reflect pre-existing representations and discourses but actively produce and reproduce them anew in each media text. There is accordingly always a risk of

Table 5.1

Aristocratic	*Capitalist*	*Social Democratic*	*Oppositional*
rank	free individual	disadvantaged group	class subject
authority	free market	pluralism	power
duties	wealth creation	income/earnings	exploited labour
birth	culture	status	class
hierarchy	natural differences	prejudice	class antagonism
national tradition	national interest (economy)	national interest (social)	class interest
preservation of order	expansion of wealth	redistribution of social income	radical transformation
disobedience	criminality	extremism	class struggle

tension between institutional requirement, commercial imperative, aesthetic or technical form, and ideological strategy which may result in contradiction and even ideological incoherence.

At a simple level this can occur even within the ideological straitjacket of a television news bulletin. While the ritual royalty story might implicitly address us as 'commoners', an industrial relations story – in which both capitalist and labour ideologies may be expressed in interviews – will almost certainly be contained within an institutionalising social democratic discourse representing the dispute as being between 'the two sides of industry'. It is entirely conceivable that some audiences will both reject that institutional discourse in solidarity with other trade unionists yet never question the 'natural' appearance of yet another royal hospital visit. The teasing out of such contradictions should be a primary objective when teaching media representation of class relations.

Media classes

Unlike the education system, the media do not possess any legal sanctions to hold their working-class audience. This especially applies to television, which has to address a mass audience composed of different classes and sub-classes. Prior to the arrival of commercial television, the BBC had arrogantly assumed a seigneurial right to give its audience what it thought they obviously needed – a continual dosage of high culture occasionally sweetened with some light music on the radio. Lord Reith likened the threat of commercial television to bubonic plague, but the mass desertion of the working-class audience to ITV suggested that for most the disease was infinitely preferable to the cure. The BBC was forced to go 'down market' in order to regain its status as 'voice of the nation'.

Television is therefore the most rewarding medium to use when teaching representations of class because of the contradictions which involve a mass medium attempting to reach all the parts of its class-differentiated audience simultaneously. However, due to their different distribution practices, while the press, radio and cinema do not share this requirement to such an extent, they obviously provide valuable supplementary material. Television's 'basic leakiness' (Mike Poole and John Wyver, 1984) in terms of its representations of class can perhaps best be approached by teaching how class relations are represented and mediated within different TV genres and forms. The purpose is to analyse how relatively 'closed' or 'open' are their diverse representations of class relations, which may in turn suggest useful discussions of TV's ambiguous institutional role as a popular mass medium within a class-segregated society.[1]

Sitcom

The media reflect a world that seems to be familiar – familiar characters, familiar situations. Familiarity is the basis of their ability to sell and to give us pleasure. But this continual re-presentation of the world *as it is* can reinforce the *naturalness* of a class society: some people happen to have power, others don't – *c'est la vie*. In the media, as in life, people find themselves in particular situations because 'that is the way things are'. Often on television these situations will be comic, and that comedy is often generated by class relations. One of the principal textual dynamics of TV situation comedy (sitcom) is class difference, both between characters within the text and between the text and its inscribed audience. So teachers and students should examine how sitcoms play on class for laughs, and how that process confirms or modifies our knowledge of living in a class society.

Humour is, of course, a notorious petard on which teachers embarrassingly hoist themselves in the classroom. It is important that study of sitcom does not either degenerate into 'a good laugh' or become a puritanical innoculation against what the teacher finds unfunny. Study of individual texts could ask *why* they make us laugh and the role that class relations play in the humour. The BFI has produced a *Sitcom* teaching pack (1985) which includes slides, exercises and references to videos available for hire – *Hi-de-Hi!* and *Porridge* – which are clearly relevant to considerations of class in sitcom, although the pack's concerns are far broader. We will discuss here three sitcoms (frequently repeated as 'classics') which use a particular strategy, frequently used in sitcoms, of foregrounding the world of one particular class, and where the humour and narrative are generated by intra-class contradictions.

To The Manor Born. The narrative of *To The Manor Born* is concerned to resolve an ideological contradiction within the British ruling class, which is memorably expressed by heroine Audrey Fforbes-Hamilton (Penelope Keith): 'He's got the money. I've got the breeding'. At the end of the series vulgar interloper Richard De Vere (Peter Bowles) from Trade marries Audrey, having proved himself a gentleman who, if not literally to the manor born, proves himself as being the next best thing. The final wedding could almost be an allegory of the ability of the British ruling class to maintain its power through pragmatic liaison, to represent itself as the natural order.

Rather than immediately screening a particular episode for analysis, students could be shown some instances of other representations of the British aristocracy. The Ealing comedy *Kind Hearts and Coronets* (1949) might be screened to introduce them to the long tradition of satire of the landed gentry. Discussion might focus on whether, with a radical Labour government in power, the film's contemporary audience would have identified with Mazzini's (Dennis Price) singleminded assassination of the D'Ascoyne family, secure in the knowledge that the 'people' were at last in charge. This could then be pursued by providing students with some information on the continuing power wielded by the aristocracy.

Trevor Griffiths's *Country* (1982) reveals how the aristocracy planned to hold on to its wealth despite the 1945 Labour landslide and would be a useful complement to the Ealing film, as would *The Gamekeeper* (1979), Ken Loach's bleak view of the rural class structure. Students might also carry out some image analysis of eighteenth-century paintings of aristocrats enjoying the bounty of nature on their estates which they had appropriated from the common land (see John Berger, 1972b).

Most of us live very different lives from those of the denizens of *To The Manor Born*. So why do we find it funny? Why do we hear studio audience laughter when Audrey says, 'Who built all that [the manor] up to what it is today? I did it by my own fair hand and the sweat of my brow – at least it was me who sent the men out!' (We never see the centuries of rural exploitation that built up such manors, nor do we see the Third World workers who work in De Vere's international foodchain.) Students' answers might speculate on the character of Audrey herself. Undoubtedly she is a 'strong woman' who is determined to hang onto 'her' property and to dominate completely all the men within the series. Lacking her class power, women might enjoy this vicarious gender domination. Yet the male audience will feel secure in the knowledge that Audrey will be 'tamed' by De Vere in marriage. She will move back into *her* house as *his* wife. So the narrative offers pleasures of gender identification which, because they cross class boundaries, naturalise the class differences between characters and audience.

The focus could shift to the other characters such as the vicar and Bassinger the butler, who are treated as menials by Audrey and as wage labourers by De Vere. However, by the end of the series De Vere comes to recognise the value of the feudal organic society and the advantages of the 'bonds' (in both senses of the word) which tie the rural 'community' together. It is his, and our, *éducation sentimentale*. There is no character who voices opposition to the Audrey or Richard De Vere power-axis. Our response to the programme is complex: are we laughing because we feel superior to the 'manners' of the gentry or because we gain 'guilty' pleasure from sharing their view of the world? The considerable stress on the visual fetishes of the aristocratic lifestyle – a Rolls, hunting crop and shotgun appear in the titles – suggests that the programme's dominant discourse is an aristocratic ideology which seeks to familiarise us with an unfamiliar upper-class world. We can laugh at them but we must accept them. Our laughter is, in fact, a mark of our acceptance.

The Good Life. Analysis of the classic 'middle-class angst' sitcoms such as *The Good Life* and *The Fall And Rise of Reginald Perrin* introduces students to how comedy can mediate tensions within the ideological formation of a particular social class – in these instances the professional middle-class who occupy a contradictory class position as being both subordinate to the owners of the means of production yet the beneficiaries of capitalism's material benefits. Both these sitcoms are concerned with middle-class alienation from this situation and their ideological project is to suggest that it can be ameliorated by changes in individual lifestyle but not resolved through social action of any form.

Comedy in *The Good Life* is generated from the conflict between a middle-class (capitalist) ideology of independent self-sufficiency (the Goods almost parody the Robinson Crusoe myth in their attempts to go it alone) and the middle-class reality of being dependent on wages in the labour market. The Goods try to live by barter within a consumer society based on money and commodity exchange – they learn to value material possessions according to their use-value as opposed to their exchange-value. The narrative demonstrates this to be absurd, yet also provides a moralistic critique of the materialistic Jerry and Margo. Resistance to the values of consumer capitalism is transformed into the idiosyncratic lifestyle of the harmless Goods. The Avenue is no escape route, but an ideological cul-de-sac.

Once students have thoroughly analysed the differences between the two couples and how the narrative in each episode reworks them, discussion could concentrate on assessing how the programme's humour might work (or not work) on a non-middle-class audience, which may lack the 'corrupting' consumer durables, and the 9-to-5 job so loathed by the Goods. Does the series redeem the middle classes by asking everyone to laugh at the Goods' antics in suburbia, or does *The Good Life* show how the middle classes are just wage slaves of the system like us, rather than its ambivalent beneficiaries?

Whatever Happened To The Likely Lads? The humorous ideological work performed by *The Likely Lads* sitcoms is the resolution of two contradictory male responses to their working-class position. While Bob aspires to middle-class status, Terry retains his traditional macho working-class identity, and, while extremely scathing about Bob's ambitions, is occasionally jealous of the material benefits, such as a mortgage, which Bob is busily accumulating. As with *The Good Life*, it would not be difficult for students to analyse the differences in clothes, language and attitudes to 'proper behaviour' which differentiate the lads and occasion most of the humour. The series seems to position us with Terry's view of the world, as he normally enjoys the last laugh over Bob, whose aspirations are gently ridiculed in the series. However, Terry's irreverent cynicism amounts to a negotiating oppositional ideology in his refusal of the work ethic and in his 'don't let the bastards grind you down' resistance to the status quo. Yet his lack of success in the job market is clearly related to this attitude: if he wants to get on he will have to become like Bob. This class and cultural dilemma is central to the narrative, which clearly always holds open the question: will Bob and Terry's different trajectories polarise their respective class affiliations to the point where their friendship is destroyed? The narrative manages to transform this threat into a question of gender rather than class relations by designating Bob's fiancée Thelma as the 'class enemy'. The male solidarity of The Lads infinitely postpones the moment of class reckoning and disruption. Yet finally, when Bob and Thelma marry and Terry is left on his own, it is difficult to avoid the conclusion that we are meant to perceive this isolation as a form of punishment for his refusal to 'grow up', to stop being a lad, to get stuck in. In the end the working-class stay where they are because they like it.

A course of work on sitcom and class is concerned with asking what representations of class relations does the sitcom form produce and which does it suppress or marginalise. Their humour clearly often depends upon mediating class-based tensions through representations of stereotypical individuals within specific class *milieux*. The resolution of these tensions is indefinitely delayed until the end of the series, when either marriage (a gender-based resolution) or an individual's departure (Fletch leaves jail) ends the narrative. Our pleasure in sitcoms is partially dependent upon our own class-based competencies in reading the codifications of class differences, relations and tensions. We would argue that while most sitcoms confirm and validate those competencies, they rarely challenge the social bases which generated them. At best we can enjoy the occasional triumph of a negotiated oppositional discourse triumphing over the institutional and respectable – Fletch over Mackay, Terry over Bob, Ted Bovis over Geoffrey Fairbrother in *Hi-de-Hi!*. But Fletch remains in jail, Terry on the dole, Ted in camp: so who gets the last laugh?

Quizzes and gameshows

Television quizzes and gameshows are ritualised forms of conflict that mediate fundamental social tensions through a highly structured and ordered form which provides pleasure. Given that class is a primary determinant of social tension, these programmes provide suitable texts for the teaching of the representations of class.

One fruitful approach would be for students to watch extracts from several different shows to assess whether class plays a role in the way that they are produced. Programmes such as *Mastermind*, *Call My Bluff*, *Family Fortunes* and *The Price is Right* all use visual and cultural codes which are radically different and are suitable for this form of work. The hierarchical (even authoritarian) atmosphere of *Mastermind* is constructed through its mix of Outside Broadcast academic institution location, lighting codes, 'cultured' presenter, hushed audience and isolated contestant – a different world from the hurly-burly of *The Price is Right*, in which we 'come on down' with Leslie Crowther, who generates an inclusive warmth between audience and contestants by encouraging vocal participation, where all is presided over by the deified consumer goodies on never-ending display. Alternatively, *Call My Bluff* is obviously designed to resemble nothing so much as a middle-class parlour game with its intimate closed circle of repartee.

Students can progress to comparing the types of questions involved and the answers expected. What forms of knowledge do these programmes expect from their audiences and contestants?

The purpose of such comparisons is not only to suggest how different class audiences are addressed through different cultural codes by the television institutions, but, more importantly the assumptions about the forms of knowledge deemed appropriate for those audiences and about the forms of reward that contestants are offered. The knowledge which merits the prestigious award of 'Mastermind' is that of the 'informed citizen' combined with the arcane specialist knowledge of any area of high culture – knowledge which is possessed rather than constructed. Within this discourse knowledge is its own reward, unless you're Fred Housego, the taxidriver winner who has become a media personality as a result of being both working-class *and* having a brain.

Not so in *The Price is Right*. The show is predicated upon the assumption that while most people have a detailed knowledge of the prices of consumer goods, they do not have the financial means to use that knowledge by actual consumption. The 'narrative' of *The Price is Right* is generated by that increasingly real disruption between the ideology of the free market in which we can all 'choose' what we want but lack the means of effecting that choice. The knowledge needed is one of the utilitarian skill of survival in consumer jungleland; the reward is the ownership of some of those consumer commodities. The narrative resolution is a precise re-enactment of the central myth of capitalist ideology: that material benefits are achieved by those with the knowledge, skills and luck to attain them. The losers remain just that – losers . . . but the price is always right. Television constructs 'knowledge' as a possession individuals can acquire. Rarely is knowledge considered or evaluated as useful in terms of how it might be collectively produced, socially shared, economically transforming. Instead they 'naturalise' the unequal distribution of knowledge and cultural capital as being merely a process of cultural differentiation. Questions about education's role in class relations are implicitly raised by such programmes, but their answers are unlikely to change it in any way.

Soap

'Soap operas' are a dominant television genre at the moment, and provide a continual source of copy for the popular newspapers and magazines. Given this popularity, they form an essential component of media teaching, and the consideration of their representations of class must clearly be part of such study. It is perhaps useful to distinguish between British-produced weekly serials of potentially infinite length such as *Coronation Street*, *Crossroads*, *EastEnders* and *Brookside*, and the US-produced melodramatic soap operas such as *Dallas* and *Dynasty*. Not only are their representations of class very different but they also provide different forms of pleasure.

UK soap. Teaching representations of class from the main UK soap serials could clearly involve many strategies. There is the BFI teaching pack on *Coronation Street*, which provides a number of useful ideas. However, one tactic might be a comparative analysis of different serials in terms of their *realism* and how this affects their representations of class relations. All these serials claim to be *reflections* of daily British life in different regions. Much of this 'reality effect' is achieved by references to common cultural events at the time when they are occurring in real life: we enjoy a vicarious Christmas party at the Rovers or at the Motel before moving on to a real one. As the number of soaps increases, each serial has to produce and maintain its audience by representing the familiar while being sufficiently different from the others to provide its own distinctive pleasures; this can prove difficult, as Granada discovered with *Albion Market*.

One pertinent form of analysis is to compare Channel 4's *Brookside* with either *Coronation Street* or *EastEnders*. *Brookside* consciously set out to be more 'realistic' than previous soaps in its reflection of real life. Phil Redmond, deviser of the series, considered that other series had 'failed . . . to cope with realistic issues and everyday problems . . . people will accept and actually want programmes that tell the truth and show society as it really is' (quoted in Christine Geraghty, 1983). Redmond insisted on having real houses instead of studio sets, but was forced to cut out the 'realistic bad language' of early episodes. Students might begin by observing some of the ways in which *Brookside*'s textual strategies work to declare its difference from *Coronation Street* or *Crossroads*. *Brookside*'s brand of realism has had its textual consequences: more location work, single-camera shooting, narratives based on individuals or their families cut together – and because families tend to resolve their own crises (while they are often resolved by the 'community' in other series), *Brookside* displays class antagonism more overtly.

However, *Brookside* has its critics who argue that its concern for a naturalistic realism has led to a decline in the number of strong female characters and a loss of the sense of community generated by having such 'communal' locations as the Rovers' Return and the Motel (see Geraghty, 1983). The issue raises an interesting dilemma about representations of working-class life. Can representation of a 'community' in a class-based society only be achieved through the nostalgic filter, associated especially with *Coronation Street*?

> Class as materially determined in relation to the means of production, and much less as self-realised in political and social action, is still either absent or (often comically) marginalised. Women's strength and endurance is celebrated, but as the inevitable and given lot of women rather than as socially determinant. The *nostalgic tone of the serial consigns any lingering effective class consciousness to something that, to all intents and purposes, is in the past.* (Richard Dyer *et al.*, 1981, p.5, emphasis added)

There is also the counter-argument that the 'utopian' element in such serials provides a collectively based critique of the system's class relations, 'the assertion of a vivid image of how life should be' (Dyer *et al.*, 1981; see Geraghty, 1983, for the argument in reference to *Brookside*). There are no 'answers' to these issues, but we would argue that there is unlikely to be a more accessible route into discussion of realist versus non-realist asethetics and the implications for a more progressive representation of class relations in popular culture for secondary level students. Finally, it is worth noting that *EastEnders* provides an example which achieves both a sense of community and of 'realism', much to the disgust of Mrs Whitehouse.

US soap. While British-produced soaps stimulate the pleasure of familiarity, 'reflecting' everyday life, the pleasures of watching *Dallas*, *Dynasty*, *Falcon Crest* and their ilk are precisely the opposite. It is their representations of a class whose lifestyle is totally *dissimilar* to ours which is the main source of audience pleasure. Teaching might begin by analysing some of the coverage these serials merit in the tabloid press and womens' magazines, especially their play upon fantasy (see Photograph 9). Analysis might centre on how the press continuously reworks the question: are the star actors' own characters similar to their dramatic roles? If they were identical, there would be no story, so there has to be some difference, yet the ideological project of such coverage is to convert the difference of the rich into the domestic and the familiar: we learn about the tragedy beneath the smile of success, the mother beneath the vamp.

Productive preliminary exercises when considering how class relations are represented by US serials would be the playing of a business simulation game in which students would learn about some of the structural requirements of capitalist business – and class – relations.[2]

> Both *Dallas* and *Dynasty* deal with the economics of multinational corporations but they do so in terms of the familial conflicts which control the destinies of these companies. This is typical of the domestic melodrama's oft-noted tendency to portray all ideological conflicts in terms of the family. (Jane Feuer, 1984a)

Students should be encouraged to consider ways in which these serials can render the class (and gender) relations of their transnational audiences problematic. The obsessive ostentation of wealth and restless manoeuvring of sexual desire (including the incestuous) clearly constitute a contemptuous transgression of bourgeois ideologies of hard work, thrift, romantic monogamous marriage. However, they may also allow a middle-class audience the luxury of looking down on these sinful people with moral rectitude, or a working-class audience to note with relief that the rich are satisfyingly unhappy (see Feuer, 1984a, for this debate).

While a feminist progressive reading of the US soaps is clearly possible (due to their problematisation of the family), their representations of the international ruling class are perhaps more irredeemable. It is true that *Dallas* especially represents individuals as being structurally trapped by the profit imperative whatever

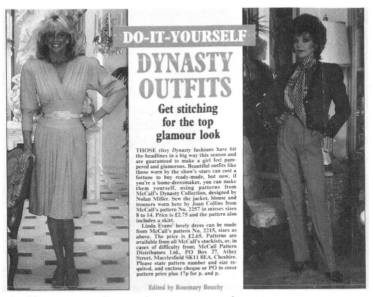

9 If stars are ordinary, then anyone can be a star

their own worthy intentions: Bobby and Ray support JR when the chips are down. This is represented only within the terms of the family feud, as wealth creation is narrativised as the outcome of the actions of individuals rather than classes. This not only allows the audience to distinguish between the 'good' capitalists and the 'bad capitalists' (Bobby Ewing or Blake Carrington versus JR or Adam Carrington and Alexis), thus implying that the process of capitalism in essence is benign; it also mystifies the actual process of multinational wealth creation. When Bobby Ewing strikes oil in Canada or Blake Carrington gets an oil licence in the Far East, this is represented as a personal triumph, a narrative climax. Yet the extra Ewing or Carrington wealth will be generated from the labour of classes and countries which are underdeveloped or subordinated by US imperialism. They will watch *Dallas* and *Dynasty* on their Japanese TV sets drinking Coke, but their labour, their lives will not be represented. Labour and work is conspicuous by its absence on such programmes. The dirt of imperialism has been washed out by soap with barely a stain left behind. It is hardly surprising that the multinational oil firm British Petroleum exploited the *Dallas* image in its 1985 advertising campaigns.

'Social problem' documentary

Within the whole range of documentaries in which television purports to represent 'life on earth', there is a specific tradition which may be designated as the 'social problem' documentary. This form of documentary, in its different stylistic variants, can be found both in the current affairs slots such as *Panorama* and *World in Action* and in the prestige documentary feature slots such as *Real Lives*, *40 Minutes* and *First Tuesday*. This type of documentary normally identifies a specific instance of suffering and deprivation which television then brings to our attention. Given that many of these ills will be the outcome of present class relations, we can recognise that they beckon our pedagogic attention when teaching representations of class.

A fruitful introduction could be the screening of some early pioneering examples of this tradition of documentary film, which are mainly the products of John Grierson's GPO Film Unit (later to become the Crown Film Unit), which was set up in the early 1930s. These films are invaluable in teaching because they represent the founding moments of both the visual rhetoric and positioning of the audience which have continued into the dominant practices of TV documentary. Students will find it easier to analyse these textual processes with unfamiliar material which will also distantiate them from the now thoroughly naturalised TV documentary conventions.

Housing Problems (1935) is characteristic of social problem documentaries in purporting to take an objective look at the problems of poor inner-city housing. It takes an investigative stance, and consists largely of interviews with the slum dwellers. The film insists on their plight being a social responsibility, but suggests that the solution lies in a programme of rehousing, the way in which we as a caring society can put right an obvious wrong. Like many such documentaries it can powerfully, even poetically, deal with the *effects* of a class society, but not with the underlying causes of poverty. The approach is essentially paternalistic, suggesting that with 'help' and 'planning', people's lot can be improved. But they themselves are not apparently expected to play a part in changing their lives – they simply wait to be rescued. Students can analyse conventions, such as the use of establishing shots of the slums, which clearly position the audience *outside* the slums, *above* the experience of the problem, a view of a class's life set out for another class to watch. The film was praised by Grierson because it attempted to avert revolution – 'a bloodier solution' – and because it 'touches the conscience' (Forsyth Hardy, 1966).

The development of British documentary film practice was only part of a more general development of a 'social democratic' discourse in the 1930s, which called into being the new social category of 'the citizen'. 'Film can really bring the outside world alive to the growing citizen . . . It really can serve an interpretative function . . . it can, if it is mastered and organised, provide this necessary umbilical to the community outside' (Forsyth Hardy, 1966, p.23). While some of these films may be remote to secondary students, short extracts from films such as the aesthetically innovative *Coalface* (1935) or *Industrial Britain* (1931) would be sufficient for them to analyse how this documentary tradition represented the work and conditions of the working (male) classes. For just as the films address an audience as 'citizens', so they represent the working class as victims, often expressively lyricising the heroic dignity of labour as an aesthetic spectacle. Above all, these films appeal to our social conscience, which involves 'a persistent sense of a quite clear line between an upper and lower class . . . it is a matter of social conscience to go on explaining and proposing at official levels, and at the same time to help in organising and educating the victims' (Raymond Williams, 1980, p.155).

Teachers can then screen some later developments of documentary. Humphrey Jennings' *When Fires Were Started* (1943), is an account of the work of the Auxiliary Fire Service in the Second World War. It provides an instance of an official commentary on the firemen which is patronising but nevertheless also gives them sufficient space, without commentary, to develop an 'unofficial narrative [which] resists any cultural disposition to wrap these men of a different class in an environment of social victims or undress them in a workplace of physical heroes' (Colls & Dodd, 1985, p.31). *We Are The Lambeth Boys* (1959), an example of the Free Cinema movement, also displays similar tensions between an official narrating voice and the unofficial voices of the South London teenagers observed in the film.

The documentary practices of television in the 1980s are obviously rather more sophisticated, partly due to the introduction of lightweight cameras, faster filmstock and synchronised sound. However, we would argue that the 'social democratic' discourse remains dominant in the social problem documentary. Teachers can ask students to analyse one or two examples, noting the differences (particularly pronounced is the use of handheld camera and the greater use of interviews) and similarities between old and modern forms. The similarities might include the use of a middle-class voice or reporter, an appeal to social conscience and state intervention rather than to the need for political struggle. Attention should also be focused on noting the differences between 'victim testimony' (shot size, cutaways of a victim's daily life, a confessional interview mode) and expert analysis (wider shot size, static interior location interview, no personal dimension, an evaluative and analytical interview mode). This constitutes a discursive hierarchy which, given present class-based access to information and knowledge, almost invariably reproduces a class hierarchy between a working (or non-working) class which suffers, and a middle class which defines, evaluates and prescribes. Students might enjoy making a video or tape-slide 'social problem documentary' on the middle class which employs some of the same aesthetic conventions normally used in representing the working class as a social problem.

We should add that we are not arguing that progressive teachers should dismiss the achievements of the social problem documentary. Spaces for even this type of work are rapidly disappearing and need to be guarded and, if possible, developed. Students should also be shown documentary films from the Third World, the independent sector, and such past film-makers as Paul Rotha and Joris Ivens, who admirably summed up the fundamental dilemma of the social problem documentary when commenting on *Housing Problems*:

There have been cases in the history of documentary when photographers became so fascinated by dirt that the result was the dirt looked interesting and strange, not something repellent to the audience . . . In my opinion certain of the early British documentary films, for example *Housing Problems*, fell into this error of exotic dirt. You could not smell these London slums . . . If the British Films could have been sponsored directly by social organisations fighting the bad housing conditions instead of by a Gas company, they would have closed in on such dramatic reality as rent strikes and protest movements. (Joris Ivens, quoted in Julian Petley, 1978, p.13)

Social drama

Student's understanding of television's representation of class can be extended through engaging with some examples of the TV drama tendency which Alan Lovell (1984) has described as British Social Drama. This tendency includes work ranging from the early episodes of *Z Cars*, the early plays of Dennis Potter, David Mercer, Trevor Griffiths (including the 1976 *Bill Brand* series), Jim Allen, the films of Ken Loach and Tony Garnett, and the *Boys From The Blackstuff* series by Alan Bleasdale. This body of work is distinguished by its naturalist/realist aesthetic and its commitment to the portrayal of working-class life which together aim to exploit the television medium in order to expose social injustice to a wide audience.

Study of some of these plays is valuable because it is probably fair to say that they contain some of the most oppositional representations of class relations in Britain which the mass media have ever produced. We hasten to add that we are not advocating the presentation of a 'right-on' corpus of texts which students should sit back and admire; quite the opposite, in fact – these texts should be subject to the same critical rigour as any other. A critical focus can be gained from the initial screening of one or two of the British 'New Wave' films of the late 1950s. *Saturday Night and Sunday Morning* (1960), *A Taste of Honey* (1962) and *This Sporting Life* (1963) are perhaps the most famous of this group of films, which were very influential in establishing a visual rhetoric for the representation of working-class life yet which share the problematic approach outlined in the discussion of social problem documentary. The representations of the urban working class, in films such as *Kes* (1969), were 'poeticised' ones of grime and hardship. The 'poetic' features of these films were widely praised by contemporary reviewers. Isabel Quigley in *The Spectator* wrote: 'Richardson [in *A Taste of Honey*] has used the place and its objects as he uses people, moodily, lovingly, bringing beauty out of squalor'. We would argue that these particularly British 'poetic' representations debilitate rather than liberate. They invite a moistening of the eyes, heavy sighs and then a shrugging of shoulders. They invite us to ask, in the end, a defeated question: 'Well, in the face of all that, what can anyone do?'

Unlike the Free Cinema directors such as Lindsay Anderson and Tony Richardson, the writers of 'social drama' have generally had working-class roots. However, this does not mean that their work has not raised far more issues about representation of class relations than we have space to discuss here. Two examples of the kind of issues which could be raised with students however, are:

1. The fact many of the plays critically endorse the patriarchal nature of working-class institutions and culture. One critic has noted, for example, that in *Boys From The Blackstuff*, 'women are never seen as unemployed people in their own right; they are depicted only in their relationships to men (as wives, mothers, etc.)' (Kevin O'Sullivan, 1984). However, the *Blackstuff* plays did constitute a major departure from the tendency's tradition of mainly representing working-class lives through an almost exclusive focus on the family (see also David Lusted's article in the same dossier – Paterson, 1984).

2. The fact that the implicit endorsement of working-class culture's less progressive features is part of a more general aesthetic problem in the tendency's commitment to naturalistic realism. Trevor Griffiths probably speaks for all these writers when he says:

When you're trying to speak to large numbers of people who did not study literature at university, because they were getting on with productive work, and you're introducing fairly unfamiliar, dense and complex arguments into the fabric of the play, it's just an overwhelming imposition to present those arguments in unfamiliar forms. (Mike Poole and John Wyver, 1984, p.3)

However, whatever the dramatic strengths and weaknesses of this commitment, there is little doubt that it imposes a lack of analysis of the causes of the injustice which have been so eloquently and emotively portrayed. For instance, in *Cathy Come Home* (BBC, 16 November 1966) and *Kes* it is the welfare state institutions of the housing authorities and the school which become the narrative 'enemy'. This is not to defend these particular institutions, merely to comment that the films cannot analyse how the welfare state's agencies have been transformed from being major historical gains for working-class people to being the instruments of their domination – which is, of course, how they are experienced in the films. Realist plausibility necessitates experience being the only way in which these institutions can be represented. Students could actually compare the representations of welfare state officials in these films with those offered in the later *Blackstuff* plays. The dramatic problems of political analysis for naturalistic realism are indicated in these plays by the fact that the two political activists, George and Snowy Malone, have died by the end of the series. However, students should also be encouraged to discuss how *Blackstuff* departs from naturalism in *Yosser's Story*, particularly through devices such as a dream sequence, extreme camera angles and the appearance of real people such as Grahame Souness, the Liverpool football player.

A further crucial issue that students should be asked to consider is why this form of political drama is produced by television. One answer, of course, is that oppositional work can only appear in those institutional spaces sanctioned by the culturally prestigious categorisation of 'art television' or the product of an individual 'author' (see John Caughie, 1981). Whatever its limitations, the social drama represents one of the high-water marks of progressive television and accordingly is increasingly threatened by the intensifying industrialisation of TV. The problem which oppositional ideologies of any sort pose for television is indicated by the following interchange between Sue Lawley and Shaun Sutton, the Head of BBC Drama, when the controversial Ken Loach/Jim Allen series *Days of Hope* was transmitted in 1975:

SL: Shaun Sutton, you haven't answered Bill Deedes' point when he says that there are things about plays like this, with this sort of 'propaganda' in them, which the BBC – or people within the BBC – would not notice were left-wing.

SS: I am quite capable of noticing that they are left-wing. I think any large artistic group will always contain a certain number of people of left-wing persuasion. This is absolutely inevitable, and I think it is perfectly right. In the last two years, we have presented less than ten plays of this nature, before *Days of Hope* – less than ten out of 850 original drama transmissions. That seems a very fair proportion to me.[3]

And those were the good old days!

This discussion of different TV genres and forms is obviously far from exhaustive. We have not mentioned 'literary classic' drama, historical drama, arts programmes (clearly signified as being the province of high culture), variety, or news. Yet even this brief discussion indicates the immense range of representations of class relations which exist, at least at an empirical level. We have noted the relative exclusion of oppositional discourses and representations, but also that popular forms such as soaps and sitcoms contain elements of a critique of dominant class ideologies. Teaching the representation of class in individual texts is perhaps only the 'micro' level of analysis. We also need to introduce students to a 'macro' level of media representation of class relations. Above all, this entails asking students to consider the ways in which the media displace representations of class conflict into representations of 'the nation'.

Teaching 'the nation'

Under the all-embracing banner of 'the national interest' or an image of *Britishness*, the media are able to represent class relations and differences merely as so many facets of the whole. These can be interesting, funny, tragic, emotionally wrought, part of a 'social problem' or whatever, depending upon the emphasis of the text. They are nevertheless subsumed under a national identity. The idea of documentary balance plays a part in this process by presenting the different arguments about some 'problem' but within a framework which takes for granted the existing social order. Any argument questioning that order itself is not on the agenda. The national whole is always greater than its parts.

As teachers we clearly have to address this 'imaginary coherence' (the term is from Nicos Poulantzas, 1978, p.214). So can teacher, the ideological warrior, debunkingly stab the nationalist and chauvinist dragon's heart and release helpless students from the scales of false consciousness? We would argue that such an approach would be an inevitable pedagogic failure, but also a misunderstanding of how 'the nation' works as an ideological category. Clearly the nation state, as embodied in a range of national and international juridical, military and economic institutions, practices and discourses will materially exist for some time to come. What should concern us as media teachers is how the media represent a version of 'the nation' that is congenial to particular (national and international) class interests and hostile to others. Owing to the incomplete nature of the capitalist industrial revolution in Britain, the 'national interest' or 'nationalism' has historically been identified with the interests of the aristocratic and capitalist formations and not with the 'national-popular will' and not with the voice of the 'people' as in numerous European and Third World countries (see Tom Nairn, 1981).

Our pedagogic strategy, then, must be to encourage students to analyse how 'the nation', 'Britishness' and 'the national interest' are constructed in the media and to distinguish which class ideologies are favoured in the process. Do the media marginalise oppositional representations of 'the nation' which might challenge the dominant constructions of it? Consider, for instance, the removal of American defence installations or the 'nationalisation' of multinational capital. Since the 'nation' as an ideological category is constructed through an entire range of media discourses and representations (including racist ones) which only cohere into an 'imaginary coherence' after considerable ideological work, this is a huge field. We will therefore briefly discuss just three crucial areas in this process: royalty, history, and the national economic interest.

Royalty

If there is one area where the teacher will never run short of texts for analysis it is media coverage of royalty. Such is their bewildering profusion that the main difficulty is where to begin. The Royal Family is *the* symbol of national unity, and no one has ever improved on the description of its ideological role by Walter Bagehot:

> It never seems to struggle. It is commonly hidden like a mystery, and sometimes paraded like a pageant, but in neither case is it contentious. The nation is divided into parties but the crown is of no party. Its apparent separation from business is that which removes it both from enmities and from desecration, which preserves its mystery, which enables it to combine the affection of conflicting parties – to be a visible symbol of unity (to those still so imperfectly educated as to need a symbol). (*The English Constitution*, 1867)

How is this unity constructed? Rosalind Brunt (1984) has commented on how the media represent royalty as ' "both just like us" and "not at all like us" '.

A viable teaching strategy would be to analyse with students media texts which perform a *familiarity* function and then those which perform a *distance* function. For it is within the contradiction between these two forms of representation that their ideological role becomes more apparent.

Familiarity. The popularity of the Royal Family has been partially built up by media representations of the Royals in their domestic surroundings, and as a family just like our own 'families'. This partly stems from the joint BBC–ITV production *Royal Family* made in 1969, which gave us all an 'inside view' of the Royals at home. But there are also the 'working mum of today' profiles of the Princess of Wales, the stress on how hard working the Royals are, and the family crises which remind us that they have the same human emotions as everyone else. Rosalind Coward has commented upon how the Royal Family's popularity for the media partly stems from their potential for narrativisation as an ongoing soap opera, with Princess Margaret the wicked sister, Prince Andrew the bad sheep (Randy Andy), etc. (Rosalind Coward, 1984). Students might well be able to chart some of the affinities between media coverage of the Royals in terms of stereotyped roles with that of US soaps.

Distance. However, if the Royal Family *were* 'just like us' they would lose all their interest. Accordingly, many media texts stress their distance from the humdrum lives of us ordinary mortals, their transcendence of political and social divisions. This is orchestrated through TV coverage of major royal events such as coronations and weddings, their regular appearance on television news as 'the good news' story to heal the fracturous body politic which has featured earlier, the 'horror' stories of people such as Michael Fagan and Michael Trestrail 'contaminating' the royal presence, the reporting of oracular pronouncements on social matters by Prince Charles, the privileged institutional status of the Queen's Christmas broadcast to 'the Nation and Commonwealth'.

Of course, teachers can also raise the absences in this coverage: no scrutiny of royal wealth, of their role in the maintenance of an anachronistic class formation, of their family connections with exiled reactionary heads of state, of their actual material 'uselessness'. As Rosalind Brunt wisely points out, the popularity of the Royal Family can only be accounted for if we recognise that they meet 'real social needs' for enjoyment, disinterested recognition of merit, for fellowship and unity. How else these needs could be met might, of course, also be discussed with students.

History

There is obviously a considerable overlap between representations of royalty and those of 'history'. It can occasionally seem that British television is still fixated upon a recitation of the 'Kings and Queens of England' view of history. Royalty, of course, is represented as the dominant living embodiment of 'our' history which has been almost reduced to a tourist commodity. Colin McArthur (1978) has shown how television specially 'cannibalises' history by returning to the British past for source material for spectacular costume drama (often aimed at the US TV market). Not only does this represent history as being the product of a

few 'great individuals', but it also constitutes an effective
ideological intervention in the maintenance of present class
relations. Students could (possibly in conjunction with a
sympathetic History teacher) work on some of the texts that have
played a key role in the 'nostalgia boom'. *Chariots of Fire*,
Upstairs Downstairs, *Days of Hope* and *Shine on Harvey Moon*
might be compared as representations of a particular period in
history which has become established as a golden and settled era
by media nostalgia. How do these representations of class in the
past modify our perceptions of class relations in the present? Are
we relieved that we don't live in such a hierarchical society, or
are we attracted to that seeming stability? Are we reassured that
we now live in a classless society?

Teachers might choose to follow up some of the work done on
representations of the 'nation at war' in the BFI's *National
Fictions – World War II in British Films and Television* (Geoff
Hurd, 1984). This collection demonstrates how the need for unity
in the war precipitated a major propaganda intervention by the
state in funding films to urge all classes to do their bit for the war
effort. This entailed a strategy of allowing relatively progressive
representations of the working classes to ensure their identification
with the official messages of the narrative, which was just part of
a much wider move towards creating a classless society after the
war. Screenings of *Millions Like Us* (1943) and *Listen to Britain*
(1942) will engage students in analysis of the manufacture of a
'national identity' and class unity. The teacher could then screen
films such as *The Dambusters* (1954) from the 1950s to illustrate
how once the war was won the working class (and women) were
returned to their subordinate status and history was left to
middle-class men to win once more. Analysis could then turn to
more contemporary images of the war such as *Dad's Army*
(1971), where the war is used to summon up a nostalgic past
community, or *The Imitation Game* (1980), which questions that
assumption (some say in a very sexist way). This project could
finish with some texts from the Falklands/Malvinas conflict, which
consciously evoked a Churchillian rhetoric about the Dunkirk
spirit and our finest hour.[4]

Analyses of representations of the Second World War are
particularly valuable because during the war an embryonic
oppositional definition of the 'nation' as the expression of the

popular will came into being and was then subsequently suppressed. Its remoteness as a period enables students to engage with the concept of the 'nation' as an ideological construct whose meaning is never finally fixed.

The national economic interest

Given that nearly 20 per cent of UK manufacturing output is controlled by foreign multinational corporations, one might question the continuing validity of the term 'national economic interest'. One would certainly use it with more qualification than the media. However, notwithstanding the undeniably huge inequalities in ownership of wealth in Britain, the media continue to represent our different and conflicting economic interests as being unproblematically subsumed into the 'national economic interest'. Within the terms of this discourse profits are always 'good' (even if they mean redundancies) and strikes are disruptive even if they are pursuing a 'national economic interest' which might be differently perceived from how the state or employers define it – as happened in the coal dispute where the NUM were trying to put the case for a national energy policy that would include a major role for coal.

Study of media representations of strikes will introduce students to representations of class conflict at its acutest. After all, strikes are the most overt manifestation of the clash of class interests at the workplace. The coverage will concentrate on the effects of the strike rather than its causes, characteristics which have been documented by the Glasgow University Media Group in particular (see Glasgow University Media Group, 1982). Teachers might introduce this topic by screening *Making News* (1984) or *Why Their News is Bad News* (1982) (available from the Campaign for Press and Broadcasting Freedom), which set out, quite accessibly, the 'norms' of television news reporting of strikes. This could be complemented by the screening of past films such as *I'm Alright Jack* (1959) which shows the embryonic formation of the stereotype of 'the man in the middle' victimised by greedy workers and blinkered management.

Documentation of the coverage of the year-long coal dispute is already growing and will doubtless have increased by the time this book appears. The Campaign for Broadcasting Freedom's pamphlet, *Media Hits the Pits* (1985), provides ample evidence of the media coverage of the dispute. The *Miners' Campaign Tapes*, a series of six videotapes made through the resources of the independent film and video sector and representatives from the National Union of Mineworkers – winners of the 1984 BFI Grierson Award – provide an unusual and valuable teaching resource. The videos do not make any attempt to be balanced; instead they are clearly agitational and morale-boosting devices aimed at a specific audience – the mineworkers themselves and other trade unionists whose support was being lobbied. With these tapes it is possible to see the considerable distance between mainstream output on the dispute and the potential alternatives: the tapes have a narrowly defined audience, not a general one; they have an explicit political message, not a hidden one; and they are intended for public consumption within meetings, not within the domestic confines of one's own home. The tapes, when juxtaposed with the social democratic/capitalist discourse of mainstream television news and current affairs, not only indicate the limited diversity of representations of industrial disputes available in our media; they also point to the possibility of very different representations of both 'class relations' and 'the national interest'. They also point to the possibilities of challenging dominant representations of 'class relations' and 'the national interest'. It is these possibilities which learning about media representations should discover.

6 Gender

'A girl is a girl. It's nice to be told you're successful at it' – Rita Hayworth

If by gender we mean the ways in which femininity, masculinity, relationships and sexuality are conceptualised in any society, then we must acknowledge the power of the media to construct gender in ours. How do we learn to be female or male? How do we become 'naturally' one or the other? How do we become 'unnaturally' neither or both ? Discernible biological differences between the sexes appear to naturalise the social and economic positions in which girls and boys, women and men are unequally placed. So while oppression is directly experienced by women and by gay people as a result of those unequal positionings, it is not necessarily conceptualised as such. Instead, sexist oppression is accepted without question as being part of the way things are. 'That's Life!' The media, alongside other socialising agencies, are constantly constructing that apparently natural 'reality'.

Any teaching about the ways in which media representations construct gender will be immediately and continuously required to negotiate the problems of confronting accounts of personal experience which are often both firmly rooted in the 'way things are' and yet also at odds with it. Offered glamorous prospects for their femininity by the media, girls are also made aware that they are 'naturally' equipped to fulfil socially useful roles. Glamour girl, housewife and mother are a few of the limited and contradictory options open. Women can acquire power and exert it within these designated identities. Brushing hair and painting nails is quite often used to resist teacher interference in the classroom – and how often have anti-sexist strategies been met with 'What's wrong with wanting to look attractive?' or 'Someone's got to look after the kids, haven't they?'. Stereotypical images of male prowess and of female sex kitten are frequently adopted by students and used subversively within the determinations of their social class and their schooling. For many girls, having been elbowed out on to the edges of the playground and into the depths of the kitchen sink, 'femininity' may well appear to be a uniquely valuable asset. In *Learning to Labour* (1977), Paul Willis shows how laddish behaviour at work allows the subordination under capitalist modes of production to become bearable. However, in spite of the potential men and women can gain through socially approved roles, that power is limited, especially in the case of women and of gays and lesbians, who are either on the precariously defensive or courageously trying to determine positions and identities for themselves.

A teacher who begins to investigate representations of gender by using students' personal experience as a referent will soon have to confront mixed reactions of confusion and resentment. Apparently straightforward and simple questions of gender problematise the personal, making it political. The bedrock of commonsense assumptions as to what constitutes homo- or hetereosexuality is fissured: ideas about sexuality are contradictory and changing. The 'buddy' films of Howard Hawks, *Starsky and Hutch*, the football players who fawn over each other have 'scored', these both affirm conventional ideas of tough, capable masculinity, but can also be seen to negotiate difficulties and uncertainties. The dumb sex object that we have come to equate with media representations of women is not to be found in the film *Nine to Five* (1980), in *Widows* (at least in the first series) or in *Cat's Eyes*. To the rules society lays down about our gender, there are variations and exceptions. These rules and exceptions which the media represent usually confirm notions about the status quo, but occasionally construct different ways as to how we might be able to consider the positions which the social formation has engendered for us.

Little is learnt by comparing what teachers too often assume to be the generally considered 'stereotypical' images with another state of affairs which is assumed to be 'true'. The objective of any media study should be to understand *how* and *why* media representations of gender efface, resolve or, more unusually, expose the contradictions which beleaguer our commonsense understanding. Beyond the simple identification of gender differences we should aim to bring into recognition the systems of oppression which ensure that homo- and heterosexual women, men and children have unequal relations.

We accept that there are few heads capable of engaging with a study of narrative, of institutional determinants, of audiences and of representations of race, age, class and gender. For the sake of intellectual clarity, conceptual isolation can save unnecessary headaches. Nevertheless, it has to be recognised that the chapter headings we have used in this book to designate particular objects of media study are more often than not inseparable. Studying Don Siegel's *The Killers* (1964) in order to discover the principles of its narrative construction will also inevitably raise questions about the narrative function and the representation of Sheila Farr, and may even require teaching about her *film noir* antecedents. Teaching about representations of gender and of race in *Burning an Illusion* (1981) or the *Pictures of Women* (1983) series on Channel 4 should not ignore the contexts of their production or circulation.[1]

In our investigation of how the media construct gender, no essential woman- or manhood can be presumed. If we take sexism to be the systematic oppression of women by men and of homosexuals by heterosexuals, then we must also recognise the various oppressions suffered and exerted. Working-class and middle-class women, black women, lesbian and heterosexual women share recognitions of sexist oppression in sisterhood, but the ways in which race and class temper that solidarity also need to be acknowledged. Black and white men might share features conventionally recognised as masculine, but white men are not subjected to racism. These qualifications are not intended as constant postponements, interminable difficulties which obstruct the business of teaching about representations of gender in the media. We recognise that it is not enough to acknowledge that one complex question will propagate multifarious others. But if media representations of gender are going to be taught then the complexities briefly described here cannot be ignored. To enable students to understand both general patterns and particular instances of media representations of gender we have tried to suggest approaches and strategies according to categories which will mainly confine our discussion to representations of women. This means that we cannot deal adequately with representations of gays, lesbians and men. We recognise, however, that assumptions of heterosexuality need to be questioned throughout, and we would wish to point to the recent work on representations of men which has usefully broadened concerns about how our notions of gender are constructed.[2]

Our discussions of representations of gender are categorised in the following ways:

1. woman as body;
2. women in domestic labour;
3. women in paid work;
4. adolescence and romance.

Woman as body

Men have broad shoulders and narrow hips, and accordingly they possess intelligence. Women have narrow shoulders and broad hips. Women ought to stay at home; the way they were created indicates this, for they have broad hips and a wide fundament to sit upon, keep house and bear and raise children. (attributed to Luther, in O'Faolain and Martines, 1979)

Pictures of women's bodies are used to sell a vast range of products: cars, magazines and newspapers, computers, alcohol, perfume, package holidays. Pictures of men's bodies are not used in the same way, nor to the same extent. To assume a moral consensus among students as to the unfairness of this practice is to assume too much, especially when teaching mixed groups. From boys the reaction is often, 'Well, if this is the case, so what?', leaving the teacher with apparently little else to do than impose a 'personal' opinion.

What have to be pointed out here are the power relationships which represent women as objects to be fixed by the camera, generally the equivalent of a male gaze. Who is this image for? Why is the woman there? What effect would be produced if a man was represented in that image in that way? Questions along these lines do not focus on descriptions of the image, outraged or salacious, but they begin to make rather less natural those representations which reduce women to their bodies, sexual objects for men.

In 1956 we launched a car known in Sweden as the Amazon.

People joked you had to be one to drive it and they've been telling the same story ever since.

Now for 1982 we're introducing power-assisted steering as standard on all our big Volvo saloons and estate cars. It'll be funny not hearing those jokes anymore.

AMAZON

245 DL

VOLVO

PRICES FOR THE 1982 VOLVO ESTATES START AT £7985. SALOONS AT £6068 (EXCLUDING DELIVERY & A NUMBER PLATES). ALL PRICES CORRECT AT TIME OF SIGNING TO PRESS. SALES TEL: (0494) 33444. SERVICE TEL: (HIGH WYCOMBE (0494) 33444. PARTS TEL: (HIGH WYCOMBE (0494) 33444. OR WRITE TO DEPT. R1/22, VOLVO CUSTOMER SERVICES, HIGH WYCOMBE, BUCKS. HP13 3PH.

10 Bodies selling bodies

Representations of women in advertisements have traditionally provided a 'good way in' to media studies. However, quite apart from the problems involved in using sexist images, an investigation of this kind may not do much more than teach students what they already know. The term 'sex object' is already laden with values and associations which have in themselves become conventional. A different starting point might be to look at the ways in which ostensibly 'scientific' and 'neutral' representations of women's bodies lay them bare to the scrutiny of male beholders, powerful in that they, as doctors or scientists, are self-proclaimed possessors of knowledge. Not only are women surveyed and represented by male professionals and writers, but they are 'fixed' in those representations which apparently discover the 'complications' of the female body, a body which nevertheless houses ineffable processes. Thus, even in the most professedly 'objective' representations, woman's body, her visible form, is represented in terms which have naturalised, through centuries, contradictory social positions: glamour girl, wife, mother. Sexual, social and economic subordinations are what these positions share.

An image currently belying these notions of subordination is the one of the woman 'working out'. Jane Fonda has epitomised this representation of a woman who can become liberated not so much through political activity and consciousness (although her own history lends the 'work out' a 'right-on' resonance) but more through pushing her own body through the paces. It is interesting that the liberating control which aerobics promised necessarily involved pain. You have to 'feel the burn'. Videotapes and books on aerobics have all the scientific trappings to make them convincing – opening the heart and lungs, a glowing complexion, a zest for life. 'Our bodies are our own' has long been a slogan of the women's movement, and women are gradually beginning to win the struggle to take their health into their own hands. However, in the videotape of her 'workout', Jane Fonda makes no such political claim. Her poses, whilst denying sexuality, are undeniably sexual, as the costume of leotards and legwarmers testify. Her crotch is often the focal point of the frame, and Fonda is face to camera most of the time. This establishes an ambiguous relationship with the audience. For other women watching and working out Fonda may simply be showing them what to do. But as the woman who has achieved glamour, slimness *and* liberation she is also representing what they *haven't* done (perhaps cannot do!) in conventionally sexist (even pornographic) photographic codes.

Woman as body is problematic for the dominant look of the (male) camera, and perhaps that is why she is so often subjected to it (Laura Mulvey, 1975). Greater mastery over women and their bodies takes place when they are partially represented. The parts of women's bodies most often represented in still photographs (apart from pornographic ones) are faces, looking to be looked at. Different contexts will demand different photographic codes, but one context accessible to classroom study is the women's magazine. On the covers of women's magazines, women's faces are metonymic: they not only signify the identity of the magazine, they also signify the whole woman.

Selling Pictures, a teaching pack produced by the BFI,[3] offers rich possibilities for students learning about representations of gender. Among other materials the pack includes a set of slides and a poster of a range of front covers from women's magazines. The differences of race, class and age can be ascertained by comparing the covers (*My Weekly* with *Harpers Bazaar*, for instance) but there are also similiarities between them, as though they commonly denominate women in general. Whatever class, age or race of women these magazines address, the faces on their covers are pleasant and alluring. The allure differs from the sophisticated and sexual to the more open *joie de vivre*. But unlike advertisements (although this is what magazine covers are), these representations are not ostensibly produced for men. Here, the women represented on the covers look invitingly at women who will purchase them. The power relationship is still one between product and consumer, and, of course, male photographers, photo-editors and layout designers have produced the representation in the first place. But women represented on women's magazine covers construct a particular, if ambiguous, address to their audience.

The alluring faces represent an image with which a female consumer can identify. These disembodied faces are not so much to be scrutinised by men (though, of course, that may well happen) but they invite women consumers to turn that scrutiny upon themselves. The representations are internalised. They represent women to women as how women would like to look

and be looked at. In his discussion of nakedness and nudity, John
Berger succinctly expresses this internalisation:

> Men look at women. Women watch themselves being looked
> at. This determines not only most relations between men and
> women but also the relation of women to themselves. The
> surveyor of woman in herself is male: the surveyed female.
> Thus she turns herself into an object – and most particularly an
> object of vision: a sight. (John Berger, 1972b, p.47)

The beautification of anatomical curves is not a simple matter of
'aesthetic appreciaton'. Once this internalisation of the male gaze
is understood by students, it goes some way towards explaining
why women are themselves caught up in those representations
which use their bodies as sexual objects.

Berger's analysis implies that the female viewer internalises the
male gaze which oppresses her but does not recognise that
oppression as such.[4] However, this is not always necessarily the
case. That these representations of women's faces are alluring
means they are also alluring to women. The 'surveyor of woman
in herself' need not necessarily be male. She could be female,
and the possibilities exist for these women's magazines, albeit
produced within and reinforcing the confines of sexism, to
articulate a desire between women and the representations of
themselves which is far from heterosexual. The possibilities for
discovering this alternative gaze in the classroom are not as
remote as might immediately be thought. Ask girls why they
think the faces on these covers are 'lovely' or 'beautiful'. Instead
of dismissing their responses as part of their 'false consciousness'
within a sexist and capitalist formation, the teacher may well be
validating otherwise forbidden pleasures and desires by asking
such a question.

If teaching about representations of women as body can
tentatively discover alternative relations of power between
representations and their audience (in this case who they
represent) then what has to be recognised is the *limited range* of
representations made available. Representations of *both* women
and men are no less limited in that the same stock of types are
repeatedly represented. It cannot be denied, however, that
women have less power than men to produce and circulate their

own representations. When women do construct critiques of the ways in which they are represented by the dominant media, the results are powerful. An extremely useful and short film to use in this respect is the animation film *Give Us a Smile*, produced and distributed by the Leeds Animation Workshop. Perhaps the most objectionable representations of women as bodies are those of black women. Ask students to describe the ways in which black women are most commonly represented, and they will usually outline three typifications. One is the 'beast of burden', the black woman as oppressed worker and to Western eyes stripped of her sexuality. Another might be the 'lovable, plump mammy', the role Butterfly McQueen eventually refused to play but which may be resurrected in the persona of Rustie Lee. Most prevalent are those representations of black women as exotic bodies, the doubly 'forbidden fruit'. Airline commercials sell countries as tourist havens by associating them with the women who will 'take you there'. Once again, like the anatomical drawings these commercials represent, the black woman's body is represented as a mysterious landscape which can be discovered by those with the right sense of adventure and the right size wallet. To ask why these particular representations of black women are dominant is to take study of the media into study of an imperialist history. Here gaps between the ideological and the material can be bridged as the power relationships in both become critically exposed.

Women in domestic labour

Ask students where domesticity is mainly represented and their answers will list those media products with women as their target audiences – TV commercials for detergents, *Homes and Gardens* soap operas, women's magazines. The domestic connotes woman. Women in domestic labour are usually represented in the media as (house)wives and mothers, rarely as sex objects. Even so, domestic women are still seen to be smiling. They smile differently from the *Cosmopolitan* or *Honey* cover girl because they now have responsibilities, but they are nevertheless contented with their lot. The home (where a man's heart is) is, of course, the woman's place. Female students may recognise domestic labour as 'work', but then the smiles of contentment so often represented make the domestic seem a leisured space. A useful introductory task to set students is to ask them to collect representations of the domestic which focus on work. The task will seem fruitless (and for that reason a fairly stringent time limit should be set) because few images answering that description will be found. Representations of work are generally absent in media representations of class, but here the absence seems particularly pertinent. The reproduction of labour is apparently effortless. Photographs show food as the completely prepared meal, beds are made, shoes and socks tidied away from view. Commercials for irons show them powerfully steering themselves across yards of the most resistant-looking fabrics. Students might well feel cheated when asked to look for signs that are not to be found, but the absence is in itself significant. Why is domestic labour invisible? An invariable answer is because people don't want to be reminded of the humdrum, dirty and boring. Precisely. If domestic labour was represented it would have to be recognised as the unequal share most women have to do. In *Dallas*, Puerto Rican maids can be seen dimly in the background. The white women have their work done for them by other women who are rendered invisible.

Single parents, bad housing, inadequate childcare, these absences from dominant representations of women at home are thrown into sharp relief by a slide pack called *Who's Holding the Baby?*, produced by the Hackney Flashers.[5] An exercise using these slides with students might entail asking questions as to how the Hackney Flashers constructed their photographic messages. What images and slogans are recognisable from the mainstream media? How have these been changed? Juxtaposition and montage in these photographs not only deliberately expose the ways in which they have been constructed, but also reveal the social structures which ensure the maintenance of inequality. They also point to ways in which those oppressed by media representations can collectively use the media in oppositional ways. Questions then raised as to why these kinds of images are difficult to find will show that dominant representations are not as 'natural' as they first seemed.

Part of the work around representations of women in domestic labour should be concerned with the ways in which the media position women as domestic and isolated workers in their schedules. Mid-morning and early afternoon programmes position women as consumers, and their productive and re-productive functions are constructed in terms of their domestic concerns. A typical day's mid-morning and afternoon programming will demonstrate this point. On the afternoon of Friday 7 February 1986, audiences at home could choose from the following: *News Afternoon*, *Pebble Mill at One*, *King Rollo*, *Bric a Brac*, *Count Me In*, *Heathcliff the Cat*, *The Railway Children* and *Secrets Out* on BBC1; schools programmes and *World Bowls* on BBC2; *Benny*, *Rainbow*, *Here to Stay*, *News at One*, *Thames News*, *Friday Matinee (Love in Pawn)*, *Mr and Mrs*, *Thames News*, *Sons and Daughters* on ITV; *A Question of Economics*, *Dance Matinee*, *The Chord Sharp*, *Fragile Earth* and *Countdown* on Channel 4. With a few exceptions the domestic afternoon audience is constructed in terms of its childish or romantic interests.

Students might be asked to reschedule programmes and to invent new ones for a domestic audience which might be conceptualised differently. It could quite plausibly consist of the growing numbers of unemployed, nightworkers and the retired, as well as parents with toddlers. Alternatively, students could be asked to write treatments for programmes for women at home which would serve their needs very differently from the ways in which the daytime hours are filled at present.

Motherhood, so often represented as a state of instinctual bliss, also needs to be understood as a social construction. A simple practical exercise might be to send students out to photograph parents with their babies and toddlers in the streets, queuing at the bus stop or in the post office. Juxtaposing these with images from *Mother and Baby* or Mothercare catalogues is not to evoke a recognition of what is more 'realistic', but to pose questions about the functions which representations of ideal motherhood in our society perform. Pleasant it may be to look at images of beaming mothers and gurgling babies, but far from enabling women to recognise and change their subordinate positions as unpaid domestic labourers, these representations of ideal motherhood not only disguise that subordination by suffusing it with a 'natural glow', but they also engender anxiety and a sense of inadequacy. The gap between the reality of dirty nappies and a house to clean and the media representations of fair young mothers helping their look-alike daughters in Hygena kitchens is constantly oppressive. The mothers represented have finished cooking and cleaning, but for those unrepresented the work is never done.

In the award-winning *Kramer vs. Kramer* (1979), motherhood is gradually edged out of the narrative in an ostensible 'progressive' move towards promoting representations of a more capable paternity. By the end of the film the mother has relinquished the claim to the custody of her child. Her submission is the ultimate gesture of altruism. By losing her child she becomes what every mother ought to be. The son and the father can get on in the world together.

Students could display images of motherhood from different times and places to show that the ideal motherhood so dominantly represented in our media is one determined by middle-class notions. That women have successfully brought up children without having to be trapped in the singular role of motherhood makes apparent different ways of being. For adolescent students, especially girls for whom marriage and motherhood have been constructed as the acme of achievement, this may well provide part of a more optimistic education. Motherhood is a social construction which is constantly under review, and study of newspaper articles will reveal what problems are currently negotiated. At the time of writing, articles on the Gillick case, Enoch Powell's Protection of the Unborn Child Bill, surrogate motherhood, children in care and the births of royal babies jostle to claim our attention and moral verdicts. In comparing such newspaper articles questions should ask what is being assumed about motherhood. What kinds of motherhood are being advocated? Are the implicit moral judgements contradictory? Fertility and childcare, apparently still so intrinsically part of female 'nature', are still not under women's control.

Women in paid work

To step outside the domestic role (even when necessity dictates) can invite retribution, as Mildred Pierce discovered (see E. Ann Kaplan, 1978, p.76). Media representations of jobs deemed suitable for women are often determined by the wider economy.

SUNDAY PEOPLE, April 28, 1985   27

Margaret Forwood

THE BEST READ TELEVISION COLUMNIST IN BRITAIN

MY TV WEEK

Give us the Avengers or Angels—not C.A.T.S. in mufflers!

THE THREE stars of C.A.T.S. Eyes, I hear, were chosen not only for acting ability (tee-hee) but also for their very different sexual appeal.

Apparently TVS carefully worked out that every male viewer would fancy either elegant uppercrust redhead Rosalyn Lander, or they'd prefer cheerful cockney blonde Leslie Ash, or else their taste would run to brunette...

CHILLY: Leslie, Jill and Rosalyn. Woollies spoil their sex appeal.

11

A study of women's magazines during and after the world wars will bear this out, and the BBC series *Inside Women's Magazines* is a valuable resource. In *The Life and Times of Rosie the Riveter* (1980) four American women relate the tales of their own working and domestic lives within the changing requirements society made of them. Soap operas, the 'women's genres', are rich material to analyse in terms of how women are represented in their domestic *and* working lives. In *Coronation Street*, Mike Baldwin's machine shop, the Rover's Return and the shop are the places where women work, but they are rarely seen to be working. Instead, work features as a space where women congregate to pass comment on each other, on events in the street.

The BFI pack, *Teaching 'Coronation Street'*,[6] organises approaches to teaching about the serial in terms of its narrative structures and in terms of how its women characters are represented. In *Coronation Street* work provides a forum for more important things outside. In Channel 4's *Brookside*, however, work is in itself an important part of women's wide-ranging conversation. Karen Grant ditched Andrew, her boyfriend, because she wanted to go to university; Annabelle Collins sets up her own catering business in spite of her chauvinist husband; nursing, for Kate, was (literally) her life, and Heather Huntingdon is determined to be a successful accountant in spite of the men who harass and compromise her. Bobby Grant's trade union principles are challenged by Sheila and Karen for their failure to make the personal political. In the *Brookside* narratives, work in the lives of the women characters poses enigmas. How can work be pleated into the domestic or romantic? How can a woman at work prove she is as good as, or better, than the men? For men there are problems at work – between union and management, for instance – but work, or the lack of it, does not problematise their gendered roles in society. How is Heather Huntingdon's or Sandra's work articulated with other strands in the narrative? How does Bobby Grant's or Paul Collins's work make them question their male roles? These comparative questions are fruitful ones to ask because they will not necessarily provoke straightforward answers. Students might argue that women and their work in *Brookside* are narrative devices upon which are hung various other issues of narrative or 'social' significance. They may, however, argue that the 'progressive' realism of *Brookside* allows audiences to question and to debate issues of gender which dialogue and narrative set up and spin out. The continuum of soap operas (some say that 'nothing ever happens in them') perhaps imitates the ways in which women think about their lives. Problems are never single, nor are they solved with the arrival of an armed policeman. In most women's lives one thing does lead to another, and this requires sequential negotiations and temporary resolutions.

In spite of more 'progressive' representations of women since Channel 4's programming, the types of work in which women are represented are still extraordinarily limited: nurses, secretaries, models, waitresses and policewomen. Where women are ostensibly given responsibility (in other words, when they are not doing working-class jobs) they are represented as sexual objects on display first, and as efficient hard-thinking people second. If they are 'too good' at their professional jobs then they are not proper women. If they are proper women then they cannot possibly do a difficult job well. There are, of course, welcome exceptions, and however dramatic narratives are encoded, women in the audience will more than likely decode them in more positive ways. Students could be asked to compare the working relationships of male protagonists in *The Sweeney* or *Miami Vice* with those of female protagonists and their colleagues in *Juliet Bravo*, *The Gentle*

Touch or *Cagney and Lacey*. The women may lack the muscle and hardware of which the men make aggressive use, but they do not lack daring, tact or cunning. Joyce and Lucy get on with the jobs they have to do in *Hill Street Blues*. They pull their punches, take no concessions and are witty with it.

Adolescence and romance

These limited representations of adult women in the media demarcate gender boundaries in our society. This is not to say that women have not effected changes either in their social positions or in the ways in which they are represented by the media. Women's publishing, for instance, has become the major growth area for publishing in the 1980s, and the journal *Spare Rib* now enjoys national distribution and a large circulation. Nevertheless, publications such as *Outwrite* and *Mukhti* continue to be produced on shoestring budgets and are not always easy to buy, especially outside cities. Production and distribution of women's video and film is constantly obstructed and marginalised. It is not hard to understand why acceptance of dominant representations of women and of 'the way things are' continues. For girls and young women, representations of gender show that sexuality has to be marshalled and fixed, and it is during girlhood and adolescence that the contradictory preparations for the various states of oppressed womanhood are made.

There is now no shortage of material which teachers can make available. An investigation of sex stereotyping in the images and texts of books across the school curriculum would alone provide enough work for a term. But the learning students should have acquired about the ways in which women are variously represented will serve to contextualise work which deals with representations of their own gendered histories. Images and texts in gender-differentiated comics and magazines – *Bunty* and *Victor*, *My Guy* and *Shoot!* – may be providing students with 'what they want', but at the same time any teaching about the media should begin to show that these 'wants' are themselves constructed and that the lack of alternative representations means that other 'wants' are more rarely articulated. In magazines for both sexes the heroes and protagonists are always white. Black girls don't apparently fall in love, and they are certainly never the objects of desire. White men know how to blitz grass-skirted savages and slit-eyed 'nips'. To point to the racism in these publications is to begin to contradict the notion that they provide what their readers want, for to read them in those terms would mean denying the existence of a multiracial society, even though black students must constitute a fairly large percentage of their readership.

If 'wants' are constructed, how is this achieved? Students might trace the representations of girls in a comic such as *Bunty* with those in *Jackie* or *My Guy*. In the former, girls are often resourceful, brave and plan things out together, even though they are usually the boarding-school types. Class boundaries in sisterhood are built early. In the latter, girls walk alone, wistful in autumnal rain, or they are wracked with jealousy of their best friends. Adventure, permissible in girlhood, is scaled down for young women, but it is a requisite for boys who are going to be men. We do not deny that this kind of work is very difficult to undertake, especially in a mixed class of adolescents for whom sexuality may be proving exciting, but hazardous, to negotiate. Perhaps our teaching about representations of gender should be concerned to make these negotiations more exciting, but also more thoughtful. When investigating representations of gender in girls' magazines, a class should *not* just be asked to define the positions which representations of girls construct for girls reading them. Questions as to what positions are not made available should also be asked and, perhaps more importantly, the class should be asked to examine the ways in which girls' magazines represent boys.

A possible exercise is to give the class a brief photo-story from an IPC publication and to ask students to re-write the thought and speech bubbles that have been blanked out. Students could also prepare the next week's episode of a photo-story, changing the opportunities for a distressed or boy-crazed heroine and allowing her, for instance, to wreak her vengeance and proudly walk into a sunset of her own making.

Top of the Pops is a programme which provides countless complex representations of young women behaving as they 'know' they can in the context of a pop programme. However, even a programme as blatantly sexist as *Top of the Pops* offers itself to alternative, if subdued, readings. The 'star' heroes, from Donny Osmond and Adam Ant to Boy George and Marilyn, signify an ambiguous sexuality. Is it an encoded femininity which girls go wild about, an 'outrageous' heterosexual display which disguises desires still more illicit? Sheryl Garratt argues the case:

> The people most attracted to the ideal of the hard, hairy, virile hunk of male are, in fact, other men, who form the majority of the audience at any heavy metal gig. Women seem far more excited by slim, unthreatening, baby-faced types who act vulnerable and who resemble them. Androgeny is what they want: men they can dress like and identify with, as well as drool over. With so few women performers to use as models, perhaps girlish boys are the next best things. (Sue Steward and Sheryl Garratt, 1984)

Garratt also explains that the popularity of the 'baby-faced' stars does not depend on a mindless heterosexual adulation. On the contrary, it has much more to do with girls' sociability: 'Our real obsession was with ourselves; in the end the actual men behind the posters had very little to do with it at all'.

Music programmes have yet to provide feminists with 'representations of women performers to use as models', but TV programmes such as *The Tube* have admitted a much wider representation of gender. Their outlandishness allows all kinds of barriers to be transgressed but these transgressions are nevertheless confined by other, socially constructed boundaries. After all, it is only the 'young' who can get up to such antics, who can flaunt an ambiguous sexuality and get away with it. These representations of gender which are not oppressively determining are recuperated into a politics of style by the dominant media. Magazines such as *The Face* and *I-D* simply translate the politics of 'gender bending' into what's 'cool' or 'naff'.[7] To be a boy and wear feminine, styled clothes might signify a contempt for conventional 'masculinity'. On the other hand it may signify no more than success in a trendy cosmopolitan world where comparatively few are permitted their eccentricities. After all, dressing flamboyantly does not in itself cure men of their chauvinism. What teachers have to investigate with students is what liberations the politics of style offer. How can they be incorporated into the less glamorous, ordinary lives that most people lead? Why are such liberations necessary in our ordinary, 'normal' lives?

'Youth' as an audience category is one specifically addressed by radio and television music programmes and by the fashion industry, and in that category the interests of young women are usually subsumed. Youth is generally represented as male. This is even more likely to be the case as unemployment continues to push women back into the home and young men out on to the streets. If there are only a few programmes for 13–18 year-olds then there are even fewer for young women. Why? At this point analyses in the classroom need to inquire more deeply into the structures of broadcasting and publishing. Who controls what? How are decisions made? How can we win the struggle to make our representations visible? In this section we have tried to show how questions about media representations of gender can lead directly to questions about the structures of our social formation.

7 Race

'the concept of childhood . . . being developed between the seventeenth and eighteenth centuries introduced specific determinations of dependency which are bound up with a mercantilist phase of territorial expansion. Childhood, in short, is exportable well beyond the confines of the family, as it may be attributed to entire races presumed not to have reached a civilised status. Immaturity and primitiveness are contemporary notions, indeed, discoveries actually made, which circle around a whole complex of unresolved questions: what is human? *When* is one human? In a pre-civilised state? Only in a civilised state? To ask the question "what is human" is two-edged and poignant at a time when the slave trader supplied the answer' – Richard Appignanesi (1979) p.189

Contexts

A press photograph taken at Notting Hill Carnival in August 1978 (Photograph 12). A scene of pleasure. A fine day; music and dancing; food and drink; young policemen enjoying the fun with young female revellers. Given that newspapers present images of gloom and doom much of the time (most news, by definition, is bad news) it might seem churlish to do other than applaud such an image of multi-racial harmony. However, to read the image in this way is to read it superficially, purely as it is in itself; it is not to see it within the flow and existence of all news photographs in general, and in particular in the flow of those that include representations of black people. Before indicating what the context for the photograph is, let us look at it a little more closely.

12

First of all it is interesting that the policemen are not wearing
their jackets – this was no doubt officially sanctioned due to the
warm weather, but nevertheless it is useful for the informal
approach being adopted after the confrontations of the previous
two years. This context makes the easy informality and friendliness
of the photograph – shirt sleeves rolled up, arm in arm with
young black girls, (some) broad smiles, postures that would
almost seem to suggest sexual availability – all the more striking.
At the same time it is useful to recognise another context – that
of the history of press reporting of the carnival. Every year for
the last fifteen years most national daily newspapers have carried
such pictures; the carnival has become the one annual press event
for portraying racial harmony between the police and black
people. This careful construction just happens to be doubly
marked in the case of this photograph: note the hand and camera
of a photographer on the left-hand side of the image, and note
also at whom the policeman with the broad smile is looking!
 A further context is provided by the accompanying UPI (United

Press International, one of the big four Western news agencies) caption:

08/27/78; LONDON. Policemen join in the fun of the first day of the 14th Nottinghill gate carnival [*sic*], the predominantly West African and Caribbean festival which attracts an estimated 250,000 people over two days.

A similar picture for the next day, with an almost identical caption, concludes: 'last year it ended in mugging and robberies' [sic]. Thus are set the terms of reference of the photograph for newspaper picture editors both in Great Britain and overseas.

But what about the wider context? If we investigate previous images of Notting Hill Carnival in the years that preceded and followed 1978 we find the following. The years 1976 and 1977 saw the tension between the police and the black community in the area coming to a head and generating the worst conflicts that took place in the 1970s. By the middle of the decade young black people were no longer prepared to go on accepting the treatment their parents had received, and the state was becoming increasingly anxious, as indicated in the White Paper on racial discrimination (September 1975) which initiated the 1976 Race Relations Act; immigration controls were becoming even tighter; certain chief constables and police representatives were taking an unusually active role in public debates (including the new head of the Metropolitan Police, Robert Mark, who gave the BBC's Dimbleby Lecture in 1973); and there was the moral panic about mugging, the flames of which the media had fanned since 1972.[1] Now while the media unthinkingly adopted the police position in 1976 and 1977 without investigating the cause or the roots of the trouble at those events, it was also clear to the police that they had to adopt a more careful strategy in response to the black community if there was not to be a return to the relations that existed at the time of the Notting Hill riots in the late 1950s, and the Mangrove raids, which met with a more organised and politicised resistance, in the 1960s. This 'care' was also part of the debates about 'community policing', which led to the police deciding to have their own band in the 1984 carnival!

It is impossible to teach about representations of race and to discuss their contexts of production and circulation without also teaching about the histories that structured racial inequality, which used racial differences to mask social, economic and political oppressions. A colonial history of the West, and of the British Empire in particular, will render invisible the millions of Africans and Asians whose labour created the imperial wealth on which 'greatness' was founded. This has important implications when, rendered visible again as starving victims of 'natural' disasters, the people of the Third World are represented not in the 1980s as marauding hordes but the deserving poor whom the West can afford, through its prudence and progress, to help.

13   *Sanders of the River*

1. Do you think photograph 13 is a news photograph?

   'Yes' answers will probably argue that the power relations and its 'dramatisation' makes it newsworthy. 'No' answers will emphasise the deliberate staginess of the 'tribesmen' and of the obviously risible colonisers.

2. Why was this an acceptable representation, to many people, of racial difference in 1935? (The film was a huge box office success.)[2]

3. Would you expect to find such an image in a film made today?

14   *The Guardian*, Tuesday 27 August 1985
                                              (picture by Martin Argles)

1. Who is the central focus of the newspaper photograph shown
   as Photograph 14?

2. How can you tell?

3. Why do you think Neil Kinnock is posing with his arms around
   two young black children?

When teaching about representations we need to question the
functions they serve and the political contexts for their use.

Social classification of racial difference

Any work on 'race' has to pose the questions of what 'race' and
'racial difference' are and what we mean when we use the terms.
Are there *biological* differences between peoples with different
colour skins? Of course not. The differentiation of peoples by
skin colour was part of eighteenth-century physical anthropology,
which then became intertwined with nineteenth-century social
and political thought and fed into the creation of a typology

based on 'racial' differences. The concepts of 'race' and 'racial difference' function as systems of *social classification*. They have no biological or socio-biological validity whatsoever. Given that 'race' has come to be used as a natural, obvious category over the last two centuries, it is hardly surprising that the media accept, and maintain, the classification of race. As Stuart Hall notes,

> the media are . . . part of the dominant means of *ideological* production. What they 'produce' is precisely representations of the social world, images, descriptions, explanations and frames for understanding how the world is and why it works as it is said and shown to work. And, amongst other kinds of ideological labour, the media construct for us a definition of what *race* is, what meaning the imagery of race carries, and what the 'problem of race' is understood to be. They help to classify out the world in terms of the categories of race. (Stuart Hall, 1981)

When discussing race generally, and race and the media in particular, it is commonly assumed that 'race' means black people. However, while we will mainly refer to peoples of Afro-Caribbean origin, our analysis in many cases will also hold true for any group which is outside the ethnic and cultural mainstream of Anglo-Saxon society.

If the definition of 'race' and 'racial difference' is biologically invalid, how are we to understand the tensions, antagonisms, hatred and oppression that black peoples have experienced the world over? Why are there still many countries which possess regimes built on a deliberate policy of the subjugation, torture and murder of black, brown and (in many cases) indigenous peoples? In order to answer these questions an analysis of racism in historical, political, economic, cultural and social terms is clearly required – an analysis that understands racial difference as a social construction and how the 'scientific' validation of physical anthropology has given rise to centuries of struggle, warring, plundering and subjugation. Racial difference – and racism – are then seen as a 'required construction', a construction required by societies determined to exploit and dominate other cultures, other lands. These constructions, and social justifications, are possibly seen at their most contorted in the situation where one culture tries to dominate another culture, e.g. British attitudes to the Irish in the maintenance of an ideological control through the use of 'humour'.

Racism does not necessarily require a difference of skin colour: all that skin differentiation offers is a shorthand form of visual recognition in order to define who to delimit and distinguish from oneself – otherness. Where such racial characteristics do not exist, such as in the example of British attitudes to the Irish (and other Western European countries have similar relations, e.g. the French and the Belgians, the Swedes and the Finns), aural clues are mobilised, i.e. speech differences, accent, dialect.

These social and political constructions of racial differences come, in their particular conjunctures, to be acceptable. It is not enough for a nation to conquer and subjugate another culture, it also has to justify this domination not just to others *but* to itself. After all, the subjugated must be 'inferior' or 'primitive' or they wouldn't have succumbed. Economic and political domination can be supported culturally so that, after a time, not only can the dominant accept their position as natural, but the dominated also accept their inequality fatalistically. After centuries it is easy to see why things 'have always been like this'. Roland Barthes (1972) offered an illuminating example:

> I am at the barber's and a copy of *Paris Match* is offered to me. On the cover, a young Negro [sic] in French uniform is saluting, with his eyes uplifted, probably fixed on a fold of the tricolour. All this is the *meaning* of the picture. But, whether naively or not, I see very well what it signifies to me: that France is a great Empire, that all her sons, without any colour discrimination, faithfully serve under the flag and that there is no better answer to the detractors of an alleged colonialism than the zeal shown by this negro in serving his so-called oppressors.

Nevertheless, however these relations of dominance and of subordination are maintained, they are also subject to stresses and changes. There are attempts to resist, to clamp down more firmly, to permit a more charitable humanitarianism.

This is where the role of the media is crucial both in enabling dominant and racist understandings of racial difference to continue within a social formation and in this contradictory ideological role, allowing limited challenges to that dominance. This complex ideological functioning of the media has been debated by many analysts of the media.[3] As Reeve and Stubbs point out, the media

> have to select and structure their ideological representations from those available in a specific social formation. In regards to racism, this would lead us to expect that we will not find a single cohesive, ideological representation of race in the media: we will, however, expect to find a set of representations which are articulated with other elements in media discourse. (Reeve and Stubbs, 1981)

In teaching about media representations of race we need to make our students aware of *how* and *why* these 'sets of representations'. We shall investigate what we perceive as four significant sets of media representations of racial difference. We have chosen to categorise these representations in terms of the differences they are dominantly used to invoke: the exotic, the dangerous, the humorous, the pitied. Before investigating these categories in more detail, however, we will make a few observations about two concepts within which much conscientious teaching about race has become tangled and trapped: 'prejudice' and 'the stereotype'.

Whilst being seen in negative terms within our culture, the term 'prejudice' nevertheless helps to mobilise racial difference as a valid notion. However, it attempts to offer an explanation but no analysis of racial hatred. Drawn from psychological discourse, the concept of prejudice offers a simplistic explanation of racism which is inaccurate in its implication that individuals possess *innate* sensibilities and attitudes which are either 'right' or 'wrong'.

The 'stereotype' is a closely related concept, and psychologists' interest in the notion is part of a general concern with people's attitudes – their origin, how they change, and why some seem to be more resistant to change than others. Stereotypes, like prejudice, are also seen as reflecting a type of attitude that is particularly difficult to change.

The implication of 'prejudice' is that individuals pre-judge the real world and base their judgements on firmly held beliefs or dogmas rather than on either experience or intellectual analysis. The stereotype is often seen to represent the shorthand descriptive form which explains the nature of the prejudice to others. Projected on to particular persons or groups, the stereotype reveals more about the holder's beliefs or personality than the reality described. Stereotypes in this scheme are thus simple, negative and inaccurate, and because they are so loosely related to the 'real world', they are not easily changed by alternative evidence.

Thus stereotypes and prejudice are characteristically seen as rigid attitudes held by an individual which express hostility towards a particular minority, usually in a weaker social position. The stereotyped views of a 'prejudiced' person are, in the final analysis, seen as a kind of personality disorder.

A sociological account, on the other hand, is concerned to see the wider implications of stereotyping, and raises questions such as 'who benefits from the stereotyping of certain groups?' Prison warders often stereotype prisoners as 'animals' because this perspective serves a purpose. It becomes quite 'reasonable' to treat prisoners as less than human because 'that is what they are'. Many people feel that the police hold a stereotyped view of black people as 'muggers', petty 'criminals' and 'rioters'. The obvious function of this belief is to make acceptable the criminalisation of black people in general and, having made black people visible as criminals, they are then, inevitably, more easily victimised.

The validity of a sociological or a psychological perspective on racial difference can be assessed by considering the following report:

The Virk brothers were attacked by several white racist youths and had to defend themselves. But when police were called to the scene, *they* were the ones arrested. They were later convicted solely on the basis of police evidence, and sentenced to varying terms of imprisonment by Judge Michael Argyle on 19 July 1978. Passing sentence, the judge condemned the brothers for trying to 'introduce racial prejudice' as a factor and rebuked the defence for asking the white youths whether they were members of the National Front. (Peter Hain, 1984)

Here one sees the usual reference to 'racial prejudice', but this time being used by the judge to impugn a 'chip on the shoulder' attitude on the part of the (Asian) brothers. In effect the judge was stating that the brothers merely possessed a personality problem and at the same time refused the possibility of wider structural and political issues being raised.

By accepting police definitions (they are, after all, the upholders and defenders of 'our' society), the media inadvertently support this process in news bulletins.

In his book, Hain indicts the institutionalised racism of our society. However, while books constitute one of the media, that kind of book will have a miniscule audience compared with the truly *mass* media. So what are the roles of television and the press and cinema in regard to the question of racial difference? While we may argue the invalidity of the concepts 'prejudice' and 'stereotype', the media continue to accept them as commonsense terms.

We think that to investigate how the media represent different groups as other than ourselves will help to inform us about how we perceive and understand both 'ourselves' and those who, as that word implies, do not 'belong'.

The 'Exotic'

The mercantile Europeans of the sixteenth century came across 'wondrous' lands and peoples in their quests for more plentiful resources. Those who inspired their 'wonder' were marked as 'other', which served a useful purpose when later the search for resources and markets became so rapacious that the 'other' had to be subjugated, robbed, controlled. The occident's sense of the 'other' alternately disturbed and amazed. Whenever the wonderful 'other' disturbed the occidental order, then that challenge had to be met with force; and when it amazed, then it confirmed, by its 'primitive' decorousness, the occident's superior nationality.

Black people have been represented as wondrous and strange by white Europeans, Americans and Australians. Rituals, dress, language, artefacts and food are not understood as parts of complex cultural and social formations but are extracted, exoticised and revered by naive Western eyes. The 'other' as 'exotic' continues as a racist discourse in dominant media representations of black people, but the discourse itself is rarely perceived as strange, out of order. While writing this paragraph

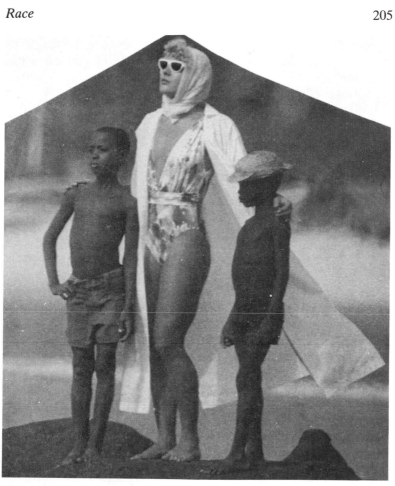

15

we switched on the television to find Anneka Rice on Thames's
Wish You Were Here . . .? (31 December 1985). She was sampling
a holiday to the Victoria (!) Falls, peppering her commentary
with such terms as 'in darkest Africa' and could talk about
Livingstone 'discovering' the Falls without a qualm. In an issue of
the *TV Times* (25–31 May 1985) ITV publicised its major Saturday
Sports programme with a photographic feature article. In it,
Shirley Strong (British Olympic hurdler) modelled swimwear on
a beach in Sierre Leone (see Photograph 15). Her arms rest on
the shoulders of two young black boys who are wearing old cotton

shorts. One presumes that the copy writer and editor thought the heading 'Racy Shirley's Shore Winners' a clever play on words, but the picture depends upon the acceptability of colonial relations. White European athlete-cum-fashion model meets Third World children in Sierre Leone. We are informed, furthermore, that 'Shirley Strong tries out some of the eye-catching styles on the beaches of Sierre Leone, on Africa's West Coast, *to the delight of the locals*' (our italics). This is not our reading of the image, nor could we imagine that the boys' shorts would be admired in the same way as the swimsuits are: 'both will show off a bronzed body to perfection'.

The 'exotic' is also a constant thread running through the regular international tours made by members of the Royal Family when visiting 'their' Commonwealth. These trips, and their televisual reportage, have become ritualised through the tribal dance welcome and entertainment offered by dancing black people dressed up in ancient tribal clothes. The accompanying commentaries invariably refer to the 'rhythm' of the people – a quality that is used to identify the essential and 'primitive' roots of the culture. Apparently it is a Rousseauesque quality lost to the peoples of the 'developed' Western nations.

It is also a 'mythic' quality that the media perpetuates in contemporary drama and light entertainment programmes. Witness, for examples, the role of LeRoy as the star dancer in *Fame*, or Ben Vareen from *Roots*, who is noted for dancing on request in chat shows. Similarly, it is in singing and general musical performance roles that black people gain a media visibility, *but* inevitably one that simultaneously maintains the rhythm myth. Britain has had many black entertainers – Kenny Lynch, Shirley Bassey, Cleo Laine, Joan Armatrading, and an increasing number of pop and reggae groups – but it is in America in vaudeville, the theatre, the concern hall, cinema and television that black people have been allowed, within limits, to become stars and even originators of new musical forms. Nevertheless, it is important to remember that for all the successful entertainers – Sammy Davies Jnr, Louis Armstrong, Sidney Poitier, Quincy Jones, Diana Ross, Stevie Wonder, Michael Jackson, Paul Robeson, to name but a few – it is a success that has been built on the marginalisation of literally thousands of black performers. Decades of the marginalisation of the Blues (only becoming more widely known after white singers such as Elvis Presley began making a great deal of money by singing them) as an innovative and original musical form for example, not to mention the appalling eyeball-rolling and 'mammy' stereotypes of the cinema played by performers such as Stepin Fetchit and Hatty McDaniels, form the bedrock of the success of the few.

In a recent Channel 4 programme, *I Love Quincy!*, the black composer Quincy Jones mentions laughingly how when he first went to Hollywood doubts had been expressed about whether a black man could write film music! Presumably the racist 'lack of reasoning' here was the notion that the 'innate' quality of black people's music was uncontrollable and therefore inapplicable to the precision timing of film music. But it is the life and work of Paul Robeson that offers the most poignant reminder of the dangers and difficulties of being a successful *but committed* American black performer. Committed to equal rights – and standing up for them – the polymath Robeson (brilliant law graduate, actor, singer, football player, etc.) was, for years, not allowed to work or tour abroad due to his political views.[4] Black stars are accepted, and even celebrated, just so long as they do not stray too far into the political arena.

The other main arena in which black people *are* allowed to be 'wonderful' – and revered as such – is sport. Many of the world's greatest soccer (Pele, Eusebio) and cricket (Sobers, Lloyd, Richards) players have been both black and lauded by the media. It is important not to forget, however, (a) that many media reports of their performances rely upon conventional racist discourse – there is continuous reference to the 'natural' fluidity and rhythm of their ball control, etc.; and (b) the regular racist barracking of black footballers currently playing soccer in the English League. But it is, of course, boxing which provides the most significant stage for sporting black superstars. World titles, particularly in the heavyweight division, have come to seem the prerogative of black boxers. In no other sport is the combination of 'primitive' rhythms and barbarism better united than in the 'noble' art of pugilism. Most black boxers have accepted their role and fate and have been grateful for the money and fame that has accrued from their status. For example, Britain's current European heavyweight champion, Frank Bruno, has refused to question the political ramifications of fighting the white South African boxer,

Frank Bruno
'I wanted to learn to tap because I knew that, as a heavyweight boxer, it would help my timing in the ring if I was fast on my feet. The first time I came to Roy for a lesson, everyone seemed so good, but I realised that, once you get the rhythm, you can learn very quickly. People still think it's funny, but I do it for fitness and pleasure.'

Susan Penhaligon
'I was seven when I started at dancing school. I learnt ballet and modern dance, but I loved tap best. My teacher said I was "not a great talent" but I scraped through exams and left when I was 15. My whole childhood was spent loving Fred Astaire and Gene Kelly films and my ambition is to dance the "Singin' in the Rain" routine. I think Roy can help me with that!'

Hot tap

16

Gerry Coetzee, and the fact that he is thereby contributing to the justification of the white racist regime. This refusal to confront these implications is all the more striking given recent media coverage of the latest black upsurge in the struggle against apartheid and the fact that the media have now been banned from going into any trouble zones. It also means that Bruno (presumably) unthinkingly allows the now perennial 'rhythm man' construction as presented in the issue of the *TV Times* already referred to (see Photograph 16).

This image also has the racist 'advantage' of displaying the 'brute animalism' of the man in terms of his size, but it is a power that is 'controlled' by the posture, clothes and text. When such power is not controlled by society, however – as in the case of the career of Muhammed Ali, who was stripped of the world heavyweight crown – an attempt at marginalisation soon follows.[5] It is at such points of confrontation that the 'exotic' becomes the 'dangerous'.

The 'Dangerous'

Having expropriated other people's lands, possessions and human rights, colonising cultures are bound to encounter great danger. The 'cost' of colonisation is the 'risk' of defeat, and many forms of control – both physical and ideological – have to be instituted to maintain power. Thus the British slavery system in the Caribbean involved complex methods of control and subjugation such as the plantation system, insistence on the use of English, and the banning of traditional means of communication such as drums. The enslaved were constructed as potentially dangerous. It is a construction that, in a reformulated guise, operates to this day and is re-presented by the media in two distinct narrative modes: non-fiction and fiction.

Non-fiction. The ending of slavery, the Empire, and the consolidation of trading arrangements for the Commonwealth might have meant the demise of the physical oppression of black British people, but it didn't remove the ideological framework of black = danger. And the need for a substantially larger and able bodied workforce in Britain after the Second World War meant that black people were needed, and thus invited, to come and live and work in Britain. Immigration meant that suddenly this 'danger' was not 4,000 miles away but 'over here'.

Emigration since the war has always been at a higher level than immigration, so the 'problem' of immigration is not a question of figures as so often proclaimed by politicians and reported by the media. Immigration is an *ideological* 'problem' in that the cultural residue of antagonism to the ex-colonised has been re-formulated to be appropriate for post-war Britain. Immigrants were soon assumed to be black, a term no longer connoting 'primitive', 'uneducated' and servile, but which has come to serve as a metonym for scrounger, mugger and rioter.

These racist ideological constructions have shifted and changed over the last four decades; the media's representation of immigration has similarly changed, but also ranges from quite explicit racist attitudes to the more subtle forms of 'inferential racism'.

As an example of the former, consider the now infamous case of the front page of *The Sun* dated 4 May 1976 (see Photograph 17). It is important not only because of the falsity of the reporting, but also because at the time it led to such a shock response that the Campaign Against Racism in the Media was formed as a result. Geoffrey Sheridan (1982), CARM's first secretary, wrote about the incident as follows:

> There was nothing ambiguous about the article, which concerned two Asian families expelled from Malawi, less their possessions. On their arrival in Britain, the local authority had placed them temporarily in a hotel, hence the £600 cost. On May 5, the *Daily Mail* hit on another angle: 'We want more money, say the £600 a week Asians'. This was their reply to the question: 'Do you need more money?' – hardly a surprising response when both were large families being paid £46 a week by social security.
>
> Behind the story was British imperial globe-trotting. Asians had originally been brought to East Africa as indentured labour to build the railways, and then left to their own devices. But that wasn't of interest to the *Sun* or the *Mail*. The 'scandal' broke at a time of increasing activity by the fascist National Front, when physical attacks on blacks in Britain were fast

17

becoming a daily occurrence. Anti-racists in the National Union
of Journalists considered that Fleet Street's front pages were
fuelling this violence.

These are particularly horrific examples of newspapers deliberately
misreporting *and* being explicitly racist, but, despite the work of
CARM and other groups and activisits engaged in the struggle
against the racism of the national and local press, explicit
examples of racist attitudes abound.[6] Furthermore, it is not just
that the content of so many of these stories is racist but that the
frames of reference of the reporting are racist. In the case of *The
Sun* story just quoted it is not so much a problem that the paper
ran the story – it is after all an outrageous situation – but rather
that it never occurs to reporters and newspapers that there are

alternative ways of describing the situation. It is possible to write about this story without resorting to racist categories: for example, it would have been possible to ask why the country has an immigration service that operates in such a haphazard and sloppy fashion (if it is assumed that we have to have an immigration service).

As an example of a more subtle (if racist attitudes can ever be described as subtle) or inferential racism consider the following case. A cursory glance through another issue of the *TV Times* (1–7 June 1986) revealed a letter, the racism of which is not confronted by the weak reply:

> Several weeks ago I visited a person who was deeply disturbed when ITV televised a Muslim service on a Sunday. It was doubly unfortunate, as the BBC had no service at that time – it was televising the London Marathon. I appreciate that we have many immigrants and mixed cultures, but we do have a Christian heritage, and many people believe that Sunday should be a day of Christian praise and worship. Could not ITV consult with the BBC and make sure that one Christian service is available?

The reply came from the religious adviser to the Independent Broadcasting Authority, who wrote:

> We know many elderly and housebound people rely on these services for spiritual sustenance. However, it is our responsibility to reflect religious traditions in Britain, which are predominantly, but not exclusively Christian. In our multi-racial society there are now a million Muslims – a greater number than either Methodists or Baptists. We try to liaise with the BBC, but it is not always possible. (*TV Times*, 1–7 June 1985)

But this inferential racism can be more overtly seen when the media cover an explicitly 'racial' story. For example, documents recently released by the British government throw an interesting light both on governmental attitudes in the key 1950s period and on media attitudes in the 1980s. Immigration was one of the areas of discussion in the confidential Cabinet papers covering the years 1952–5 which were made public on 1 January 1986. The next day the *Daily Mail* ran a two-page feature on the documents and led with an article on 'immigration', the whole tenor of which is based on a 'them' and 'us' attitude and, as usual, on black people constituting a 'problem': 'Ministers spent much of 1955 trying to *summon up courage* to curb immigration . . . The cabinet commissioned a report on the *problems caused* by the growing influx of coloured workers' (our italics). It is so much a part of the racist discourse of the *Mail* that it never occurs to the paper to assume that the readership might be anything other than white and thus would unthinkingly see the curbing of immigration as being a courageous act. Immigration is never conceived of in terms of white people (witness the positions taken by the paper over Zola Budd), nor is emigration ever discussed.

What the story is fundamentally concerned about is the history of a weak government signalled by the headline: 'Ministers talked and then did nothing'. In fact, the legislation considered to be too extreme by the then Tory government is what is now embodied in the 1981 Nationality Act. Then, they were worried that 'the administration would be subject to criticism for discriminating between different categories of British subject' – not an area of criticism over which the current government displays much concern![7]

Overall, what is most striking about the *Mail*'s discourse is a complete lack of interest in questioning or interrogating the documents released; thus they simply accept and report the fact that Lord Home had 'warned that the influx of working class Indians could become a "menace" unless it was checked'! Instead they indicate that they had asked Lord Home about this issue the night before and that he had replied: 'It was evident that something would have to be done at some stage'. Lord Home has the last and final word, he is quoted without comment, and the paper is therefore seen to agree with his analysis, which is that he was proven correct in his (racist) views.

Fiction. The black = danger equation is less explicitly played out in recent media fictions although it is still there. However, the history of the fictional representations of the 'dangerous' is long and extensive. It is to be found in such a venerated canon as

Shakespeare's plays (and note how prestigious productions of
Othello, complete with the white actors Laurence Olivier and Ben
Kingsley 'blacking up', have attempted to read the play liberally
by emphasising the nobility of this 'simple' and 'naive' man).
Hollywood, too, has produced a long stream of films which
present black people as offering a threat to whites. But it is in
Hollywood's most famous area of myth-making that the most
appalling racism of the film industry is portrayed: the Western. In
the vast bulk of the films depicting the westward movement of the
pioneers we see the almost total genocide of the indigenous
peoples of the North Americas. The 'Indians' are depicted as
'wild', 'savage', 'primitive', 'dangerous', 'marauding' and can be
unthinkingly killed without a single moral or political qualm. It
was not until near the end of his distinguished career that the
great Western director John Ford made the following statement
and attempted to begin to redress the balance by making
Cheyenne Autumn (1964):

> I had wanted to make it for a long time. I've killed more
> Indians than Custer, Beecher and Chivington put together, and
> people in Europe always want to know about the Indians.
> There are two sides to every story, but I wanted to show their
> point of view for a change. Let's face it, we've treated them
> very badly – it's a blot on our shield; we've cheated and
> robbed, killed, murdered, massacred and everything else, but
> they kill one white man and, God, out come the troops.
> (quoted in Peter Bogdanovich, 1971, p.104)

Other films were to follow such as Arthur Penn's *Little Big Man*
(1970), but by this stage there were new and contemporary
enemies – Vietnam and communism. The earlier period of Cold
War movies was to give way to the hysteria of the films that
followed the loss of the Vietnam War. From the crudity of films
like John Wayne's *The Green Berets* (1968) through to the relative
sophistication of movies like Francis Ford Coppola's *Apocalypse
Now* (1979) and Michael Cimino's *The Deerhunter* (1978),
Hollywood has replayed and reworked the fears and anxieties
engendered by losing a war to a foreign and militarily weaker
(but by implication physically and racially weaker) nation.
Furthermore, more than a decade later not only is that 'failure'

bitterly remembered but it provides even more grotesque cinematic fictions in the form of the *Rambo* movies – significantly starring Sylvester Stallone who, fictively as 'Rocky', is the only white American who has vaguely looked like winning the world heavyweight boxing crown since the days of the real 'Rocky' (Marciano) in the 1950s.

In all these cases the ideological function of the narrative fictions would seem to be to massage the national consciousness into an acceptance of the rectitude of such levels of killing, death and destruction. The massacre of the indigenous peoples of North America has been narratively 'justified' in the name of progress, so that a loss like Vietnam cannot be contemplated in Latin America or in the Arab world if there are still Americans like Rambo who have a will to win against all the odds. In *Back to the Future* (1985) a teenage boy and a scientist who fools around with plutonium make sure that Libyan terrorists get their come-uppance. Another way in which white fears and anxieties about racial difference have been handled has been to displace physical into sexual danger by the creation of the stereotypes of the 'exotic' women and the 'virile' men. Here the 'otherness' of black people is defined in terms of the fatal sexual allure of the woman and the danger of a sexual potency of the man, both of which provide a threat to the peace and domesticity of family life.

In the cinema, examples of the former would include the role of Chihuahua (Linda Darnell) in John Ford's *My Darling Clementine*, where she embodies the mystery and danger of Mexico against the pure Clementine from the East and from Doc Holliday's pre-alcoholic past. In the same year King Vidor's *Duel in the Sun* (1946) has Jennifer Jones playing a 'half-breed' who is the cause of all the trouble between Gregory Peck and Joseph Cotten. This construction of the exotically and erotically dangerous black woman is also an important thread running through the stage persona of a whole range of popular singers, e.g. Eartha Kitt, Shirley Bassey, Tina Turner, Grace Jones.

Cinematic examples of the latter would be a film like *Mandingo* (1975), where the theme of miscegenation was justified by the director Richard Fleischer on the basis that 'The black characters do have more character and more dignity than any of the whites!' Black male sexuality provides a crucial narrative motivation through the role of Jim Brown in a film like Tom Gries's *100*

Rifles, as Jim Pines notes: 'Actually, one of the purposes of the film is the violent copulation-confrontation between Jim Brown and Raquel Welch, super-stud versus super-sex symbols in the contemporary American movie' (Jim Pines, 1975, p.93). But examples of this construction of black male sexuality generally exists as a barely discernible undercurrent, something that is *too dangerous* to allow to come to the surface except in pornography. As far as television is concerned, the fictional handling of the 'sexual dangers' of 'racial otherness' are only played out through humour, particularly in situation comedies.

The 'Humorous'

By definition, comedy is a licensed zone, disconnected from the serious. It's all 'good, clean fun'. In the area of fun and pleasure it is forbidden to pose a serious question, partly because it seems so puritanical and destroys the pleasure by switching registers. Yet race is one of the most significant themes in situation comedies – from the early Alf Garnett to *Mind Your Language*, *On The Buses*, *Love Thy Neighbour* and *It Ain't Half Hot Mum!*. These are defended on good 'anti-racist' grounds: the appearance of blacks, alongside whites, in situation comedies, it is argued, will help to naturalise and normalise their presence in British society. And no doubt, in some examples, it does function in this way. But, if you examine these fun occasions more closely, you will find, as we did in our two programmes, that the comedies do not simply include blacks: they are *about race*. That is, the same old categories of racially-defined characteristics and qualities, and the same relations of superior and inferior, provide the pivots on which the jokes actually turn, the tension points which move and motivate the situations in situation comedies. The comic register in which they are set, however, protects and defends viewers from acknowledging their incipient racism. It creates disavowal. (Stuart Hall, 1981)

It is not just that 'race is one of the most significant themes in situation comedies', but that in the area of humour generally there is an almost obsessive engagement with the 'question' of race. To the short-list offered by Stuart Hall one could add a long string of titles: *Till Death Us Do Part*, *The Fosters*, *Rising Damp*, *In Sickness and in Health* to name but a few. These are significant not only because of their popularity but because many of them were sold on a format basis to the USA where they were re-made for the American market. Such programmes neutralise the 'threat' and 'danger' of the 'otherness' of black people by making them and their situation comic and laughable. In *Mind Your Language* one encountered a classic example of a programme which insisted on the superiority of white British people. None of the foreign students (and every racial stereotype exists in its crudest form within that classroom) could speak English properly, a source for hilarity not dissimilar to the scenes involving Manuel in *Fawlty Towers*. This is indeed ironic in a country which is not exactly famous for the facility of its people to speak other languages!

It Ain't Half Hot Mum! contained the conventional stereotypes of Indians living under colonial rule as the source for mirth, but as Stuart Hall quietly observed in the CARM programme *It Ain't Half Racist, Mum!*, 'For those on the receiving end of the British Empire it was no joke'. In all these programmes it is possible for television to confront and engage with its own fears and anxieties on behalf of the audience and always in such a way as to re-affirm the innate superiority of the British way of doing things.

This is nowhere more evident than in the 'humour' of stand-up comics. Some white comics such as Jim Davidson rely for much of their material on making malicious 'jokes' about other cultures and races, particularly the Irish, Asians and black people generally. The racist attitudes of such comics are quite explicit and proudly displayed. More complicated are the black comics like Charlie Williams and Lenny Henry. Lenny Henry in particular still adopts an appalling white stereotype of an African tribal chief complete with 'funny' accent, eye-rolling and cries of 'Katanga!', much to the guffaws of the audience. And this was after he was quoted in the *Radio Times* as currently paying more attention to not being racist in his humour!

What we have here is not the self-lacerating and questioning humour of the classic Jewish comedian like the other Lenny (Bruce) but instead the perpetuation of the myth of the savage bogey man identical to the cartoon cannibal with which Kenny Everett used to open *The Kenny Everett Television Show*.

Since the inception of Channel 4 the company has expressed a
commitment to a non-racist policy and employs a commissioning
editor for multi-racial programming. Whilst this policy obviously
represents an important step in the development of British
broadcasting, it is unfortunate, to say the least, that Farrukh
Dhondy is also responsible for co-authoring the Channel's black
situation comedy *No Problem!* The humour of the series, while
not depending on conflict between black and white, nevertheless
arises out of the depiction of a number of extremely conventional
stereotypes including the Victor Romero Evans character
'Bellamy' who lives, close to nature, in a tent in the garden! *'No
Problem!* is a problem![7] However, a more urgent problem – and
one that the media have taken a great interest in recently – is the
one we categorise as the 'pitied'.

The 'Pitied'

1985 was the year of representations of famine. Television and
the press have intermittently paid attention to the 'needy' of the
world, but not on the scale of 1985. Charitable organisations such
as Oxfam and Save the Children have also adopted a fairly high
media profile in the past in terms of constant advertising
campaigns. Nearly all the images of black people – in particular
mothers and children – represent them as victims and sufferers.
Passively unable to help themselves, the images emotively
encourage us to send a donation and to relieve the suffering not
of the person in the image (who is quite possibly already dead)
but of black people generally.

What these advertisements and news stories never offer is any
form of explanation of the causes for this suffering beyond
'natural' disasters such as floods, earthquakes and drought, with
occasional references to either incompetent or malevolent
domestic rulers. What is never offered is a historical account of
how such persons find themselves to be in the plight they are, *nor*
of the role of a country such as Great Britain has played in creating
those situations.

Having plundered, expropriated and enslaved the African
continent, the 'Western' world now observes the results – famine
and devastation – and pities the sufferers. The media thus present

us with images of swollen-bellied babies and pitifully thin adults but rarely offer an account of the virtual holocaust that led to this state of affairs. One of the very few accounts of this history is to be found in *Ten 8* magazine, no. 19 (1985), entitled 'Famine and Photo Journalism'. An article by Barbara Dinham and Colin Hines opens as follows:

> Africa was once self sufficient in food, and yet today most African countries face food shortages. Sub-Saharan Africa, in particular, is the only region in the world where food production has declined over the past 20 years – this against a background of record wheat crops in the 1980s elsewhere in the world. Africa grows little wheat: in 1984 the continent had to pay out £900 million in foreign exchange for its wheat imports. And yet at the same time, Africa was still a major exporter of agricultural products, and a source of many crops that we consume daily in the UK. These include coffee, cocoa, sugar, groundnuts, and palm oil. Africa is also a major producer of rubber, cotton, tropical hardwoods, and increasingly a source of cattle, vegetables and fresh flowers.
>
> Clearly, Africa is not agriculturally destitute, and the connections between export-oriented agriculture on the one hand and poverty and famine on the other are not coincidence.
>
> Agriculture is crucial to the economies of many African countries. More than half of the 43 sub-Saharan countries are almost totally dependent on agricultural exports, and only six earn less than a quarter of their foreign exchange from agriculture. And many countries are dependent for most of their export income from one or two commodities. These countries are vulnerable. They have no control over the commodity markets, the market structure and world trade systems. And they have no control over the prices which they must pay for imported capital equipment and consumer goods.
>
> Before the colonial era, African agriculture was geared to food production, and most societies were self-sufficient and secure. The technology of subsistence agriculture was on a par with much of Europe, using iron tools; irrigation, terracing, crop rotation, green manuring, mixed and swamp farming. On a continent where the soils were extremely fragile and easily destroyed by intensive use, farmers had an intimate knowledge

of soil potential. All the same, surpluses were common, and were traded along the many trade routes criss-crossing the continent.

The colonial take-over changed all those patterns for the worse. By the end of the nineteeth century, the mining and concession companies had staked their claims, along with settlers and the colonial governments. African societies, already destroyed or weakened by 300 years of slave trade, were faced with demands for land and labour which further shattered their economic, social and political structures. (Barbara Dinham and Colin Hines, 1985, p.10)

This account reminds one of the realities of the Irish potato famines of the nineteenth century: in that case there was no lack of food production, but what was produced was transported to England by the British.

Obviously, it must be recognised that the increased media coverage of countries like Ethiopia have led to a much greater public awareness of the problems currently being experienced by the peoples of those countries, which in turn has undoubtedly generated greater contributions to the aid agencies. Furthermore, the efforts of Bob Geldof and Band Aid and Live Aid have clearly helped thousands of people to survive who would otherwise have died. Geldof in particular has also helped to expose the hypocrisy and idiocy of elements of the EEC's agricultural policy. However (and it is a very large however), it is nevertheless the case that this championing of 'charity' (a highly patronising concept) helps to perpetuate a dependency created by the original domination of those lands. The Live Aid logo (see Photograph 18) figuratively proclaims the dependence of a whole continent on the leisure, technologically enabled, of those who can feel better singing for others' suppers. It diverts attention from the international policies of governments, so that charity becomes the new justification for the nature of the relationship between the First and Third Worlds. Self-congratulation replaces the brute force and oppression of earlier epochs and serves as the ideological function of these representations of black people deserving pity and help. In a society that has ostensibly made the more overt forms of racism unacceptable, notions of charity preserve the

18

old relations of dominance and subordination. As Anne Simpson elucidates, in the same issue of *Ten 8*:

> Aid is projected as the humanitarian solution to the sad situation in which the underdeveloped countries are unable to provide for themselves. It is the duty of the humane and privileged white developed world to offer help. And if only there was enough of this help, all would be well. More seeds, more tractors, more experts to 'help them help themselves' would put things straight.
>
> Such idealism is fundamentally flawed because it rests on a potent racist myth: that the crisis of Third World countries are caused by a lack of Western seeds, tractors or experts; and that their poverty is due to their own inadequacies. This projects Third World people as helpless victims and Westerners as saviours, neatly ignores the fact that Western agents created the basis for under-development in the first place through colonialism – and that they continue to profit from that same underdevelopment today. Aid would be better termed

repatriated profit – because the net flow of resources is from the Third World to the West.

The myth also ignores the actions and proposed solutions of Third World people themselves – and the Western-sponsored repression and destabilisation that such efforts often meet. The world is conveniently divided into two, along Brandt's snaking red line, ignoring the real links between elites around the globe and the shared need for change among the poor. The 50 million who go hungry in the United States have everything in common with the hungry elsewhere. The distribution of land ownership in Britain and El Salvador is exactly the same, with two per cent of the population owning 60 per cent of the land. (Anne Simpson, 1985, p.21)

These relations of dependence between the West and the 'Third World' are rarely represented. Instead, the most visible representations of black people (particularly on school notice boards and in assemblies) are those which inform European children of their superiority simply by virtue of their ability to help. And while those helped are to be pitied, the helpers can, of course, only be applauded.

No education should omit the teaching of respect and compassion towards others, but the dangers are that in emphasising the 'positive' aspects of our own children we accentuate the 'negative' aspects of others'. In her *Ten 8* article, Anne Simpson goes on to describe how these media images of the 'Third World' inform the consciousness of 'First World' children, especially through children's television:

A group of third form pupils in an ILEA secondary school, when asked about their images of the 'Third World' listed the following: poverty, babies dying, monsoons, war-devastated crops, starvation, disease, drought, refugees, flies, death, Oxfam, dirty water, India, Cambodia, curries, beggars, malnutrition, bald children, large families, insects, stealing, poor clothing, bad teeth, kids with pot bellies, mud huts, injections.

When asked where these images came from the class said that *Blue Peter* had many appeals for blankets and water pumps to help poor people in poor countries: *John Craven's Newsround* often showed pot-bellied children eating rice; TV programmes about wars and refugees provided some more of the images. One girl wrote: 'our images come from programmes like *Blue Peter*, the *News*, *Village Earth* and special films. In most of these films they show sickening sights of poor people. In *Blue Peter* they ask for donations to help these people. They always have an appeal to send thousands of bags of rice to Cambodia yet again. And wherever Simon, Peter, Sarah or Janet go off to find out more about "what's going on in Cambodia" they always show screaming pot-bellied kids having injections from white doctors in short sleeved shirts with other kids waiting in queues for the same thing, or screaming babies getting weighed by nurses that look like nuns.' (Anne Simpson, 1985, pp. 22–3)

Many of these images are extremely emotive. Media teaching has to confront these horrific images directly, though, if students are to appreciate the history which generates such suffering. An oblique approach is to compare those forms of coverage of Third World affliction with the media's (rather rare) investigations of racial violence in Great Britain. It will be noted that the category of the 'pitied' extends to Asian families helplessly waiting in their homes to be attacked in London's East End. Students can also be asked to assess how the media report black people's resistance as being of 'concern' to its white (liberal) audience – whether it be Asian self-defence groups in Newham or guerilla warfare in Latin America or Africa.

Discussion of the representation of race has to be a discussion of absence, of invisibility. Relatively few black performers are employed by television, and when they do appear on television it is predominantly in the traditional roles of sports people or singers and dancers. It is almost unknown for a black person to be consulted as an 'expert' on the EEC, on nuclear power or on science, for example.

Since the inception of Channel 4, London Weekend Television took on the responsibility for 'ethnic minorities' programme production for the minority channel, with *Black on Black* and *Eastern Eye*. Channel 4's anti-racist policy has in fact led to a range of broadcasting decisions, including not only programmes for British black communities but also regular transmissions of

Third World films, providing the British audience with a less
ethno-centric view of the world.

As a result, Channel 4 has opened a range of spaces for black
acting, writing and programme-making, and the innovativeness of
some of this production has forced into the open the barrenness
of the bulk of British television broadcasting. However, this is
not to say that it has managed to solve single-handedly what we
would consider to be major shortcomings within this area.

When teaching it would be interesting, for example, to pose
questions about whether the *Bandung File* productions on
Grenada and Viv Richards offered a more valuable and important
account of questions of race and politics in the Caribbean and in
Britain than had the more traditional LWT programmes which
they replaced. To invite this comparison is not to value one above
the other but to argue that, significant as they all are, they
nevertheless do no more than skirt the edge of the area with
which this chapter attempts to engage. Until this area is confronted
more in terms of the four categories we have chosen – the
'exotic', the 'dangerous', the 'humorous', the 'pitiful' – it will,
unfortunately, continue to possess a currency and a validity which
a few programmes on Channel 4 will never manage to overcome.

The struggle over race is not just to eradicate racist attitudes
and practices, but also to generate a field of operation where
'blackness' is not, of necessity, the issue at stake. For people to
work and operate within the media institutions where their race is
not the determining space within which they are constrained is to
forge a fundamental re-thinking and a conquering of the racism
of a white social formation.

8   Age

'Society cares about the individual only in so far as he is profitable. The young know this. Their anxiety as they enter in upon social life matches the anguish of the old as they are excluded from it. Between these two ages, the problem is hidden by routine. The young man dreads this machine that is about to seize hold of him, and sometimes he tries to defend himself by throwing half-bricks; the old man, rejected by it, exhausted and naked, has nothing left but his eyes to weep with. Between youth and age there turns the machine, the crusher of men – of men who let themselves be crushed because it never even occurs to them that they can escape it. Once we have understood what the state of the aged really is, we cannot satisfy ourselves with calling for a more generous 'old-age policy', higher pensions, decent housing and organized leisure. It is the whole system that is at issue and our claim cannot be otherwise than radical – change life itself' – Simone De Beauvoir (1977) p.604

Tempus fugit. We all grow older. While our students envy us for the independence and authority which age seems to bring, some of us idly dream of our lost youth. Between us stands the insurmountable barrier of age, the generation gap which refuses to be bridged. But why is it there in the first place? How is it created and maintained? And who gains from its existence, since old age comes to us all in time?

Ageism remains teasingly invisible as a form of oppression, at least until old age creeps up on us from behind. Commonly perceived as only afflicting older people, ageism is far more extensive in its ideological ramification. We all go through the inevitable and individual biological process of growing old, yet

225

our experience of ageing is profoundly social. Ageist ideology helps to legitimate our whole way of life or social formation through allocating us particular functions and roles to fulfil throughout our lives. We spend our childhood and adolescence between play or leisure and education or training for when we 'grow up' to work and raise children. Our old age will be spent in retirement, another form of play. Such a 'natural' biography is, of course, both historically recent and extremely specific to Western industrialised societies, but the myths of ageism allow us to believe differently.

In most Third World countries, children and old people work to ensure economic survival. Even in Britain 2½ million children have part-time jobs, and 10 per cent of those have two jobs.[1] Yet childhood and old age are almost invariably represented as periods of economic dependence. Our contemporary expectations of what is 'natural' at any given age have been structured by several long-term historical processes. The traditional role of children and old people in economic reproduction was eroded or marginalised by the capitalist factory replacing the family as the main site of production. Old people have become especially isolated as the middle-class nuclear family has gained dominance over extended family and community-based forms of social organisation.

The formal state education system has institutionalised a rigid division between education for the young and work (or unemployment) for everyone else. Furthermore, these shifts have been accompanied by a range of institutional discourses and practices (such as juvenile law, paediatric and geriatric medicine, youthwork, gerontology) which serve to construct *age* – or at least childhood, adolescence, and old age – as problematic, as social problems to be defined, organised and controlled.[2]

Ageist representations re-present our historical and political definitions of age as the intrinsic and natural essence of the ageing process. The ideological is transmuted into the biological. Just as women are dominantly represented as 'passive' and black people represented as 'primitive', so all children are 'innocent', adolescents 'rebellious', old people 'sexless' and 'helpless'. However, such stereotyping is increasingly challenged as the number of people over pensionable age rises to over 9 million and numerous middle-aged and young people discover the joys of enforced 'leisure' and early retirement due to the drastic restructuring of the capitalist economy.

However, ageist representations perform ideological work other than the marginalisation of old and young. They also conceal how our experience of ageing is determined by our class, race and gender. We all grow old but in different ways. A higher percentage of black older people need supplementary benefit than white. Working-class people will not have accumulated a nest-egg through private pension funds. Older women will not receive a golden handshake after decades of domestic labour. The depiction of old age as a time of helpless dependence allows mildly ameliorative 'old age policies' to be projected as the solution to the 'problem of old people', rather than changing the economic and social relations which systematically position certain groups of older people into years of degrading dependence after a life of labour.

Young people also inhabit a representational realm outside social and economic relations. Karel Reisz's *Momma Don't Allow* (1955, co-directed with Tony Richardson) begins with a group of teenagers (that invention of the 1950s) escaping from their places of work into the jazz club where identities – classes, races, sexes – dissolve into a celebration of universal youth. The youthful hero of Colin McInnes's *Absolute Beginners* tells us that

> the great thing about the jazz world, and all the kids that enter into it, is that no one, not a soul, cares what your class is, or what your race is or what your income, or if you're boy, or girl, or bent, or versatile, or what you are.

The creation of a vast and lucrative youth leisure market was an essential part of this process of making *youth* the primary source of identity for the young. Therefore we need to differentiate between those representations of youth within media products addressing the young, and the rare and usually sensational appearance of young people in the mainstream media. (A similar process is now happening in the USA as companies seek to create an 'old age' market through the use of more positive images of older people.) For in the latter, young people are reduced to a spectacle of rebellion (or victims of the 'recession'), revolting youth doing its thing. Sociologists have demonstrated that the codes and insignia of youth sub-cultures – Teds, mods, skinheads, punks, Rastas – represent a complex reworking of elements drawn from mass popular culture and from class and racial traditions which amount to a form of stylistic 'resistance' to the dominant culture. The media, however, incorporate this resistance by converting the signs of rebellion into mass-produced commodities or, more subtly, by trivialising and exoticising them into a motiveless, arbitrary spectacle.[3] Not only does this exclude the majority of young people, especially young women, from media representation; it also enables more serious forms of revolt to be dismissed as a 'youth crisis' rather than a serious critique of the social system. The 1981 riots in Britain were represented as an exceptional instance of youth alienation rather than as part of a working-class tradition of rioting at times of acute social crisis.

Another function of ageist ideology is the representation of fundamental social antagonisms as being some form of eternal generation power game. Traditional forms of informal oppositional education are disrupted as political opposition comes to be expressed as a battle between the young and the old, as in this childhood memory of the East End in the 1930s:

> Becton Road corner used to be called the East End's university. The Labour League of Youth, the ILP, the Communist Party, they all used to put up speakers regular, Wednesdays of an evening and Sunday afternoon. I used to go up there with my mates to bunk off Sunday School. We used to go to hear Will Thorne he was an old man then, but still a fine speaker. These places, stumping grounds we called them, they were traditional, passed on from generation to generation and the law knew well enough not to interfere. (quoted in Phil Cohen, 1984b, p.104)

Ageist metaphors permeate our political discourse. Often they combine with racism in discussion of relations between the West and the Third World:

> The concept of childhood . . . being developed between the seventeenth and eighteenth centuries introduced specific determinations of dependency which are bound up with a mercantilist phase of territorial expansion. Childhood, in short, is exportable well beyond the confines of the family, as it may

be attributed to entire races presumed not to have reached a civilised status. (Richard Appignanesi, 1979, p.189)

Consequently Third World countries are *young* and *immature*, and have to be guided by the 'older' nations of the West. An ageist conception of the intrinsic dependence of the young serves to justify colonialism. (One could compare Mrs Thatcher's comparisons between children and the striking miners on her South East Asia tour in April, 1985.) Often the Left inverts this form of ageism and assumes that youth is synonymous with revolt and old age shorthand for reaction (despite the steady decline of support for socialism in the young), as in 1984 when the old age of Ronald Reagan and Ian McGregor often became symbolic of their reactionary incompetence.

It is all too evident that the Left is in desperate need of political dialogue between generations. Old and young, whether working-class, blacks or women, have far more in common in both their oppression and media representation than might be thought. Therefore we would argue that teaching about ageist representations should focus on their similarities as much as their differences. This should be educationally beneficial in putting some distance between students and some representations which are inevitably bound up with their own personal conflicts of identity and development.

Children

Modern representations of children emerged with the changing social and economic role of children during the transition to industrial capitalism. Students might be defamiliarised from contemporary images of children by seeing some examples of pre-eighteenth century art in which children, usually those of the aristocracy, are depicted as miniature adults (Marlin Hoyles, 1979). Our present construction of childhood is derived from shifts in the conceptualisation of children during the eighteenth century, epitomised in Rousseau's inversion of the doctrine of original sin into childhood innocence. Children's literature dates from this period, indicating an awareness in the middle class of

19 *Portrait of Miss Haverfield* by Thomas Gainsborough

20 *Playmates* – a print issued by Pears Soap

children as a separate audience. Their male children went to boarding schools in special uniforms, beginning the sartorial separation of children from adults.

For the Victorian patriarch his non-working child was as important a status symbol as his non-working wife. The 'special needs' of children provided the ultimate rationale for the nuclear family unit of caring mother and bread-winning father. (A legacy of this is the role of children in films about divorce such as *Kramer vs. Kramer.*) The Victorians focused special concern on childhood sexuality, which was both acknowledged and yet vehemently denied due to the cult of childhood innocence, an ambivalence caught in the popular print of the time shown in Photograph 20. Despite anthropological evidence of childhood sexuality being culturally acceptable in other societies (see Mike O'Donnell, 1985), this ambivalence has persisted into the twentieth century, possibly because, as Jacqueline Rose argues, we have ideologically invested in a particular representation of adult sexuality:

> Sexuality persists, for all of us, at the level of the unconscious precisely because it is a question which is never quite settled, a story which can never be brought to a close. Freud is known to have undermined the concept of childhood innocence, but his real challenge is easily lost if we see in the child merely a miniature version of what our sexuality eventually comes to be. The child is sexual, but its sexuality (bisexual, polymorphous, perverse) threatens our own at its very roots. Setting up the child as innocent is not, therefore, repressing its sexuality – it is above all holding off any possible challenge to our own. (Jacqueline Rose, 1984, p.4)

The construction of sexual innocence in children allows some media products to offer the exploitative *frisson* of portraying children involved in 'adult' sex and violence. The Brazilian film *Pixote* (1980) won numerous international awards, possibly due to the novelty of having its 10 year-old protagonist involved in murder and prostitution, which would be unexceptional in other exploitation films. It is also worth mentioning that child pornography is a billion dollar industry in the USA. The pornographic representation of children does not challenge the cultural misrepresentation of childhood sexuality, but merely confirms children's passivity within the usual exploitative and voyeuristic male domination of pornography's visual regime.[4]

Childhood innocence extends beyond sexuality, however. Analysis of images of babies and very young children with students can lead to discussion of how representations of children are deployed to naturalise and universalise different aspects of the social formation (see Photograph 21). Childhood can be constructed as a form of universal reference point transcending class, race and gender – a human essence untainted by the marks of economic and social relations. No wonder that politicians are so keen to be photographed kissing babies. Babies can be used to naturalise institutions as diverse as the family and royalty. The tendency to abstract children from their historical context is most pronounced in images of starving children in the Third World (see Photograph 22). Patricia Holland has written of how in the flow of images of Third World disaster we:

rarely see any child older than about six and few women who

Australia $1.50 New Zealand $1.60 Malaysia $5.25

MAY 1985 70p

mother

THE MAGAZINE THAT CARES FOR YOU AND YOUR CHILDREN

YOUR BABY

BIRTHS–HOME OR HOSPITAL?• KEEPING COOL IN SUMMER•HOW TO CARE FOR TEETH• WE TEST BUGGIES

21

FAMINE KNOWS NO BORDERS

There cannot be anyone who has not been deeply
affected by the sheer horror of the famine in Ethiopia. But that
was just the tip of the iceberg as the famine took its
relentless path across Africa.   International Christian Relief
have teams in two of the stricken countries, Kenya and Uganda,
caring for the starving and the homeless particularly
children. But we need your help urgently. Just £10 a
month will keep a child alive. Not a penny will be
wasted or misused.

Will you buy a young life —
please? Fill in the coupon
and send it to us — today.
The need is so great.

Yes, I would like to sponsor a needy child in Kenya ☐ Uganda ☐ Please tick your choice.
I would like to send in my sponsorship money ☐ yearly (£120) ☐ quarterly (£30)
☐ monthly (£10)   Enclosed is my first donation of £. . . . .
☐ I cannot be a sponsor at this time, but would like to help where most needed.
Here is my donation of £ . . . .
☐ (Please tick if you would like a receipt)

Name . . . .

Address . . . .

. . . .   Postcode RT18/85

Cheques should be made payable to:
INTERNATIONAL CHRISTIAN RELIEF
PO Box 180, St. John's Hill, Sevenoaks, Kent TN13 3NP.
REGD. 270659   Tel: Sevenoaks (0732) 450250.

22

are not burdened by children. The condition of the Third
World is appropriately expressed by and encapsulated in
pictures of children . . . We may pick at random between the
thousands of sick, emaciated, lost, pathetic, dying dark-skinned
children. Suffering, whether from war, famine or liberation
struggle, tends to be offered to us in pictures which express
suffering alone. Suffering is condensed into the figures of
children; backgrounds tend to be erased or played down.
(Patricia Holland, 1981, pp.97–8)

ke Goldwater/Network

23

Images of children actively engaged in political or even military struggle are extremely rare and can be used to throw doubt on the cause they are involved in, as it is assumed that they would not be acting from their own volition (see Photograph 23). Our culture only recognises children as the objects and never the subjects of history.

Children obviously are more vulnerable to the vicissitudes of history due to their relative lack of physical maturity. But this biological condition is used to justify the effective denial of child agency, despite such historical events as the Children's Crusade or the Children's strikes of 1911. (In 1978, between 16,000 and 18,000 children were given drugs to control 'hyperactivity'.) The following Liverpool reminiscence seems totally alien to our expectations of children:

I came rather late to politics – when I was 13. I knew kids of 11 who were more politically advanced than me. We used to

organize public meetings in the streets, by ourselves, without
any adults at all. We would get up and talk about unemployment
and injustice and the threat of fascism. We used to get quite a
crowd around us. There were lots of arguments and hecklers.
Some grown-ups would come to take the piss, but sometimes
they stayed to listen. I think they were impressed that we knew
what we were talking about, even if we didn't win them over.
Yes, we were only 12 or 13 then, still at school. It seems ever
so young by today's standards, but in those days it wasn't.
(quoted in Phil Cohen, 1984b, p.105)

While the media do acknowledge the significance of children's
political action abroad in events such as the 1976 Soweto riots,
when this type of scene takes place at home on the streets of
Belfast or Liverpool it becomes a crisis in social discipline.
Families are exhorted to get their children back where they
belong – in the home, dependent and dependable. Press reports
on the 200,000 children who went on strike for a day in April
1985 emphasises that 40 (out of 200,000) had gone 'on the
rampage' and proceeded to dismiss the demonstrations as either a
joke or manipulation by the 'lunatic Left'. The anxieties children
might feel about their bleak and unemployed future are reduced
to a 'giggle' (see Photograph 24).

Children's television provides useful teaching material, as
secondary pupils are sufficiently distanced from it to be able
efficiently to decode some of its assumptions. Jacqueline Rose's
comments on children's literature could be equally well applied to
children's television:

Children's fiction is impossible, not in the sense that it cannot
be written (that would be nonsense), but in that it hangs on an
impossibility, one which it rarely ventures to speak. This is the
impossible relation between adult and child. Children's fiction
is clearly about that relation, but it has the remarkable
characteristic of being about something which it hardly ever talks
of. Children's fiction sets up a world in which the adult comes
first (author, maker, giver) and the child comes after (reader,
product, receiver), but where neither of them enter the space
in between. To say that the child is inside the book – children's
books are after all as often as not *about* children – is to fall

ʼaily Mail, Friday, April 26, 1985

— Kinnock gets a caning from militant MP behind the demos —

Let's play strikes!

Thousands join the truant marches – but don't know why

THOUSANDS of children grabbed a chance to play truant yesterday and went on strike.

And by the end of the day, many were under arrest for rowdy behaviour.

Groups went on the rampage through several towns, shouting abuse, trampling gardens and throwing stones.

The strike had been condemned by both the Prime Minister and Labour leader Neil Kinnock but was publicly

By CLIVE EDWARDS

supported by more than a dozen Left-Wing MPs, some of whom took part in rallies.

The action was part of a Hard Left campaign against the Government's Youth Training Scheme.

But many children had no idea why they were taking part in marches. 'I'm just here for a laugh,' was a common cry as youngsters held up posters and placards.

For most it was just a game, joking with friends and some smoking their illicit cigarettes.

The rallies were bizarre to watch. Hundreds of young children shouting slogans of political hatred and division.

They copied perfectly the aggressive chants learned from the TV news with screams of Maggie Out and the miners' anthem Here We Go.

And while pupils took to the streets, a key organiser of the strike, Militant MP Dave Nellist, was caning Labour leader Neil Kinnock for his lack of support.

Mr Nellist, MP for Coventry South East, said : 'Neil Kinnock seems to be developing a sad tendency that if something moves he shoots it.

'He is in danger of making the same mistake about the

anger and frustration of school students as he made about the miners last year.'

In Reading 40 schoolboys were arrested after stones were hurled at teachers and gardens trampled.

In Coventry, about 200 children held a rally and later ran noisily through the city centre, scattering shoppers.

In London, 500 children turned up for the main rally to march to the offices of the Manpower Services Commission. They were led by Labour MPs Ernie Roberts and Harry Cohen.

In Woolwich, South London, children went on the rampage after their march was banned.

Daily Mail, 26 April 1985

straight into a trap. It is to confuse the adult's intention to get at the child with the child in portrays. If children's fiction builds an image of the child inside the book, it does so in order to secure the child who is outside the book, the one who does not come so easily within its grasp. (Jacqueline Rose, 1984, p.1)

Teaching can focus on two dominant and interrelated themes:
1. What representations of children are produced for children?
2. What image of the child audience do the broadcasters have?

1. Although children form a significant part of the general TV audience, they only appear in any quantity in children's programmes. However, there is an extremely limited repertoire of roles made available for children in 'their' programmes. Analysis of non-fictional programmes such as *Blue Peter*, *How Dare You*, *CBTV*, *Superstore* and numerous quizzes can begin with noting just how few roles children can occupy, and the stereotyped relationships with the controlling adults that are permitted. Children are usually either audience spectators or participants in various games and competitions. Occasionally they

will be featured more prominently, but only when they have accomplished some meritorious task. Students might also examine the class and racial composition of the children who are featured and the types of activity which the programme-makers consider suitable and representative of what children do. (Just as work is a key absence in adult programming, so is critical examination of school in children's programming.) Fictional programmes such as *Grange Hill* can be subjected to narrative analysis, scrutinising how particular storylines are resolved to ensure that deviance is never ultimately rewarded (with the glorious exception of *Marmalade Atkins*). Press coverage of *Grange Hill* can also be studied to reveal stereotyped assumptions of how manipulable children are by screen images of deviance.

2. Analysis of assumptions about the child audience made by the broadcasters can focus on what forms of presentation and content they consider appropriate for children. Generally, non-fictional children's TV is mediated through the in-vision presenter, who is almost invariably adult. Students can discuss what some of the criteria might be for choosing these presenters and how these would differ from those for an adult programme. Most presenters are frenetically cheerful and pose as being on 'the side of the kids', as in *How Dare You*, where they help the children throw gunge at their teachers. Yet their presence, although suitably big brother or sisterly, is also a reminder that however much licence the children are allowed, there is always an adult on hand to restore order. The adult is the possessor of knowledge in the programme, whether compering a quiz or demonstrating some worthwhile activity.

Children's television presents an immensely restricted representation of the world to its audience. Interesting comparisons can be made between the issues permissable within the 'fictional' format of drama, with its indirect form of address and the sanitised representations which address children directly through programmes such as *Blue Peter* and *John Craven's Newsround*. Then there are absences to consider: menstruation, family violence, contraception. While types of knowledge which many children may intensely desire are deemed inappropriate for discussion in 'non-fictional' programmes the programme-makers do not hesitate in their paternalistic hectoring of the audience to be 'up and doing things' (usually assuming the resources of a middle-class family with which to perform them). An adult audience would be indignant at such treatment, but children are assumed to be passive and not engaged in economic production (an erroneous assumption), so they have to be exhorted to perform pointless pseudo-artisan activities to occupy them. Analysis of the world represented to children reveals what children are represented as : inactive, apolitical, asexual, classless, raceless, and, above all, totally dependent.

Youth

The strategy of teaching about representations of children prior to, or in conjunction with, teaching about images of youth helps to provide a critical focus for studying an area of representation which directly impinges on the lives of secondary students. Moreover, the way in which young people are represented is directly related to the representations of children discussed, because the 'crisis of youth' is precisely the refusal of adolescents to be contained within the regime of representation in which they have lived so far. Economic and sexual autonomy is strived for, and in the process the demands of young people throw into question the economic and social relations which are denying them that autonomy. The legitimacy of the social order is momentarily challenged before the 'kids' grow up to accept the status quo. Representations of youth therefore construct adolescence as a period of natural and individual rebellion (especially when it is in a sub-cultural form) which can be dismissed, rather than allowing such critiques to be seriously engaged with in the arena of 'adult' political discourse. This is particularly pronounced with the present level of unemployment, as the government's plans to extend and make compulsory the Youth Training Scheme directly conflict with young people's desire for economic independence. Indeed, the 'new vocationalism' now transforming so much of education is predicated upon representations of young people lacking the social and life skills which the 'adult' world requires (Phil Cohen, 1984b).

A stimulating beginning to a course of studying images of youth can be made by screening some of the major Hollywood 'youth' films which were first made in the 1950s when the young audience for mass media products was being created. Coinciding with the emergence of rock'n'roll, these films constructed the essence of the stereotypical image of 'youth' which has continued ever since. *East of Eden* and *Rebel Without A Cause* (Warner Brothers 'challenging drama of Todays Teenage Violence') both appeared in 1955 and launched James Dean as the symbol of a generation. Teaching the construction of Dean as a 'star' could focus on how the external determinants of 'youth rebellion' such as economic change, the rise of consumer culture, changes in institutions such as the family and education, were interiorised into the 'teenage psyche' which Dean as loner, misfit and outsider embodied. With this historical perspective gained, some more recent films could be engaged with, posing the question why most of them are still preoccupied with the youth mythology of the late 1950s. In particular *American Graffiti* (1974), *Rumble Fish* (1983), *The Warriors* (1979) and *Streets of Fire* (1985) – see Photograph 25 – are films which continually recycle the iconography of an historical form of youth revolt without any reference either to contemporary young people or to the historical conditions which created such icons in the first place (see Photograph 26). Jonathan Kaplan's *Over The Edge*, a US independent film, provides a valuable comparison in that its reconstruction of a real youth riot in which teenagers in a small town beseige a school because of their treatment by the community, does engage with some contemporary concerns, but still displaces its political critique from an indictment of the overall system on to the heartless older generation.

The programme on 'Youth' in the *Viewpoint 2* series provides a useful introduction to representations of young people in the rest of the media, as it engages with how negotiations with gender role can be reduced to the stereotyped conventions of 'young love'. The popular press can be relied on to provide numerous texts on deviant youth which can be examined to establish what the acceptable parameters of behaviour are for the young. Television programmes made for a youth audience are now on the decline, following an increase on all channels during the first year of Channel 4. Youth television programmes can be subjected to similar forms of questioning as children's TV. What is the companies' image of their youth viewer? How often do young people have access to youth TV programmes such as *Riverside*, *Earsay*, *Oxford Road Show*, *Whistle Test*, or *The Tube*, without

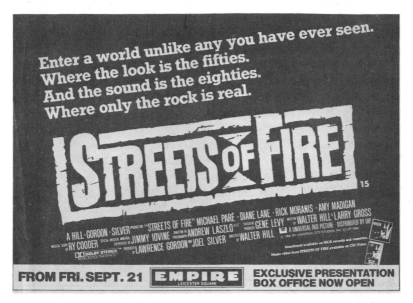

Enter a world unlike any you have ever seen.
Where the look is the fifties.
And the sound is the eighties.
Where only the rock is real.

STREETS OF FIRE 15

A HILL-GORDON-SILVER PRODUCTION "STREETS OF FIRE" MICHAEL PARÉ · DIANE LANE · RICK MORANIS · AMY MADIGAN and LARRY GROSS MUSICAL SCORE BY RY COODER SPECIAL MUSICAL MATERIAL BY JIMMY IOVINE DIRECTOR OF PHOTOGRAPHY ANDREW LASZLO A.S.C. EXECUTIVE PRODUCER GENE LEVY DIRECTED BY WALTER HILL A UNIVERSAL-RKO PICTURE · DISTRIBUTED BY UIP IN DOLBY STEREO SELECTED THEATRES PRODUCED BY LAWRENCE GORDON AND JOEL SILVER DIRECTED BY WALTER HILL © 1984 BY UNIVERSAL CITY STUDIOS, INC. Soundtrack available on MCA records and cassettes. Music video from STREETS OF FIRE available on CIC Video

FROM FRI. SEPT. 21 EMPIRE LEICESTER SQUARE EXCLUSIVE PRESENTATION BOX OFFICE NOW OPEN

25

the mediations of institutionalised presenters? What aspects of young people's lives do the media concentrate on? What do they exclude? How often are the products of the music industry critically assessed as opposed to being continually circulated between music press, radio and television? How is the hierarchy between the producers and consumers of music and fashion, which punk challenged, reinforced and reworked? How often do young people have access to TV and radio outside the ghetto of youth programming ? Finally, teachers could begin to ask students to compare media representations of youth with the images of young people that appear in the manuals of social and life skills training such as *The School Leavers' Book*. These books are explicitly concerned with inculcating 'impression management' in young people to make them more acceptable to employers and provide an admirable instance of ideological discourses being produced and circulated through different institutions of the social formation.[5]

Such a course of work will not reveal one monolithic representation of youth: there will be discovered a range of representations and discourses in circulation which combine,

26   A studio publicity still of James Dean

often contradictarily, to position young people ideologically,
which invite them to accept their allotted space in the social
formation. There are acceptable ways of being young in the 1980s
and there are unacceptable ways. The role of the 'youth media' is
continually to rework the boundaries between them. The 'youth
viewer' of *The Tube* or *Soultrain* is not addressed as if they were
the hooligans, rioters, muggers, or freaks on *News At Ten*. While

this position is not the same as that reserved for children – a *certain* amount of independence is allowed for, even encouraged – it is nonetheless unambiguously subordinate.

Old age

Ageism represents growing older as the inverse of growing up. Both children and older people are represented as helpless, economically dependent, asexual, apolitical, at best the innocent victims of the historical forces which they can never influence. Images of old people taking political action are as rare as those of the young. While all societies treat their older members differently from the rest in one way or another, for us old age is represented as something grotesque, to be avoided at all costs, whereas (affluent) youth is the epitome of our heart's desire. Other cultures treat old age as the fruition of a lifetime's experience, but for us rawness is all.

Older people, unless they happen to belong to the power elite, are almost invisible in the media, and it is this major structuring absence which first needs to be drawn to students' attention. It has been estimated that people over 65, who comprise 11 per cent of the population, become a mere 2.3 per cent of the television fictional population.[6] And it is safe to bet that many of those appearances will be either comic or problematic representations. Given the stereotyped repertoire of representations of women, blacks and the working class, it will also be entirely predictable that most of the older people who appear in the media are middle-class white men. We suggest, therefore, that work on ageist representations of the ageing process could most pertinently begin with focusing on images of older women.

This approach will demonstrate that ageism operates by reinforcing distinctions already present in the social formation. Middle-class men, who sell their intellectual labour, continue to be valued well into advanced age, whereas working-class and black men are on the scrap heap as soon as their physical labour is insufficient for the needs of the labour market. Women, however, whatever their class, begin to be affected by ageism from the age of 40 onwards, because women are mainly valued as mothers or as sexual objects. Historically, older women (matriarchs) have always been represented as a threat to the male order, as witnessed by the profusion of abusive terms such as *hag, witch* and *crone* (see Florence Keyworth, 1982). Beyond the likes of 'youthful' Joan Collins, images of women over 40 are almost non-existent, unless you count mother-in-law jokes. Older women indeed constitute almost a sub-class within older people, as they often lack the occupational pensions of men and also live considerably longer. Women who have raised families find it almost impossible to rejoin the labour market except in low-paid jobs. Patriarchal sexual relations mean that youth is an intrinsic component to women's sexual value (whereas the older experienced and middle-class male is considered sexually attractive) so that the older woman is deemed to be, paradoxically, either asexual or rampantly frustrated. Not surprisingly, a significant proportion of the cosmetic industry's profits are made by encouraging women to keep young and beautiful.

Two classic Hollywood films of the 1940s provide a valuable introduction to an analysis of women and ageing. Hollywood was centrally engaged in the general ideological effort of post-war America to drive Rosie the Riveter and her sisters out of the factories and back into the home where they belonged. The figure of the independent older woman was represented as a threat, a potential disruption to patriarchal order. *Mildred Pierce* (1945) is a film in which the narrative is concerned both to acknowledge such a threat and to neutralise it. Mildred breaks every patriarchal taboo in the book by divorcing her husband, bringing up her family herself, becoming a successful businesswoman, and initiating a non-marital sexual relationship. The price she pays for this subversive conduct is the death of one daughter (immediately after her affair began) and having her other daughter Veda grow up to hate her and attempt to seduce her new husband before shooting him. The film closes with Mildred reunited with her previous husband. The narrative message is clear: if an older woman becomes economically and sexually independent, social chaos is unleashed.

Sunset Boulevard (1950) is perhaps the quintessential expression of patriarchal fear of the older woman. Norma Desmond's decline from the matinee idol of her era into old age and madness is represented as the inevitable price women must pay for living independently of men and the family, perhaps most chillingly in

27 The older woman threat. Joan Crawford as Mildred Pierce

28 The older woman as neurotic. Gloria Swanson as Norma Desmond in *Sunset Boulevard*

the burial of the dead chimpanzee which is her surrogate baby. Students can analyse the differences of representation between the conventional melodramatic *mise-en-scène* of the scenes between Joe and young Betty, and the expressionistic *noir* use of lighting, music and camera angles when Norma makes sexual advances towards Joe. The contrast reveals an almost paranoid attitude towards the sexuality of the older woman. Norma's refusal to admit that she is growing old is represented as hubristic individual tragedy, but the contrast between the film's treatment of her ageing and the appearance of benign patriarch Cecil B. De Mille, suggests that her tragedy is more connected with society's dual standard towards ageing in men and in women.

De-familiarisation will be valuable for when students begin to analyse contemporary images of older people. Despite the best of intentions, some campaigning charities (with the notable exception of Pensioners' Link) still represent older people as dependent and helpless victims, who are usually women (see Photograph 29). Inevitably this builds up a picture of old age itself as being a

29 A lot of old people, like Miss Elizabeth Wright live in old houses which are draughty, badly insulated and costly to heat

problem instead of scrutinising the economic and social relations which deny older people the means of economic independence. Because these are the dominant images of older people in circulation, commercial companies can make a killing by using advertising which plays upon people's fears about what happens to them when they retire, a solution which is only of use to those with sufficient surplus income to afford it. The advertising images almost invariably feature a couple, which suggests that solutions to the 'old age problem' are most likely to be found within the family, and that privatisation rather than collective care represents the best option for older people. Students can also compare these types of image with those of children, who are also manically smiling or the passive victims of circumstances beyond their control. The similarities extend to television, and one could compare the role of children in LWT's *Childsplay*, where adults have to guess what word the children are defining, and the role of older people in providing a cute laugh in the vox pops of *That's Life*. More contentiously one could argue that Channel 4's *Years Ahead* programme for older people shares much the same paternalistic mode of address as children's programmes such as *Blue Peter*.

Older people most often appear on television in roles which are (supposedly) humorous. Harry Cross in *Brookside*, Hilda Ogden and Percy Sugden in *Coronation Street*, are represented as essentially nosy busybodies who interfere with everyone else; old people are an unproductive burden on the rest of the community. Students can attempt to rewrite some of the narratives of soaps using the older characters in the storylines concerned with topics such as sexual relations, for which they are considered inappropriate dramatic material. Older people most frequently appear in light entertainment programmes such as Les Dawson, Russ Abbott, *The Two Ronnies* and *Hinge and Bracket*, or in sitcoms such as *Last of the Summer Wine*. In fact they do not often appear on these shows but are represented or impersonated by young people. Older women are especially the butt of humour in a tradition derived from seaside postcards and the pantomime dame; indeed, apart from Nora Batty, nearly all comic representations of older women are performed by men. Earlier work on *film noir*'s construction of the older woman as a threat to men should enable this ridicule to be perceived as a patriarchal strategy of containment, but obviously humour is an area fraught with problems when teaching topics such as ageism.

Humour about old age circulates obsessively around the question of sexuality, as a cursory glance at birthday cards will demonstrate. Sexuality in older women or working-class men (dirty old men) is either an impossibility or grotesquely obscene. As in childhood, sexuality in old age threatens our investment in a representation of sexuality as a performance of heterosexual intercourse between an active male (who can no longer get it up) and a passive female (whom nobody desires). Repetitive humour about men who can no longer obtain an erection or sex-starved older women betray the anxiety that the phallus, ultimate symbol of the patriarchal order, may not have the monopoly on definitions of sexuality. Ageist humour serves the same function as the myth of childhood innocence in sustaining our dominant regime of sexuality by making alternative definitions of what constitutes the sexual seem unnatural.

Ultimately, it is this exclusion of alternative conceptions of living that is the ideological significance of ageist representations. The biological fact of ageing provides a potent form of legitimation for our particular social formation, because its economic and social relations are constructed to seem as natural and inevitable as the cycles of life itself. Ageing is not represented as a process of growth but as a cyclical return to a state of childhood transcending class, race and gender. Our contention is that the way in which we grow old is as subject to representation and political change as much as any other process – that our beginning is not our end.

9 Audiences

'I assume that the person watching this programme is the sort of person who likes that type of programme. He hasn't got much alternative because if he switches over to BBC he sees a similar type of programme. So you basically aim at the widest possible audience. You assume a measure of intelligence on the part of the viewer and you also see him as someone who is interested in the same sorts of things you are interested in. I really will not create, and reject the idea that you have to create Mr Average Citizen in his back parlour and say "Would he like it?" It's much easier to say "Would I like it?" ' –

'But because I'm in the prime of life and have become middle class, a bit elitist I suppose, I try to compensate for that by not being too elitist, not too middle class. But I would consciously accept that I'm nearer to the age group that I'm broadcasting to than my team are . . . I have an affinity with [the kind of audience] who wear hats and drive Morris Minors in the middle of the road very slowly and either live in Yorkshire or Kent or Dorset and have a fairly solid attitude towards life' – Two TV producers quoted by Michael Tracey (1978) p.124

'We call our average listener Doreen. Doreen isn't stupid but she's only listening with half an ear and doesn't necessarily understand "long words" ' – a radio producer quoted in Helen Baehr and Michelle Ryan (1984) p.11

Think of as many words as you can for different groups of people: school-leavers, commuters, accountants, gays, kids, families, stamp collectors, alcoholics, Tories, motorists, Asians, housewives and strikers might constitute part of a longer and

much more varied list. Having accumulated a reasonable list of
collective nouns on the board, the teacher could ask for three
further stages to be carried out:

1. The words could be grouped into different categories so that
   instead of there being one long list, the words should be re-
   organised under various headings – hobbies, work, politics,
   gender, race. The point of this exercise is to encourage
   students to analyse the nouns and to organise them
   conceptually.
2. Each student could tick the nouns to which they feel they
   belong. The resulting list will be interesting because it will
   begin to indicate to each student that they are not simply an
   individual who belongs to only one group or even to only one
   category. It is quite possible – and highly probable – that they
   will occupy a number of positions which don't necessarily fit
   together. The additional point to make about this exercise is
   that the grouping this time is based on personal experience,
   not analytic skills.
3. Each student could then be asked to consider to which groups
   or categories they feel they don't belong.

What is the significance of this exercise and what questions are
likely to arise as a result of undertaking it?

(a) There will be a recognition on the part of the class that they
    are not just individuals.
(b) Students will begin to see that they can and do belong to
    more than one group or category.
(c) Students will recognise that although in the same classroom –
    itself a social grouping – their friends are likely to consider
    themselves as belonging to different groupings.
(d) The class should recognise that these groupings have relative
    weighting or levels of significance for them and/or their peer
    groups and families. Some groupings might be accessible to
    them, others might exclude them, and yet others might be
    highly desirable.

The point overall is that the categories possess both material and
ideological levels of significance which students could be asked to
investigate; furthermore, students could be asked to say how
some groupings bind them and how others might be open to
change.

Because this exercise is based on both experiential and conceptual premises, and because each student will have to engage between these two levels, they can begin to acquire a useful knowledge of their own social position, that of the people around them, that of people at different levels of the social hierarchy, and, ultimately, of the organisation and structure of the wider culture of which they are a part.

If these seem a rather grandiose set of intentions to be derived from such a simple exercise, they nevertheless signify our contention that both education and the media are fundamentally about addressing audiences, and that without those audiences they are redundant. We write this despite what quite a number of television producers have said in the past and despite what many teachers and educators have said over decades.

'I don't think you can plan a programme for an audience, and I don't know quite who you would plan it for.'

'I think the audience is very important. It's a pity, but they just don't come up with massive suggestions . . . We are just left to get on with it really.'

'I try to use myself as an arbiter for the simple reason that in the end I'm responsible for it. They'll fire me if they get fed up with it. So in the end I have to say "I don't like this" or "my preference is for so and so".' (A TV producer quoted by Michael Tracey, 1978, p.132)

The validity of these assertions can easily be refuted: the very act of constructing something for an audience, of addressing an audience, implies a construction and an attempt to maintain that audience. However, before working through the implications of our assertion, we will outline how both the education system and the media conceive of their audiences.

The education system

Private and state provision of schooling in Britain has meant that the educational audience has never been addressed as a single and unitary one. The different kinds of educational provision are determined by the correspondingly different rationales as to what education should achieve, what it should 'give its audience'. The expression of the individual's opinion, making decisions, memorising facts and figures, have been highly regarded in the private school curriculum, where the acquisition of skills and knowledge deemed necessary for the top end of the job market has always been taken for granted.

State schools have had to recognise an increasingly diverse audience, especially since comprehensivisation. Before comprehensive schools the tripartite structure categorised educational provision and receivers fairly neatly into those who learnt manual skills and those who learnt the means of social mobility. But in the 1960s and 1970s, what was considered appropriate or 'relevant' for more comprehensive groups of students to be learning, became the crucial concern of those providing education – inspectors and teachers alike. More recently, the views of that comprehensive audience have begun to be redefined – not by the audiences themselves, nor this time by the teachers. Instead, what the state educational audience is about to receive is what an increasingly centralised government decrees. If the history of early broadcasting reveals patrician attitudes, then they can also certainly be discerned in education at the moment.

The media system

The history of early broadcasting in Britain has been one in which the BBC was less concerned with the audience (and its putative 'needs') than with the construction and provision of 'excellence' – an excellence defined by the values of the inherited dominant culture. For the BBC, what the audience needed was the 'best' possible service, the best programmes, plays and music.

The introduction of commercial television and the competition from pirate radio questioned those values, not as a result of extensive audience research but through extensive imitations of American models combined with audience experimentation – ratings figures very quickly, indicated what was 'popular'.

In both cases, the 'audience' was treated, whether wittingly or not, with a certain cynicism. In the first instance it was assumed that there was a consensus about what was good for the people (what they wanted), and in the second instance high audience figures meant that approval of the choices could be confidently assumed. Since the ratings were empirically 'verifiable', the broadcasters' case was always 'proved'. However, the point is that neither of the attitudes engage with the complexity of what an audience *is* potentially – the totality of a social formation, complete with all the class, race, gender, age, political and economic differences to be found in any such formation.

Such changes as there have been in these conceptions of the audience have only begun to take place over the last ten years, particularly as a result of the struggles by certain groups that will have been identified in classrooms through the exercise described above. Thus, as a result of activism on the part of the women's movement, black groups, gay groups, CND, etc., there have been attempts to construct media artefacts which address audiences in different ways. Until the advent of Channel 4, such artefacts (especially the alternative or oppositional work of many film-makers) could only circulate at local and community levels and would not be *broad*cast. (There are, of course, exceptions. Both the BBC and ITV have experimented with 'access TV' and the Asian community has had specialised Sunday morning programmes on television and radio for some years.) Since the inception of Channel 4 in November 1982, a much wider range of groups and views of the world have been made available over the televisual airwaves, and this is just beginning to have an effect on the other three channels.

This movement can be seen to be changing broad-casting but also to be itself the result of a range of other factors. We have already mentioned certain political groupings that have created change, but the very ecology of broadcasting itself is changing due to technological and economic factors. The development of video recorders, the introduction of cable and satellite transmission, the rise of unemployment and the subsequent attempts to redefine the notion of 'leisure' have led to a situation where the media institutions are finding it increasingly difficult to continue to aggregate the audience as arrogantly as they once did. Hence the fairly recent introduction of the concept of 'narrow-casting' when discussing the virtues of introducing cable systems.

The current situation would seem to be an intriguing one in

which the populace is caught between two conflicting forces. On the one hand, video technology offers Western societies the possibility of the production, circulation and consumption of low-cost media products designed for highly specific groups but with no way of locking in to large-scale audiences. On the other hand, satellite technology offers the reverse. No longer do national geopolitical boundaries roughly define the limits of television broadcasting: whole continents can be swamped instantaneously with *Dallas*. Is it politicians or broadcasters who hold the trump cards?

Although both the media and the education systems are concerned with addressing audiences, there is not necessarily a relationship between these two systems of address. Nevertheless, certain fundamental questions have to be asked of both. How is the audience defined? How is the audience addressed? Who does the addressing? What is the function of the address?

While these questions are crucial ones to raise in the classroom – both about the media and the education systems – we are not inferring that there is a direct and unproblematic relationship between texts and their readers or viewers. The media and an education system may be massive, but they are *not* massively determining. People clearly read their classroom experiences and the TV programmes they watch very differently. Thus it is necessary to have a concept not of *a* reading or readings, but of *differential readings* – and these readings are going to be informed by the social positioning and ideological formation of each reader within a particular culture.

Now this notion is not one by which either the media or the education system are likely to be impressed. They both try to encourage certain responses and to discourage others. Teachers do not want their students to fall asleep or to reject actively the 'knowledge' that is on offer, and media professionals would prefer people to be entertained or unproblematically informed by their programmes and not switch off or take to the streets! Therefore at this point it would be worth investigating a little more closely how both the media and the education system have understood the concept of the 'audience' in order to help create and maintain the type of audience *they* want.

The television audience

Basically there have been three ways of understanding the audience in terms of the mass media. The first is to be concerned with the 'effects' the media have on the audience; the second involves the notion of the *construction* of an audience by the media; and the third engages with how textual operations ideologically implicate an audience.

Effects studies

Effects studies have a long history. Since the very beginnings of any media form, whether drama, books, music, cinema, television, etc., there has been a fairly rapid questioning of the effects (always on other people, never on those asking the questions) that any new media is having on the people experiencing it. In asking questions about the 'effects' of the media there are several responses to make. The first is that the quest is always for a *dominant* effect. Subordinate effects, or a multiplicity or a confusion of effects, is of little interest. Secondly, it is the negative effects that are of concern, the power of the media to encourage anti-social behaviour. Thirdly, this concern with 'effects' only lasts as long as the medium remains a mass or popular medium: once the medium becomes part of the high-art culture then its power to affect negatively seems to disappear. *King Lear* would never be censored as a 'video nasty'. Fourthly, in the early history of broadcasting it was the propaganda effects of the media that were of prime concern: the Frankfurt School argued that Hitler's rise to power was partly due to his successful use of the media. More recently, in rewarding Gordon Reece (Mrs Thatcher's PR consultant) with a knighthood, Mrs Thatcher also recognised the importance of the media in her own rise to, and maintenance of, power. Since the Second World War this type of analysis in Western Europe and America has changed its focus on to the effects the media have on the lives of children, always making clear the significance of this research to the education system. A whole set of moral fears, anxieties and panics have been the result.

Research into the effects the media might have over people's lives raises important questions. That the media have influence and that they determine our lives to at least some extent is an explicit premise of this book. Any media that have the power to influence lives, consciousness and policy-making need to be analysed in terms of the nature of their power. In the main body of effects research, however, the questions are limited, the results contradictory, and the political and moral positions which inform that work partisan in the very stridency of their acclaimed 'objectivity'.

Thus, when looking at any of the 'effects studies' that have been undertaken over the decades – and there have been literally hundreds – the first questions we would want to ask are: who commissioned the research? for what purposes? what action was taken as a result of the findings?[1] One could look at the research of advertising agencies (which represents some of the most expensive and sophisticated data gathering of this kind) and understand the answers to those questions in terms of their desire to create for their clients larger markets and greater profits. There are rather more complex and subtle reasons why groups such as the National Viewers' and Listeners' Association commission audience research. Their concern is always going to have something to do with diffuse notions such as the 'common good', or the moral or religious climate of a society. In the case of government-commissioned research, the concern might be a rising crime or drug rate – hence the number of studies of the effects of the depiction of violence on the screen on the behaviour of teenage boys, never girls.

It is difficult not to see much of this work as being designed in such a way as ultimately to reinforce the beliefs and prejudices of those who commissioned it. The work is far too expensive to conduct, for there to have been many examples of highly sophisticated, objective (if that is ever possible), disinterested research. Such research also makes all sorts of assumptions about *how* people read and respond to media artefacts and *how* people respond to the research methods adopted. They allow little scope for either complexly differential readings or for oppositional responses. And they always, by definition, have to rely on the partiality of sampling techniques. Ultimately, this research is predicated on the fundamental importance of *empirical knowledge*, of it being possible to 'know' the audience (or audiences) and to know what they like or dislike.

Constructing audiences

The Family Viewing Policy crystallises a philanthropic conception of broadcasting; it draws on the accumulated research into the 'effects' of television and the uses to which these have been put by lobbies like the National Viewers' and Listeners' Association. Thus research by both the IBA and the BBC constructs profiles of audience availability and audience type. From these an image of Family Life is derived and then is used to prescribe what should be viewable at what times. Four time bands are specified by the IBA:

1) 16.15 to 17.15 (weekdays) – children's hour.
2) 17.15 to 19.30 – family viewing time, but with all material suitable for children to view alone.
3) 19.30 to 21.00 – no material unsuitable for children viewing with their family.
4) 21.00 onwards – it is considered the responsibility of parents to decide what their children should watch; but allowance has to be made for the possibility of a large (though decreasing) audience of children.

Despite the companies' moans, these timings do them no harm. They rule out the 'unpopular' during prime time (when the highest rates can be charged for advertising) and reinforce the need for a particular kind of output for a particular audience. Thus they give coherence to programme schedules that seek out consumer groups. 'Serious' drama becomes a non-starter in peak viewing time, whereas the popular quiz show and the situation comedy – both highly accessible to the desired audience – can aggregate a large audience with significant buying power. (Richard Paterson, 1980, p.81)

The crucial change that began to occur around 1970 was a de-emphasis on numbers and a greater emphasis on 'demographics', i.e. directing television shows towards specific audience groups. (Jane Feuer, 1984, p.3)

What both these quotations indicate is the fact that while television companies in countries like Great Britain and the USA might engage in audience research, the results of that research are used to 'target' an audience. But the very act of 'targeting' an audience is going to play a part in creating that audience. In the case of the 'Family Viewing Policy' it isn't simply the fact that research discovered how (usually nuclear) families organise their domestic lives independently of television, but rather that television timings help families to decide how they will structure their daily routines. The most significant notion of audience is the one operated by advertising departments in commercial TV companies and commented upon by many analysts of the media. Audiences need to be sold by commercial TV companies to advertisers. Commercial TV companies promise to deliver a particular type and size of audience to companies who have bought advertising slots at particular times of the day or night.[2] Thus programming policy (production and scheduling) is predicated upon the principle of creating a particular audience rather than on the basis of providing viewers with 'what they want to see'.

This different way of understanding the concept of the audience involves the idea that people do not exist as an audience (or audiences) until they have been constructed as such by the media. This process of constructing an audience position can take a number of forms.

Firstly, people are encouraged to buy a newspaper, go to the cinema or watch a television channel. Secondly, there is the type of entertainment or information that is offered. By presenting a Western, a film producer and a film distributor are attracting an audience that enjoys and knows what to expect from Westerns. Thirdly, there is the mode of address adopted by the artefact in question. This involves a number of elements. Narrative structures can be used to draw the spectator emotionally and physically into the action of the story. Images can also draw the spectator into the narrative through encouraging an identification with one or more of the protagonists. Other elements of filmic or televisual construction – the use of music, colour, lighting, etc. – can all be used to encourage an audience to empathise, sympathise, criticise, feel angry or happy.

In making a media artefact, then, the producers are not neutrally or innocently concerned with simply assembling these elements to produce a discrete artefact, but are involved in the process of inscribing into the texts a limited number of possible positions which the reader/viewer can adopt. These positions cannot be determined, but they can be limited. And, so the argument runs, because of the nature of the class and social background – and the race and gender – of most media producers, the potential positions constructed for audiences historically have been remarkably limited to those for the white, male, middle-class.

It is for these reasons that there has been a strong set of arguments running through the women's movement and black groups, to name but two examples, which have posited that given the lack of access to the points of media production or distribution (or until that access has been achieved) it is an important critical strategy to try and refuse the positions offered by the majority of media artefacts currently available.

Ideological dimensions of the audience

Another approach has stressed additional determinants. Stuart Hall (1980) elaborates upon the distinctions made between different kinds of audience readings that Raymond Williams made earlier (1973). Hall contends that audience readings of texts will vary according to the social positions of the constituent individuals or groups, their political beliefs, how practices of the media professionals and institutions have encoded them. This approach conceives of the audience in more complex ways than the 'effects' approach, which suggests that particular sections of the audience (notably young working-class boys) cannot mentally 'filter' what is broadcast and that working-class children, especially those from large families, are most at risk when watching the 'nasties'.[3] But audiences are varied and so are their readings. Hall's approach refuses to lump together the media into a monolithic entity as a single enemy, so preventing a complex proliferation of media encodings and decodings from running amok. Instead, Hall defines theoretical categories which can harness a potentially infinite pluralism.

Encodings and decodings of media texts are dominant or preferred, alternative or negotiated, and, finally, they may be oppositional. A society based on distinctions and inequalities of class, race, gender and age (to mention just the few categories we have concentrated on here) and which is conceived to maintain those distinctions and inequalities, will try to present its representations and understandings of the world if not as the only ones, then at least as the preferred representations. Dominant encodings and decodings are never uncontested, however, and so if the legitimacy of their general definitions is to be maintained, they must be seen to accommodate points of view which do not necessarily agree, and to include representatives from less powerful sectors of society.

Thus the BBC defends the individual playwright when 'controversial' programmes come under fire. 'Outrageous' pop videos are made permissible simply because they belong to a genre that is defined precisely according to its departures from the norm. An analysis of discussion programmes on radio phone-ins can reveal the permissible relationship between dominant and negotiated encodings and decodings. In spite of disagreements there will usually be a basic and determining consensus in that all participants, in their agreement to differ, will be content to do so within certain agreed terms. It is only once the very terms of the arguments themselves are questioned that possibilities for oppositional practices and readings are made available. A television history of the cotton industry, for example, has accounted for the profits made for the industrial revolution in terms of adventurous pioneers who developed a fine architectural 'Southern' style. An oppositional reading would account for the same profits in terms of imperialist aggression.[4]

Image analysis and the audience

A conventional approach to image analysis in the Media Studies lesson might ask questions about Photograph 30 in terms of *how* it produced meaning and *how* those meanings might be affected by the contexts in which it appeared. These are all important issues. The next stage, however, and one often overlooked, is to introduce the notion of differential readings, to encourage students to express not only their understanding of the image but also to understand the likelihood of other readings by other audiences. For example, the following readings of this image might be

1. how unusual it is to see men and women engaged in manual labour together;
2. it is wrong to see women doing heavy manual work;

30   Graham Finlayson

3. it is good to see men and women working together;
4. hauling in the nets is only done for the tourists; most of the
   catch is hauled up by winch in the next bay;
5. it is wrong to eat fish anyway.

There are many other possible readings (see Chapter 2) which are
not simply dependent on the content or context of the image
(which in this case might be a television programme, film,
postcard, etc.) but also on the expectations of audiences, socially
and culturally positioned in specific ways. A *Portuguese* person is
far more likely to know what fish was being caught, how they
would be marketed, cooked and eaten because the photograph is
an image of Nazarré, Portugal. A British person, on the other
hand, can know that the photograph was not taken in Britain
because of the clothes and because large net fishing from the
beach does not take place in this country. Saying this is to argue
that not only are several readings possible, but also that if a
'specialist' knowledge was brought to bear upon this image then
that knowledge would provide a preferred and determining
decoding.

A Portuguese student, or someone who had been on a holiday
to Portugal, might be able to caption the photograph quite
confidently: 'Villagers in Nazarré hauling in the evening's catch'.

Again, contexts and audience expectations combine in different ways to provide different decodings. Students learning about the fishing industry would expect to learn about techniques from the photograph, while sociology students would be more likely to read it for its clues about kinship and work.

Learning about differential readings will not tell students anything conclusive about audiences. We do not believe that audience responses can be measured in definitive comprehensive ways. However, we would hope that students, having completed analytic exercises similar to those described here, would have learnt the following:

1. that their own readings of texts are not the only possible nor necessarily the most obvious ones;
2. that other readings, by other people and in other contexts, might bear more weight and be more determining than theirs;
3. that there are discernible *reasons* for those other readings.

For students to understand why there exist different and possibly more determining readings than their own, means achieving a sense of the different factors which possibly determine other people's material existence, social knowledge and ideological assumptions. If to achieve a conceptual knowledge of what other audiences might perceive and understand is not to admit to the possibilities of one's own perceptions and assumptions changing, then at least it can challenge the autonomy which any one reading might presume.

Let us take a rather different type of image. Photograph 31 is a publicity still for the film *The Eyes of Laura Mars* (1978), one of a cycle of films with narratives featuring a strong female protagonist. The image used in the still partly indicates this strength: we see a woman doing a job that is conventionally thought of as being a male occupation (being a photographer), but at the same time it indicates that the title of the film refers not to the passive, romantic eyes of a woman the audience should swoon at (Garbo), but refers to eyes (the photographer's) that are actively looking at, and constructing, images of the world.

The point about the film's poster (Photograph 32), however, is that the photographer Laura Mars has been extracted from her context, her work. Why? One answer is to do with the function of film posters generally. Needing to be more richly informative than most other posters (in the cinema films are usually consumed

31

only once), film advertising generally utilises complex images involving a number of seemingly disparate elements. Assembled thus, they invite the potential audiences to narrativise. The publicity still of *Laura Mars*, although a powerful image, is not connotatively rich enough to warrant its use as a poster. Hence the additional five images *and* the reduction of the photograph to its 'essential' element – the *body* of Laura Mars. Since a film poster, more emphatically than most images, is intended to attract (construct) audiences and to persuade them to part with their money in exchange for a narrative screened in a darkened cinema, then the questions we can raise in the classroom should begin to reveal how a differentiated audience might meet that appeal:

1. Who is this poster appealing to and how?
2. How is it encouraging people to become an audience?
3. Does the poster appeal to men and women differently?

32

There are number of enigmas posed by the still which could arouse our curiosity:

1. How is it that a woman is working as a photographer?
2. Is she in fact *working*, or is photography her hobby?
3. Why has she sat down on the pavement in the middle of a busy street?
4. Why has she adopted the posture she has, and does it suggest sexual availability?

Some possible responses might be:

1. The film looks interesting because the poster offers a powerful representation of a woman who is in control of her life.
2. The film looks interesting because the woman looks sexy.
3. The film is about a woman who has an unusual occupation for a woman.

There are a number of possible readings, some of which may be encouraged and others which may be discouraged by the organisation of the image. This is to say that not all viewers will respond in terms of the preferred reading encouraged by the distributor. For example, viewers might choose to respond oppositionally by defacing the poster.

Teachers may or may not find that gender differences account for different readings among their students. Boys might stereotypically respond in terms of response (2), while girls might go for (1) or (3). However, it is quite likely that girls might just as easily opt for (2) – they might identify with the actress, wanting to be sexy like her rather than identify with her as a strong female character. Unstereotypically, either sex could go for any one or more of these responses. Again, graffiti may or may not have anything to do with the film.

Having talked with the class about their responses and having collectively assessed the students' reasons for them, the next stage in the lesson might take the form of asking the class to write an account of the poster as if they were the advertising agency trying to sell the poster design to the film distributors. This would involve the students having to make more precise assessments as to what they suppose are the dominant and subordinate readings of the image. This exercise should begin to explore the gaps between the 'perceived' intentions of producers and distributors, and the variety of audience readings.[5]

In a classroom, the most significant objective would be the *assessment* of any perceptible gaps, of any possible variety. Do any discernible intentions override plausible audience interpretations? If so, why? If not, to what advantage can those audience interpretations be put? How important are producers? How are 'preferred readings' inscribed? Is a text which offers a wide variety of readings necessarily 'better' than one that does not? The wording of questions such as these will have to fit specific objects of study and suit the contexts of particular course objectives, but they should be designed to alert students to the possible fluidity of meanings rather than to confirm an imprisoning fixity.

As teachers we mediate knowledge and representations of the world and construct various positions for our student audiences as we do so. Intending our students to learn and enjoy what we teach, we inevitably inscribe 'preferred readings' through our choice of materials, the questions we ask, the assignments we set, the tone of our voice. The positions we offer our classroom audiences may not always be accepted, and we too will have to assess constantly the gaps between our intentions as 'producers' and the variety of student responses. In the attempts to enable students to produce and read 'oppositionally', which oppositions will we encourage, and which will we discourage, while allowing for the pleasures of variety and difference?

In this book we have argued why learning about the media matters and what kind of education that learning should aim to achieve. We recognise the difficulties of realising that aim but remain hopeful about possibilities for the future, thoroughly persuaded by the pleasures that our own media education continues to afford.

Postscript

Finally, how would your students consider the following advertisement and the subsequent questions overleaf:

Tracy Logan is a typical British sixteen year old, leaving school this year. But to Japan, and our other international competitors, she's a big threat.

That's because this year she'll be starting 2 years paid skill training on the new YTS.

She'll begin her course by trying out several different skills before she chooses the one she'll train for through to the end of the second year.

By then, she'll have a skill, a certificate to prove it, and a better chance of getting a job.

Our competitors in the Far East and Europe have been training their young people like this for years.

It's made them more efficient and more productive and it's helped them take trade away from us. But from now on they're going to have to watch out.

Tracy will be spending the next two years learning how to take trade away from them for a change. Along with about 360,000 other ambitious British school leavers.

MSC

**TRAINING FOR SKILLS. THE NEW 2 YEAR YTS.
NOW 16 AND 17 YEAR OLD SCHOOL LEAVERS CAN EARN WHILE THEY LEARN.**

1. Who is addressing who and why?
2. What narratives are told?
3. How are representations of class, gender, race and age employed?
4. How can study of this media artefact enable critical comment on the state of education?

'When they photographed me, they told me my name was too posh. They said they would have to choose one the YTS trainees could relate to. It was a choice of Tracy or Lizzie, I was told'. (Attributed to Belinda Jones, the 15-year-old model used to advertise the Manpower Services Commission YTS schemes, *The Daily Mail*, February 1986.)

Notes

Introduction

1. A concept formulated by Pierre Bourdieu; see Pierre Bourdieu and Jean-Claude Passeron (1977).
2. See in particular *Media Studies in Education* (1977) and *Media Education* (1984).
3. For further information contact the Association for Media Education in Scotland (AMES), Scottish Curriculum Development Service, Moray House College of Education, Holyrood Road, Edinburgh EH8 8AQ.
4. See Tim Blanchard (1986) *Media Studies and GCSE*, London: SEFT Occasional Paper and Chris Points (ed.) (1985) *Clwyd Working Papers for 16+ Media Studies* Wales.
5. See Tim Blanchard (1985) *Media Studies and the CPVE*, Media Analysis Paper 7, University of London Institute of Education.
6. Useful contemporary accounts are to be found in the Report of the 1985 National Media Education Conference at Bradford and the Report of the 1986 'Watching Media Learning' Conference in Birmingham. Both are available from SEFT, 29 Old Compton Street, London W1V 5PL.
7. 'Interpellate' is a term we have adopted from Louis Althusser's influential essay 'Ideology and ideological state apparatuses' (1969). He introduces the concept thus:

   all ideology hails or interpellates concrete individuals as concrete subjects . . . ideology 'acts' or 'functions' in such a way that it 'recuits' subjects among the individuals (it recruits them all), or 'transforms' the individuals into subjects (it transforms them all) by that very precise operation which I have called *interpellation* or hailing, and which can be imagined along the lines of the most commonplace everyday police (or other) hailing: 'Hey, you there!'. (pp.162–3)

8. See David Lusted and Phillip Drummond (1985) and Len Masterman (1985).
9. We should also mention that in the same period British Telecom has passed from state to public ownership in the flotation of shares on the British *and* American Stock Exchanges. This has happened as

269

part of the current British Tory government's general monetarist programme. However, the one million investors who own approximately 200 shares each control only 4 per cent of the vote. Majority control lies in the hands of the international financiers and multinationals.

10. For an introduction to this area see: Open University, 'Block 3: the audience' in *Mass Communication and Society* (1977); 'Block 3: Images of the Audience' in John Hartley *et al*. (1985); David Morley (1980).

1 Histories

1. See Television Research Committee (1966) *Problems of Television Research: A Progress Report of the Television Research Committee*, Leicester University Press.

2. Taken from the BBC's confidential News and Current Affairs minutes dated 24 September 1976 and reproduced in Glasgow University Media Group (1982), p.11.

3. All quotes are taken from the interesting account in Simon Frith (1983b).

4. See Len Masterman (1985) for an account of this important conference.

5. The Humanities Curriculum Project (HCP) was funded by the Schools' Council and the Nuffield Foundation and ran from 1967 to 1972. Its brief was:

   to offer to schools and to teachers such stimulus, support and materials as may be appropriate to the mounting, as an element in general education, of enquiry-based courses, which cross the subject boundaries between English, History, Geography, Religious Studies and Social Studies.

   See Lawrence Stenhouse (1969); Jim Hillier and Andrew McTaggart (1970); Richard Exton (1970).

6. The British Film Institute, in conjunction with Secker and Warburg, published twenty-eight titles, including such influential volumes as Peter Wollen's *Signs and Meaning in the Cinema* (1969). *Movie* magazine published twenty-three titles in the Studio Vista series, and Tantivy's series with Zwemmers continues.

7. For an account of the upheaval in English studies see Peter Widdowson (1982).

8. The phrase is taken from the title of an article written by a schoolteacher who was later to become Director of the British Film Institute – Stanley Reed – and published in the Society of Film Teachers' (later SEFT) first regular publication, *The Bulletin*, in 1950.

9. See Forsyth Hardy (ed.) (1946).

10. *Ibid.*

2 Institutions

1. Both taken by John Sturrock, a Network photographer. The first was published in *City Limits*, 29 May 1984 and the second in the *New Statesman*.
2. This section is indebted to two essays by Stuart Hall (1973 and 1980).
3. See Gill Branston (1984).
4. During the past five years, publishing about the media (most notably by Comedia, Pluto Press and the BFI) has defined the institutional, rather than the textual or authorial, as a central concern. Since media institutions are dynamic structures (more so than either texts or authors!), the need for research will be constant. At the time of writing, what different audiences do with different texts in different contexts are the greatest unknowns.
5. See Ed Buscombe (1984).
6. See John Corner (1984).
7. A useful resource for teaching title sequences is Julian Birkett and Roy Twitchin (1983).
8. There are now a range of games and simulations available for teaching about media production. See especially *Choosing the News* (ILEA English Centre), *Radio Covingham* (ILEA), *Front Page* (ILEA), *Teachers' Protest* (ILEA English Centre), *Simulating the Film Industry* (SEFT), *Moviemaker* (Parker Games), *Brand X* (Scottish Curriculum Development Council).
9. The most useful available accounts of television production are: Philip Elliott (1972), Manuel Alvarado and Edward Buscombe (1978), Stephen E. Whitfield and Gene Roddenberry (1968), Michael Tracey (1978), Manuel Alvarado and John Stewart (1985), Roger Silverstone (1985).
10. See Stephen Lambert (1982); Simon Blanchard and David Morley (1982); Eight Programme Makers, 'Channel 4 – One Year On', in *Screen*, vol. 25, no. 2, March–April 1984.
11. See Brian Murphy (1983); Paul Sieghart (1982).
12. See Christopher Hird (1983); *Who Owns Whom* (annual); BFI (undated) *The Companies You Keep*; Christopher Dunkley's (1985) *Television Today and Tomorrow – Wall-to-Wall Dallas?* is a lively, accessible and up-to-date rendition of the effects of the new technologies on the media system.
13. There is a large body of work already covering this field. In addition to works already cited, see especially John Howkins (1982); Tim Hollins (1984); Armand Mattelart *et al.* (1984); and Sean MacBride (1980).
14. For an account of this whole episode see 'The Viewpoint Controversy' in *Screen Education*, no. 19, Summer 1976.
15. See Lucy Douch (1985).
16. See in particular Chapters 5, 6 and 7 in Dorothy Hobson (1982).
17. See Richard Dyer (1979 and 1980); Alexander Walker (1970).

18. See the two issues of *Screen* which focus on the censorship question: *Screen*, vol. 23, no. 5, November–December 1982, and vol. 27, no. 2, March–April 1986.
19. See Len Masterman (1985) and John Hartley (1982).
20. See Michael Tracey (1982); Nikki Haydon and Jim Mulligan (1983).
21. See Tony Pearson (1983).
22. See the accompanying TV programme booklet produced by Thames Television (1983) *The English Programme 1983–84*; the students' workbook by Julian Birkett and Roy Twitchin (1983); and also Anthony Smith (1976) and Herman Wigbold (1979).
23. See Chris Rodrigues and Rod Stoneman (1981). To hire independent film and video productions consult, among others, the catalogues of the following organisations: The Other Cinema, 79 Wardour Street, London W1; British Film Institute, 81 Dean Street, London W1; Concord Films Council, 201 Felixstowe Road, Ipswich, Suffolk; Circles (Women's Film and Video), 113 Roman Road, London E2; Cinema of Women (COW), 27 Clerkenwell Close, EC1; Albany Video, The Albany, Douglas Way, Deptford SE8; Contemporary Films, 55 Greek Street, London W1.

3   Realism

1. See Philip Schlesinger, Graham Murdock, Philip Elliott (1983); Philip Schlesinger (1980); Cary Bazalgette and Richard Paterson (1980); Justin Wren-Lewis (1981); Bob Lumley (1981); Howard Tumber (1982).
2. See Mike Clarke and Peter Baker (1981).
3. *Principle and Practice in Documentary Progress*, BBC Handbook.
4. For example, see Dai Vaughan (1974) and (1976); Roger Silverstone (1985).
5. See 'Cinema/Sound', *Yale French Studies*, no. 60, 1980; 'On the Soundtrack', *Screen*, vol. 25, no. 3, May–June 1984; Roy Prendergast (1977).
6. For a more precise breakdown, see 'Terms' in John Tulloch and Manuel Alvarado (1983), pp.ix–x.
7. See the four books thus far produced by the group: Glasgow University Media Group (1976, 1980, 1982, 1985); see also Peter Beharrell and Greg Philo (1977).
8. *Radio Covingham* (and its television versions) is a well tried and useful exercise which requires students to simulate a day's newsgathering and a broadcast. They have to be able to justify the pieces they keep and those they reject. They may find that the pressures of time force them to include pre-recorded items even though they might wish to give air space to another item at the last moment. Students will discover that although television news is almost as much about keeping audiences tuned in as anything else,

they might consider the fact that it doesn't have to be. See Manuel Alvarado (1975).
9. See Garry Whannel (1979 and 1983); Alan Tomlinson and Garry Whannel (1984).

4 Narrative

1. Joseph Conrad (1902) *Heart of Darkness*, reprinted in 1973 by Penguin.
2. A number of theorists and critics have attempted to construct systems and typologies for the structural analysis of narratives. The objects for analysis have been oral cultures (Claude Levi-Strauss), folk tales (Vladimir Propp, A. J. Greimas), literary texts (Roland Barthes, Tzvetan Todorov), filmic texts (Christian Metz), and they have all tried to break down complete narratives into segments in different ways. Story types, linguistic structures, systems of image organisation have all been identified and categorised. The methods of a number of these theorists working within their own field have been used and applied to quite different media texts, e.g. Peter Wollen (1976); Roger Silverstone (1981); Gillian Swanson (1981). Useful books for the English class are *Changing Stories* (1985) and *Making Stories* (1985).
3. *Coma*, and strategies for teaching about the film, are discussed in the Teachers' Notes on *Genre*, part of the BFI/ILEA Film Studies Course for sixth formers. See also Elizabeth Cowie (1979 and 1980).
4. If classes wish to examine in general detail how formal codings construct positions for narratees, then teachers may find a useful resonance in John Caughie's article 'Progressive Television and Documentary Drama', in *Screen*, vol. 21, no. 3, Autumn 1980. In an assessment of the genre's progressiveness, Caughie discusses the 'rhetoric' of different looks: eyeline match, field/reverse field, point of view.
5. Distributed by the Arts Council and discussed in Gill Branston (1984).
6. John Ellis (1982) discusses the different regimes of viewing which television and the cinema have established.
7. See BFI (1981) *Teaching 'Coronation Street'* and Richard Dyer *et al.* (1981).

5 Class

1. *The Wealthy* is an accessible pamphlet produced by Counter Information Services, 9 Poland Street, London W1.
2. See Peter Lambert and Nigel Richardson (1983).

3. Transcript from BBC1's programme *Tonight* quoted in 'Jim Allen Meets His Critics', *The Listener*, vol. 94, no. 2427 and reprinted in Andrew Goodwin, Paul Kerr and Ian Macdonald (eds) (1983).
4. See *BBC Taskforce South. Malvinas 1982* (1982) offers a radical examination of the internal reasons why both British and Argentina needed a war at that time for political reasons (available from the Other Cinema). See also the BBC *Open Space* programme made by the Glasgow University Media Group (1985) and their book *War and Peace News* (1985).

6 Gender

1. See Jane Root (1984).
2. See Andy Metcalf and Martin Humphries (1985); Ken Plummer (1981).
3. *Selling Pictures* (undated) BFI, London.
4. The slide from *Reading Pictures* advertising Boots' 17 mascara illustrates this point well.
5. Hackney Flashers, available from SEFT, 29 Old Compton Street, London W1V 5PL.
6. *Teaching 'Coronation Street'* (1981), BFI, London.
7. Dick Hebdige (1985).

7 Race

1. See Ann Dummett (1973); Stuart Hall *et al.* (1978); A. Sivanandan (1982).
2. Paul Robeson, who stars in the film, had originally agreed to do it as he saw it as offering an opportunity to express African culture, but he was deeply disappointed with the result for the way in which it entirely maligned African people. Thus while it was a Western success, it was later actually banned by a number of African countries.
3. See Paul Hartmann and Charles Husband (1972 and 1974); Andy Reeve and Paul Stubbs (1981).
4. See the long chapter on Paul Robeson in Richard Dyer (1986).
5. See the interesting essay on Muhammed Ali in Eldridge Cleaver (1968).
6. It would be useful to build up dossiers of newspaper cuttings concentrating on such an item over a period of time. Pat Holland offers a useful model in her article on the New Cross fire (1981), and the BFI's teaching packs *Images of Race* and *Selling Pictures* offer useful materials on which to draw. There is also now a substantial literature about newspaper reporting and race. In addition to Stuart Hall *et al.* (1978) already referred to, see also John Downing (1980); Charles Critcher *et al.* (1975); Bob Baker *et al.* (1980); Denis

MacShane (1978); Phil Cohen and Carl Gardner (eds) (1982); and Campaign Against Racism in the Media *In Black and White – Racist Reporting and How to Fight it* (undated).
7. Quotation from a speech made by A. Sivanandan at a meeting held at the University of London Institute of Education in 1983.

8 Age

1. Richard Belfield and Su Carroll, 'Child Labour', in the *New Statesman*, 1 February 1985.
2. A historical overview is offered by Simone de Beauvoir (1977). See also Martin Hoyles (1979); Chris Phillipson (1982); and Mike O'Donnell (1985).
3. See Stuart Hall and Tony Jefferson (1976); Dick Hebdige (1979).
4. See *The Image of the Elderly on TV*, available from the University of the Third Age, 8A Castle Street, Cambridge CB3 0AQ. See also *Women and Ageism*, Women's Monitoring Network Report no. 5, available from A Woman's Place, Hungerford House, Victoria Embankment, London WC2.
5. See Karen M. Stoddard (1982) for a general discussion of the representation of older women. See also Pam Cook (1978).
6. Women's Monitoring Network Report no. 5, *ibid*.

9 Audiences

1. See Martin Barker (ed.) (1984b) and Geoffrey Barlow and Alison Hill (eds) (1985).
2. A very useful set of teaching materials on advertisers' research and targeting of audiences is to be found in *Baxters: The Magic of Advertising*, available from the Scottish Curriculum Development Service, Moray House College, Holyrood House, Edinburgh.
3. *Video Violence and Children*, a report by the Parliamentary Group Video Enquiry, London. Oasis projects, November 1983, Part One, paras 8.14–15.
4. *The Rise and Fall of King Cotton* (BBC2, 1985).
5. David Morley (1980); Michael Tracey (1985); and Armand Mattelart, Xavier Delcourt, and Michele Mattelart (1984).

Bibliography

Allen, Jim (1982) 'Jim Allen Meets His Critics', *The Listener*, vol. 94, no. 2427, reprinted in Goodwin, Andrew *et al.* (eds) (1983).

Althusser, Louis (1969) 'Ideology and Ideological State Apparatuses', in Louis Althusser (1971) *Lenin and Philosophy and Other Essays*, (London: NLB).

Altman, Rick (ed.) (1981) *Genre: The Musical: A Reader* (London: Routledge & Kegan Paul/BFI).

Alvarado, Manuel (1975) 'Simulation as Method', in *Screen Education*, no. 14, Spring 1975.

—— (1976) 'Eight Hours Are Not a Day', in Rayns, Tony (ed.) (1976).

—— (1977a) 'Class, Culture and the Education System', in *Screen Education*, no. 22, Spring 1977.

—— (1977b) 'Media Education in the United Kingdom', *Media Studies in Education*, UNESCO, 1977.

—— (1978) 'The Documentary Enterprise: Realism and Convention', in Cowie, Elizabeth (ed.) (1978).

—— (1979) 'Photographs and Narrativity', *Screen Education*, no. 32/33, Autumn/Winter 1979–80.

—— (1981) 'Television Studies and Pedagogy', *Screen Education*, no. 38, Spring.

—— (1982) *Authorship, Origination and Production* (London: University of London Institute of Education).

—— (1983) 'The Question of Media Studies', *Meridian*, vol. 2, no. 1.

—— and Buscombe, Edward (1978) *Hazell – The Making of a TV Series* (London: BFI/Latimer).

—— and Ferguson, Bob (1982) 'Teaching Viewpoint 2: Some Strategies', *The English Programme 1982/83* (London: Thames).

—— (1983) 'The Curriculum: Media Studies and Discursivity', *Screen*, vol. 24, no. 3, May/June 1983.

—— and Stewart, John (1985) *Made For Television – Euston Films Limited* (London: BFI/Methuen).

Ames, *The Media Education Journal*, Association for Media Education in Scotland, Scottish Curriculum Development Office, Moray House College, Holyrood Road, Edinburgh EH8 8AQ.

Ang, Ien (1985) *Watching 'Dallas' – Soap Opera and the Melodramatic Imagination* (London: Methuen).

Appignanesi, Richard (1979) 'Some Thoughts on Freud's Discovery of Childhood', in Martin Hoyles (ed.) (1979).

276

Apple, Michael W. (ed.) (1982) *Cultural and Economic Reproduction in Education – Essays on Class, Ideology and the State* (London: Routledge & Kegan Paul).

Associated Examining Board (1977) *Expanded Notes for the Guidance of Teachers of AEB GCE 'A' Level Communication Studies.*

Aubrey, Crispin (ed.) (1982) *Nukespeak – the Media and the Bomb* (London: Comedia).

—— and Chilton, Paul (eds) (1984) *Nineteen-Eighty-Four in 1984 – Autonomy, Control and Communication* (London: Comedia).

Auty, Martyn and Roddick, Nick (eds) (1985) *British Cinema Now* (London: BFI).

Baehr, Helen (1980) *Women and Media* (Oxford: Pergamon).

—— and Ryan, Michèle (1984) *Shut Up and Listen!* (London: Comedia).

Baker, Bob *et al.* (1980) *Read All About It: A Study of Race Reporting in Newspapers* (Birmingham: AFFOR).

Balio, Tino (ed.) (1976) *The American Film Industry*, University of Wisconsin.

Barker, Martin (1981) *The New Racism – Conservatives and the Ideology of the Tribe* (London: Junction Books).

—— (1984a) *A Haunt of Fears – The Strange History of the British Horror Comics Campaign* (London: Pluto).

—— (ed.) (1984b) *The Video Nasties – Freedom and Censorship in the Media* (London: Pluto).

Barlow, Geoffrey and Hill, Alison (eds) (1985) *Video Violence and Children* (London: Hodder & Stoughton).

Barnett, Anthony (1982) *Iron Britannia – Why Parliament Waged its Falklands War* (London: Alison & Busby).

Barnouw, Erik (1974) *Documentary, A History of the Non-Fiction Film* (New York: OUP).

—— (1975) *Tube of Plenty – the Evolution of American Television* (New York: OUP).

—— (1978) *The Sponsor – Notes on a Modern Potentate* (Oxford: OUP).

Barr, Charles (1986) *All Our Yesterdays – 90 Years of British Cinema* (London: BFI).

Barrell, John (1978) *The Dark Side of the Landscape* (Cambridge: Cambridge University Press).

Barrat, David (1986) *Media Sociology* (London: Tavistock).

Barrett, Michèle, Corrigan, Philip, Kuhn, Annette and Wolff, Janet (1979) *Ideology and Cultural Production* (London: Croom Helm).

Barthes, Roland (1964) 'The Rhetoric of the Image', in Barthes, Roland (1977).

—— (1966) 'Introduction to the Structural Analysis of Narratives', in Barthes, Roland (1977).

—— (1972) *Mythologies* (London: Jonathan Cape).

—— (1975) *S / Z* (London: Jonathan Cape).

—— (1977) *Image – Music – Text* (London: Fontana).

—— (1979) *The Eiffel Tower and Other Mythologies* (New York: Hill and Wang).

Barthes, R. (1981) *Camera Lucida – Reflections on Photography* (New York: Hill and Wang).
Bates, Tony (1984) *Broadcasting in Education: An Evaluation* (London: Constable).
Bazalgette, Gary and Paterson, Richard (1980) 'Real Entertainment: the Iranian Embassy Siege', *Screen Education*, no. 37, Winter 1980–1.
BBC (undated) *Principles and Practice in Documentary Progress*, BBC Handbook.
Beharrell, Peter and Philo, Greg (eds) (1977) *Trade Unions and the Media* (London: Macmillan).
Belfield, Richard and Carroll, Su (1985) 'Child Labour', *New Statesman* 1 February 1985.
Bell, Philip, Boehringer Kathie and Crofts, Stephen (1983) *Programmed Politics: A Study of Australian Television* (Sydney: Sable Press).
Bellini, James (1981) *Rule Britannia* (London: Cape).
Benn, Tony *et al.* (1986) *Bending Reality – the State of the Media* (London: Pluto).
Bennett, Tony, Boyd-Bowman, Susan, Mercer, Colin and Woollacott, Janet (eds) (1981) *Popular Television and Film* (London: BFI/Open University).
Berger, John (1972a) *Selected Essays and Articles – The Look of Things* (Harmondsworth: Penguin).
—— (1972b) *Ways of Seeing* (Harmondsworth: Penguin).
—— (1980) *About Looking* (London: Writers and Readers).
Bethell, Andrew (1981) *Eyeopener One* and *Eyeopener Two* (Cambridge: Cambridge University Press).
Bezencenet, Stevie and Corrigan, Philip (1986) *Photographic Practices: Towards A Different Image* (London: Comedia).
BFI Dossier No. 4 (1981) *Granada: The First 25 Years* (London: BFI).
BFI Education (1981) *Teaching 'Coronation Street'* (London: BFI).
—— (undated) *The Companies You Keep* (London: BFI).
—— (1982) *Media Education Conference 1981: A Report* (London: BFI).
—— (1985) *Teaching TV Sitcom* (London: BFI).
Bigsby, C. W. E. (ed.) (1976) *Approaches to Popular Culture* (London: Edward Arnold).
Birkett, Julian and Twitchin, Roy (1983) *Starters: Teaching Television Title Sequences* (London: BFI).
—— (undated) *Understanding Television* (London: Thames).
Birmingham Film Workshop, (1982) *Four on Four: Four open forums on the new TV channel* (Birmingham: West Midlands Arts).
Blanchard, Simon and Harvey, Sylvia (1983) 'The Post-War Independent Cinema: Structure and Organisation', in Curran, James and Porter, Vincent (eds) (1983).
Blanchard, Simon and Morley, David (eds) (1982) *What's this Channel Fo(u)r? An Alternative Report* (London: Comedia).
Blanchard, Tim (1985) *Media Studies and the CPVE* (London: University of London Institute of Education).
—— (1986) *Media Studies and the GCSE* (London: SEFT).

Bogle, Donald (1973) *Toms, Coons, Mulattoes, Mammies and Bucks – An Interpretive History of Blacks in American Films* (New York: Viking).

Bonney, Bill (1980) *Packer and Televised Cricket*, Media Paper No. 2 (Sydney, Australia: NSWIT).

—— (1981) 'Australian Media Ownership and Control', *Media Interventions*, New South Wales, Australia.

—— and Wilson, Helen (1983) *Australian Commercial Media* (Australia: Macmillan).

—— (1984) *Networking and Control in Australian Commercial Television*, Media Paper No. 2 (Sydney: NSWIT).

Bordwell, David and Thompson, Kristin (1979) *Film Art: An Introduction* (Massachusetts: Addison-Wesley).

——, —— and Staiger, Janet (1985) *Classic Hollywood Cinema: Film Style and Mode of Production* (London: Routledge & Kegan Paul).

Bourdieu, Pierre (1971) 'Intellectual Field and Creative Project', in Young, Michael F. D. (ed.) (1971).

—— and Passeron, Jean-Claude (1977) *Reproduction in Education, Society and Culture* (London: Sage).

Boyce, George, Curran, James and Wingate, Pauline (eds) (1978) *Newspaper History: From the 17th Century to the Present Day* (London: Comedia).

Branston, Gill (1984) 'TV as Institution – Strategies for Teaching', *Screen* vol. 25, no. 2, March–April.

Brecht, Bertolt (1977) 'Against Georg Lukacs', *Aesthetics and Politics* (London: NLB).

Bridges, George and Brunt, Rosalind (eds) (1981) *Silver Linings – Some Strategies for the Eighties* (London: Lawrence and Wishart).

Broadfoot, Patricia (ed.) (1984) *Selection, Certification and Control* (Brighton: Falmer Press).

Brunsdon, Charlotte and Morley, David (1978) *Everyday Television: 'Nationwide'*, BFI Television Monograph 10 (London: BFI).

—— (ed.) (1986) *Films for Women* (London: BFI).

Brunt, Rosalind (1984) 'The Changing Face of Royalty', *Marxism Today*, July 1984.

—— and Rowan, Caroline (eds) (1982) *Feminism, Culture and Politics* (London: Lawrence & Wishart).

Bryan, Beverley, Dadzie, Stella and Scafe, Suzanne (1985) *The Heart of the Race, Black Women's Lives in Britain* (London: Virago).

Bryson, L. (ed.) (1948) *The Communication of Ideas* (New York: Harper and Row).

Buckingham, David (1986) *Educational Television: Institution and Ideology* (London: University of London, Institute of Education).

Burch, Noël (1973) *Theory of Film Practice* (London: Secker & Warburg).

Burgin, Victor (1982) *Thinking Photography* (London: Macmillan).

Burns, Tom (1977) *The BBC – Public Institution and Private World* (London: Macmillan).

Buscombe, Edward (1974) 'Television Studies in Schools and Colleges', *Screen Education*, 12, Autumn 1974.

—— (ed.) (1975) *Football on Television*, BFI Television Monograph 4 (London: BFI).

—— (1976) *Making 'Legend of the Werewolf'* (London: BFI).

—— (1984) 'Disembodied Voices and Familiar Faces: Television Continuity', in Masterman, Len (ed.) (1984).

Cain, John (1985) 'A Role for Broadcasters', in Lusted, David and Drummond, Phillip (eds) (1985).

Cameron, Ian (1962) 'Films, Directors and Critics', *Movie*, no. 2, September 1962.

—— (ed.) (1972) *The 'Movie' Reader* (London: November Books).

Campaign Against Racism in the Media (undated) *In Black and White – Racist Reporting and How to Fight It* (London: Campaign Against Racism in the Media).

Campaign for Press and Broadcasting Freedom (undated) *Are You in the Picture? An Introduction to the Way Television Works* (London: CPBF).

Campaign for Press Freedom (undated) *The Right of Reply* (London: CPF).

—— (undated) *Towards Press Freedom* (London: CPF).

Carroll, Don (1981) *General and Communications Studies – Don't You Believe It!* (London: Macmillan).

Caughie, John (ed.) (1978) *Television: Ideology and Exchange*, BFI Television Monograph 9 (London: BFI).

—— (1980) 'Progressive Television and Documentary Drama', *Screen*, vol. 21, no. 3, Autumn 1980.

—— (ed.) (1981a) *Theories of Authorship: A Reader* (London: Routledge & Kegan Paul/BFI).

—— (1981b) 'Rhetoric, Pleasure and "Art Television"', *Screen*, vol. 22, no. 4, Winter 1981.

Centre for Contemporary Cultural Studies (1982) *The Empire Strikes Back – Race and Racism in 70s Britain* (London: Hutchinson/CCCS).

Chambers, Iain (1985) *Urban Rhythms – Pop Music and Popular Culture* (London: Macmillan).

Chanan, Michael (1980) *The Dream That Kicks – the Pre-History and Early Years of Cinema in Britain* (London: Routledge & Kegan Paul).

Clarke, Jane and Simmonds, Diana (eds) (1980) *Move Over Misconceptions: Doris Day Reappraised*, BFI Dossier No. 4 (London: BFI).

Clarke, John, Critcher, Chas and Johnson, Richard (eds) (1979) *Working-Class Culture – Studies in History and Theory* (London: Hutchinson/CCCS).

Clarke, Mike and Baker, Peter (1981) *Talking Pictures* (London: Mary Glasgow).

Cleaver, Eldridge (1968) *Soul On Ice* (London: McGraw-Hill).

Cohen, Phil (1984a) 'Against the New Vocationalism' in Phil Cohen (1984) *Schooling For the Dole* (London: Macmillan).
—— (1984b) 'Losing the Generation Game', in Curran, James (ed.) (1984)
—— and Gardner, Carl (eds) (1983) *It Ain't Half Racist, Mum: Fighting Racism in the Media* (London: Comedia).
Cohen, Stanley and Young, Jock (eds) (1981, revised edition) *The Manufacture of News – Social Problems, Deviance and the Mass Media* (London: Constable).
Collins, Richard (1976a) 'Media Studies: Alternative or Oppositional Practice', in Whitty, Geoff and Young, Michael F. D. (eds) (1976).
—— (1976b) *Television News*, BFI Television Monograph No. 5, (London: BFI).
Colls, Robert and Dodd, Philip (1985) 'Representing the Nation: British Documentary Film 1930–45', *Screen*, vol. 26, no. 1, Jan–Feb 1985.
Communications Group (1982) *Hunt on Cable TV: Chaos or Coherence?* (London: CPBF).
Connell, Ian (1980) 'Television News and the Social Contract', in Hall, Stuart *et al.* (eds) (1980).
Conrad, Joseph (1902) *Heart of Darkness* (Harmondsworth: Penguin).
Cook, Jim (ed.) (1982) *Television Sitcom*, BFI Dossier No. 17 (London: BFI).
Cook, Pam (1978) 'Duplicity in *Mildred Pierce*', in Kaplan, E. Ann (1978) (ed.)
—— (1985) *The Cinema Book* (London: BFI).
Corner, John (1984) 'Olympic Myths: The Flame, the Night and the Music', in Masterman, Len (ed.) (1984).
—— and Hawthorn, Jeremy (eds) (1980) *Communication Studies – An Introductory Reader* (London: Edward Arnold).
Counter Information Services, (undated) *The Wealthy*, 9 Poland Street, London W1.
Coward, Rosalind (1984) *Female Desire – Women's Sexuality Today* (London: Paladin).
Cowie, Elizabeth (ed.) (1978) *Catalogue British Film Institute Productions 1977–78* (London: BFI).
—— (1979) 'The Popular Film as a Progressive Text – A Discussion of *Coma* Part 1', *M/F*, no. 3, 1979.
—— (1980) 'Discussion of *Coma* Part 2, *M/F*, no. 4, 1980.
Crime Prevention Conference (1975) *Journalism, Broadcasting and Urban Cinema* (Chichester: NACRO/Barry Rose).
Critcher, Charles *et al.* (1975) *Race and the Provincial Press* (Paris: UNESCO).
Crofts, Stephen (1970) 'Film Education in England and Wales', *Screen*, vol. 11, no. 6, Nov–Dec 1970.
Curran, James (ed.) (1978) *The British Press – A Manifesto* (London: Macmillan).
—— (ed.) (1984) *The Future of the Left* (Cambridge: Polity).
——, Gurevitch, Michael and Woollacott, Janet (eds) (1977) *Mass*

Communication and Society (London: Edward Arnold/Open University).
—— and Seaton, Jean (1981) *Power Without Responsibility – The Press and Broadcasting in Britain* (London: Fontana) (rev. edn 1985, London, Methuen).
—— and Porter, Vincent (eds) (1983) *British Cinema History* (London: Weidenfeld & Nicolson).
Curtis, Liz (1984a) *Ireland and The Propaganda War* (London: Pluto).
—— (1984b) *Nothing But the Same Old Story – The Roots of Anti-Irish Racism* (London: Information on Ireland).
Daedalus (1985) 'The Moving Image', vol. 114, no. 4, Autumn 1985.
Davies, Philip and Neve, Brian (eds) (1981) *Cinema, Politics and Society in America* (Manchester: Manchester University Press).
Davis, Howard and Walton, Paul (eds) (1983) *Language, Image, Media* (Oxford: Basil Blackwell).
Davis, Jonathan (1986) *Film, History and the Jewish Experience – A Reader* (London: NFT).
De Beauvoir, Simone (1977) *Old Age* (Harmondsworth: Penguin).
Debray, Regis (1981) *Teachers, Writers, Celebrities – The Intellectuals of Modern France* (London: Verso).
Dennett, Terry and Spence, Jo (eds) (1979) *Photography/Politics: One* (London: Photography Workshop).
DES Report (1983) *Popular TV and Schoolchildren* (London: Department of Education and Science).
Dickey, Julienne and CPBF Women's Group (undated) *Women in Focus – Guidelines for Eliminating Media Sexism* (London: Campaign for Press and Broadcasting Freedom).
Dinham, Barbara and Hines, Colin (1985) 'Help Your Self', *Ten-8*, no. 19, Birmingham.
Donald, James and Grealy, Jim (1983) 'The Unpleasant Fact of Inequality: Standards, Literacy and Culture', in Wolpe, Ann-Marie and Donald, James (eds) (1983).
Dorfman, Ariel and Mattelart, Armand (1975) *How to Read Donald Duck – Imperialist Ideology in the Disney Comic* (New York: International General).
Dorfman, Ariel (1983) *The Empire's Old Clothes – What the Lone Ranger, Barbar and Other Innocent Heroes Do To Our Minds . . .* (London: Pluto).
Douch, Lucy (1985) 'Audience Measurement in the UK', in Alvarado, Manuel and Stewart, John (1985).
Dove, Linda and the London Women's Film Group (1976) 'London Letter: Feminist and Left Independent Film-making in England', *Jump Cut*, no. 10/11.
Downing, John (1980) *The Media Machine* (London: Pluto).
Dummett, Ann (1973) *A Portrait of English Racism* (Harmondsworth: Penguin).
Dunkley, Christopher (1985) *Television Today and Tomorrow – Wall to Wall Dallas?* (Harmondsworth: Penguin).
Durant, Alan (1984) *Conditions of Music* (London: Macmillan).

Dyer, Gillian (1982) *Advertising as Communication* (London: Methuen).
Dyer, Richard (1973) *Light Entertainment*, BFI Television Monograph 2 (London: BFI).
—— (ed.) (1977) *Gays and Film* (London: BFI).
—— (1979) *Stars* (London: BFI).
—— (1980) *Marilyn Monroe*, Star Dossier One (London: BFI).
—— *et al.* (1981) *Coronation Street* (London: BFI).
—— (1986) *Heavenly Bodies* (London: BFI/Macmillan).
Education Group, Centre for Contemporary Cultural Studies (1981) *Unpopular Education – Schooling and Social Democracy in England since 1944* (London: Hutchinson).
Eight Programme Makers (1984) 'Channel 4 – One Year On', *Screen*, vol. 25, no. 2, March–April 1984.
Elliott, Philip (1972) *The Making of a Television Series: A Case Study in the Sociology of Culture* (London: Constable).
—— (1975) *Ethnicity and the Media* (Paris: UNESCO).
Ellis, John (ed.) (1977) *Catalogue British Film Institute Productions 1951–1976* (London: BFI).
—— (1982) *Visible Fictions* (London: Routledge & Kegan Paul).
English Centre (1985a) *Changing Stories* (London: ILEA English Centre).
—— (1985b) *Making Stories* (London: ILEA English Centre).
Enzensberger, Hans Magnus (1970) *Constituents of a Theory of the Media*, in Enzensberger, Hans Magnus (1976) *Raids and Reconstruction – Essays on Politics, Crime and Culture* (London: Pluto).
Erens, Patricia (1979) *Sexual Stratagems – The World of Women in Film* (New York: Horizon).
Evans, Peter (1976) *Publish and Be Damned?* (London: Runnymede Trust).
Exton, Richard (1970) 'Film in the Humanities Curriculum Project 2: Practical', *Screen*, vol. 11, no. 2, March–April 1970.
Feuer, Jane (1982) *The Hollywood Musical* (London: BFI/Macmillan).
—— (1984a) 'Melodrama, Serial Form and Television Today', *Screen*. vol. 25, no. 1, Jan–Feb 1984.
—— (1984b) 'MTM Enterprises: An Overview', in Feuer, Jane *et al.* (1984).
——, Kerr, Paul, Vahimagi, Tise (1984) *MTM 'Quality Television'* (London: BFI).
Fiddy, Dick (ed.) (1985) *The Television Yearbook* (London: Virgin).
Fiske, John and Hartley, John (1978) *Reading Television* (London: Methuen).
Fiske, John (1982) *Introduction to Communication Studies* (London: Methuen).
Forsyth Hardy, H. (1966) *Grierson on Documentary* (London: Faber).
Fraser, Ronald (ed.) (1968) *Work – Twenty Personal Accounts* (London: Penguin/NLR).
Frith, Simon (1978) *Sociology of Rock* (London: Constable), totally revised as Frith (1983a).

Frith, Simon (1983a) *Sound Effects – Youth, Leisure and the Politics of Rock* (London: Constable).
—— (1983b) 'The Pleasure of the Hearth', in *Formations of Pleasure* (London: Routledge & Kegan Paul).
Gallagher, Margaret (1981) *Unequal Opportunities – The Case of Women and the Media* (Paris: UNESCO).
Gardner, Carl (ed.) (1979) *Media, Politics and Culture – A Socialist View* (London: Macmillan).
—— and Sheppard, Julie (1984) 'Transforming Television – Part One, The Limits of Left Policy', *Screen*, vol. 25, no. 2, March–April 1984.
Garnham, Nicholas (1973) *Structures of Television* (London: BFI, revised 1978).
Gauthire, Guy (1975) *Introduction to the Semiology of the Image*, mimeo (London: BFI).
Geraghty, Christine (1983) '*Brookside* – No Common Ground', *Screen*, vol. 24, no. 4/5, July–October.
Glasgow University Media Group (1976) *Bad News* (London: Routledge & Kegan Paul).
—— (1980) *Really Bad News* (London: Routledge & Kegan Paul).
—— (1982) *More Bad News* (London: Writers and Readers).
—— (1985) *War and Peace News* (London: Open University).
Gledhill, Christine (ed.) (1981) *Film and Media Studies in Higher Education* (London: BFI).
Glover, David (1984) *The Sociology of the Mass Media* (Lancashire: Causeway).
Godard, Jean-Luc (1972) *Godard on Godard* (London: Secker and Warburg).
Golding, Peter and Middleton, Sue (1982) *Images of Welfare – Press and Public Attitudes to Poverty* (Oxford: Martin Robertson).
Gomery, Douglas (1986) *The Hollywood Studio System* (London: BFI/Macmillan).
Goodwin, Andrew, Kerr, Paul and Macdonald, Ian (eds) (1983) *Drama-Documentary*, BFI Dossier No. 19, (London: BFI).
Gramsci, Antonio (1971) 'The Study of Philosophy', *Selection from the Prison Notebooks* (London: Lawrence & Wishart).
Grant, Moyra (1984) *The British Media – A Guide for 'O' and 'A' Level Students* (London: Comedia).
Gray, Herman (1986) 'Television and the New Black Man: Black Make Images in Prime Time Situation Comedy', *Media, Culture and Society*, vol. 8, no. 2, April 1986.
Greater London Council (1985) *The State of the Art or the Art of the State? Strategies for the Cultural Industries in London* (London: GLC).
Greenberg, Susan and Smith, Graham (undated) '*Rejoice!' Media Freedom and the Falklands* (London: CPBF).
Groombridge, Brian (1972) *Television and the People – A Programme for Democratic Participation* (Harmondsworth: Penguin).
Gurevitch, Michael, Bennett, Tony, Curran, James and Woollacott, Janet (eds) (1982) *Culture, Society and the Media* (London: Methuen).

Gutch, Robin (1984a) 'Whose Telly is it Anyway?' *Screen*, vol. 25, no. 4–5, July–October, 1984.

—— (1984b) 'That's Life', in Masterman, Len (ed.) (1984).

Hackney Flashers (1980) *Domestic Labour and Visual Representation* (London: Hackney Flashers).

Hain, Peter (1984) *Political Trials in Britain* (London: Allen Lane).

Hall, Stuart (1973) 'The Determinations of News Photographs', in Cohen, Stanley and Young, Jock (eds) (revised edition 1981).

Hall, Stuart (1980) 'Encoding/Decoding', in Hall, Stuart *et al.* (1980).

—— (1981) 'The Whites of Their Eyes: Racist Ideologies and the Media', in Bridges, George and Brunt, Rosalind (eds) (1981).

—— and Whannel, Paddy (1964) *The Popular Arts* (London: Hutchinson).

—— and Jefferson, Tony (eds) (1976) *Resistance through Rituals* (London: Hutchinson).

——, Critcher, Chas, Jefferson, Tony, Clarke, John and Roberts, Brian (1978) *Policing the Crisis: Mugging, the State and Law and Order* (London: Macmillan).

—— (1978) 'Newspapers, Parties and Classes in Curran, James (ed.) (1978).

——, Hobson, Dorothy, Lowe, Andrew, and Willis, Paul (eds) (1980) *Culture, Media, Language* (London: Hutchinson).

Halloran, James (ed.) (1970) *The Effects of Television* (London: Panther).

Halloran, James D., Elliott, Philip and Murdock, Graham (1970) *Demonstrations and Communications: A Case Study* (Harmondsworth: Penguin).

Harcourt, Peter (1965) 'Towards Higher Education', *Screen Education*, no. 26, 1965.

—— (1970) 'In Defence of Film History', *Screen*, vol. 11, no. 6, Nov–Dec 1970.

Hardy, Forsyth (1966) *Grierson on Documentary* (London: Faber).

'Hargreaves Report' (1984) *Improving Secondary Schools – Report of the Committee on the Curriculum and Organisation of Secondary Schools* (London: ILEA).

Harker, David (1980) *One for the Money – Politics and Popular Song* (London: Hutchinson).

Harris, Robert (1983) *Gotcha! The Media, the Government and the Falklands' Crisis* (London: Faber).

Harrison, Martin (1985) *TV News: Whose Bias?* (Cambridge: Policy Press).

Hartley, John (1982) *Understanding News* (London: Methuen).

——, Goulden, Holly and O'Sullivan, Tim (1985) *Making Sense of the Media* (London: Comedia).

Hartmann, Paul and Husband, Charles (1972) 'The Mass Media and Racial Conflict' in McQuail, Denis (ed.) (1972).

—— (1974) *Racism and the Mass Media* (London: Davis-Poynter).

Harvey, Sylvia (1978a) *Independent Cinema?* (Stafford: West Midlands Arts).

Harvey, Sylvia (1978b) *May '68 and Film Culture* (London: BFI).
—— (1981) 'Independent Cinema and Cultural Democracy', in Stoneman, Rod and Thompson, Hilary (eds) (1981).
Haydon, Nikki and Mulligan, Jim (1983) *Nuclear Issues* (London: Thames).
Haye, Yves de la (ed.) (1979) *Marx and Engels on the Means of Communication (the Movement of Commodities, People, Information and Capital)*, IG/IMMRC.
Heath, Stephen (1976) 'Narrative Space', *Screen*, vol. 17, no. 3, Autumn 1976.
Hebdige, Dick (1979) *Subculture: The Meaning of Style* (London: Methuen).
—— (1985) 'The bottom line on Planet One. Squaring up to The Face' in *Ten-8*, no. 19, Birmingham.
Heller, Caroline (1978) *Broadcasting and Accountability*, BFI Television Monograph No. 7 (London: BFI).
Henderson, Brian (1980) *A Critique of Film Theory* (New York: Dutton).
Hetherington, Alastair (1985) *News, Newspapers and Television* (London: Macmillan).
Hicks, Cherrill (1980) 'COW Flicks', *The Leveller*, no. 34.
Higgins, A. P. (1966) *Talking About Television* (London: BFI).
Higham, Charles (1970) *Hollywood Cameramen: Sources of Light* (London: Thames and Hudson/BFI).
Hill, Janet (1951) *Films and Children* (London: BFI).
Hillier, Jim (ed.) (1985) *Cahiers du Cinéma – Volume 1, the 1950s: Neo-Realism, Hollywood, New Wave* (London: Routledge & Kegan Paul/BFI).
Hillier, Jim and McTaggart, Andrew (1970) 'Film in the Humanities, Curriculum Project 1: Theory', *Screen*, vol. 11, no. 2, March–April.
Hird, Christopher (1983) *Challenging the Figures – A Guide to Company Finance and Accounts* (London: Pluto).
Hobson, Dorothy (1982) *'Crossroads' – The Drama of a Soap Opera* (London: Methuen).
Hogenkamp, Bert (undated) *Workers' Newsreels in the 1920's and 1930's*, Our History Pamphlet 68 (London: Central Books).
Hoggart, Richard (1957) *The Uses of Literacy* (Harmondsworth: Penguin).
Holland, Patricia (1981) 'Save the Chilren . . . How the Newspapers Present Pictures of Children from the Third World', *Multiracial Education*, vol. 9, no. 2, Spring 1981.
Hollins, Timothy (1984) *Beyond Broadcasting: Into the Cable Age* (London: BFI).
Hood, Stuart (1980) *On Television* (London: Pluto) (revised edition 1983).
—— (1983) 'John Grierson and the Documentary Film Movement', in Curran, James and Porter, Vincent (eds) (1983).
Howkins, John (1982) *New Technology, New Policies* (London: BFI).

Hoyles, Martin (ed.) (1979) *Changing Childhood* (London: Writers and Readers).

Hughes, Patrick (1981) *British Broadcasting: Programming and Power* (Kent: Chartwell-Bratt).

Hunt, Albert (1981) *The Language of Television – Uses and Abuses* (London: Eyre Methuen).

Hurd, Geoff (ed.) (1984) *National Fictions – World War Two in British Films and Television* (London: BFI).

Husband, Charles (ed.) (1975) *White Media and Black Britain – A Critical Look at the Role of the Media in Race Relations Today* (London: Arrow).

Hutchinson, Robert (1984) *Cable, DBS and the Arts* (London: PSI).

Johnston, Claire (ed.) (1973) *Notes on Women's Cinema* (London: SEFT).

—— (ed.) (1975) *The Work of Dorothy Arzner – Towards a Feminist Cinema* (London: BFI).

Jones, Andrew Millar (1948) 'Television and the Cinema', *Penguin Film Review*, no. 6, April 1948.

Jones, David, Petley, Julian, Power, Mike and Wood, Lesley (undated) *Media Hits the Pits – The Media and the Coal Dispute* (London: CPBF).

Kaplan, E. Ann (ed.) (1978) *Women in Film Noir* (London: BFI).

—— (ed.) (1983) *Regarding Television: Critical Approaches – An Anthology* (University Publications of America).

—— (1983) *Women and Film – Both Sides of the Camera* (London: Methuen).

Katzen, Mary (1975) *Mass Communications: Teaching and Studies at Universities* (Paris: UNESCO).

Keyworth, Florence (1982) 'Invisible Struggles: The Politics of Ageing', in Brunt, Rosalind and Rowan, Caroline (eds) (1982).

Kitses, Jim and Mercer, Ann (1966) *Talking About The Cinema* (London: BFI).

Kitses, Jim (1969) *Horizons West* (London: Thames & Hudson/BFI).

Knight, Roy (ed.) (1972) *Film in English Teaching* (London: Hutchinson/BFI).

Kuhn, Annette (1982) *Women's Pictures: Feminism and Cinema* (London: Routledge & Kegan Paul).

—— (1985) *The Power of the Image – Essays on Representation and Sexuality* (London: Routledge & Kegan Paul).

Kumar, Krishan (1977) 'Holding the Middle Ground: The BBC, the Public and the Professional Broadcaster' in Curran, James *et al.* (eds) (1977).

Laing, Dave (1978) *The Marxist Theory of Art – An Introductory Survey* (Sussex: Harvester).

Lambert, Peter and Richardson, Nigel (1983) 'Using Business Games with Sixth Formers', in Watts, A. G. (ed.) (1983).

Lambert, Stephen (1982) *Channel Four – Television with a Difference?* (London: BFI).

Lasswell, H. D. (1948) 'The Structure and Function of Communications', in Bryson, L. (ed.).

Lauretis, Theresa de (1985) *Alice Doesn't: Feminism, Semiotics, Cinema* (London: Macmillan).

Leab, Daniel J. (1975) *From Sambo to SUPERSPADE: The Black Experience in Motion Pictures* (London: Secker and Warburg).

Leavis, F. R. (ed.) (1933, reprinted 1976) *Towards Standards of Criticism* (London: Fokroft).

Lewis, Peter, M. (1978) *Whose Media? The Annan Report and After: A Citizen's Guide to Radio and Television* (London: Consumers' Association).

Longmans Resources Unit (1982) *The School Leaver's Book* (London: Longman).

Lovell, Alan (1971) 'The BFI and Film Education', *Screen*, vol. 12, no. 3, Summer 1971.

—— (1975) *Don Siegel – American Cinema* (London: BFI).

—— (1984) 'The Context of British Social Drama' in Paterson, Richard (1984).

—— and Hillier, Jim (1972) *Studies in Documentary* (London: Secker & Warburg/BFI).

Lovell, Terry (1980) *Pictures of Reality – Aesthetics, Politics and Pleasure* (London: BFI).

Lowndes, Douglas (1968) *Film Making in Schools* (London: Batsford).

Lumley, Bob (1981) 'Notes on Some Images of Terrorism in Italy', *Screen Education*, no. 40, Autumn 1981.

Lusted, David (1981) 'Media Education and the Secondary/FE Curriculum' in David Lusted (ed.) (1982) *Media Education Conference 1981: A Report* (London: BFI).

—— and Drummond, Phillip (1985) (eds) *TV and Schooling* (London: BFI/University of London).

McArthur, Colin (1972) *Underworld USA* (London: Secker & Warburg/BFI).

—— (1978) *Television and History*, BFI Television Monograph No. 8 (London: BFI).

—— (1982a) *Dialectic! Left Film Criticism from 'Tribune'* (London: Key Texts).

—— (ed.) (1982b) *Scotch Reels – Scotland in Cinema and Television* (London: BFI).

McGrath, Vincent (1986) 'Using Video in Primary Education', *Initiatives*, no. 3, February 1986.

McKeown, Neil (1982) *Case Studies and Projects in Communications* (London: Methuen).

McQuail, Denis (ed.) (1972) *Sociology of Mass Communications* (Harmondsworth: Penguin).

—— and Windahl, Sven (1981) *Communications Models – for the Study of Mass Communications* (London: Longman).

MacBean, James Roy (1975) *Film and Revolution* (Bloomington: Indiana University Press).

MacBride, Sean (ed.) (1980) *Many Voices, One World – Communication and Society Today and Tomorrow* (Paris: UNESCO/Kogan Page).

MacCabe, Colin (1974) 'Realism and the Cinema: Notes on Some Brechtian Theses', *Screen*, vol. 15, no. 2, Summer 1974.

—— (1980) *Godard: Images, Sounds, Politics* (London: BFI/Macmillan).

—— (ed.) (1986) *High Theory/Low Culture – Analysing popular television and film* (Manchester: Manchester University Press).

MacCann, Richard Dyer (ed.) (1966) *Film – A Montage of Theories* (New York: Dutton).

MacPherson, Don (ed.) (1980) *Traditions of Independence – British Cinema in the Thirties* (London: BFI).

MacShane, Denis (1978) *Black and Front: Journalists and Race Reporting* (London: NUJ).

—— (1979) *Using the Media – How to Deal with the Press, Television and Radio* (London: Pluto).

Martin, Angela (ed.) (1982) *African Films: The Context of Production*, BFI Dossier No. 6 (London: BFI).

Marx, Karl (1973) *Grundrisse* (Harmondsworth: Penguin).

Masterman, Len (1980) *Teaching About Television* (London: Macmillan).

—— (ed.) (1984) *Television Mythologies: Stars, Shows and Signs* (London: Comedia).

—— (1985) *Teaching the Media* (London: Comedia).

—— and Kiddey, Paul (1983) *Understanding Breakfast TV* (Nottingham: MK).

Mattelart, Armand (1979) *Multinational Corporations and the Control of Culture – The Ideological Apparatuses of Imperialism* (Brighton: Harvester).

—— and Siegelaub, Seth (eds) (1979) *Communication and Class Struggle – 1 Capitalism, Imperialism* (IG/IMMRC).

—— (1983) *Communication and Class Struggle – 2 Liberation, Socialism* (IG/IMMRC).

Mattelart, Armand, Delcourt, Xavier and Mattelart, Michèle (1984) *International Image Markets: In Search of an Alternative Perspective* (London: Comedia).

Mattelart, Michèle (1986) *Women, Media, Crisis – Femininity and Disorder* (London: Comedia).

Metcalf, Andy and Humphries, Martin (1985) *Sexuality of Men* (London: Pluto).

Metz, Christian (1975) 'The Imaginary Signifier', *Screen*, vol. 16, no. 2, Summer 1975.

Miliband, Ralph (1969) *The State in Capitalist Society – An Analysis of the Western System of Power* (London: Weidenfeld & Nicolson).

—— (1977) *Marxism and Politics* (London: OUP).

—— and Saville, John (eds) (1974) *The Socialist Register 1973* (London: Merlin).

Millington, Bob and Nelson, Robin (1986) *'Boys From the Blackstuff' – Making a TV Drama* (London: Comedia).

Minkkinen, Sirkka (1978) *A General Curricular Model for Mass Media Education* (Madrid: UNESCO/ESCO).

Monaco, James (1977) *How To Read A Film – The Art, Technology, Language, History and Theory of Film and Media* (New York: OUP) (revised edition 1981).

Moran, Albert (1982) *Making a TV Series – The 'Bellamy' Project* (Sydney: Currency).

—— (1985) *Images and Industry: Television Drama Production in Australia* (Australia: Currency).

Morey, John (1981) *The Space Between Programmes: Television Continuity* (London: University of London Institute of Education).

Morley, David (1980) *The 'Nationwide' Audience* (London: BFI).

—— and Whitaker, Brian (1983) *The Press. Radio and Television – An Introduction to the Media* (London: WEA/Comedia).

—— (1986) *Family Television – Cultural Power and Domestic Leisure* (London: Comedia).

Multiracial Education (1981) 'Race and the Media', vol. 9, no. 2, Spring 1981.

Mulvey, Laura (1975) 'Visual Pleasure and Narrative Cinema', *Screen*, vol. 16, no. 3, Autumn 1975.

Murdock, Graham (1982) 'Large Corporations and the Control of the Communications Industries', in Gurevitch, Michael *et al.* (1982).

—— and Golding, Peter (1974) 'For a Political Economy of Mass Communications', in Miliband, Ralph and Saville, John (eds) (1974).

—— (1977) 'Capitalism, Communication and Class Relations' in Curran, James *et al.* (eds) (1977).

—— and Phelps, Guy (1973) *Mass Media and the Secondary School* (London: Macmillan).

Murphy, Brian (1983) *The World Wired Up – Unscrambling the New Communications Puzzle* (London: Comedia).

Murray, Jo (1984) *The Future of Educational Broadcasting* (Scottish Council for Educational Technology).

Murray, Nancy (1986) 'Anti-racists and Other Demons: The Press and Ideology in Thatcher's Britain', *Race and Class*, vol. xxvii, no. 3, Winter 1986.

Myers, Kathy (1986) *Understains . . . the sense and seduction of advertising* (London: Comedia).

Nairn, Tom (1981) *TheBreak-up of Britain* (London: Verso).

Neale, Stephen (1980) *Genre* (London: BFI).

—— (1985) *Cinema and Technology: Image, Sound, Colour* (London: BFI/Macmillan).

Nellis, Mike and Hale, Christopher (1982) *The Prison Film* (London: Radical Alternatives to Prison).

Newsom Report (1963) *Half Our Future* (London: Ministry of Education, HMSO).

Nichols, Bill (ed.) (1976) *Movies and Methods – An Anthology* (Berkeley: University of California).

Nichols, Bill (1981) *Ideology and the Image – Social Representation in the Cinema and Other Media* (Bloomington: Indiana University Press).

O'Donnell, Mike (ed.) (1985) *Age and Generation* (London: Tavistock).

O'Faolain, Julia and Martines, Laura (1979) *Not in God's Image* (London: Virago).

O'Sullivan, Kevin (1984) 'A Look at *Boys from the Blackstuff'*, in Paterson, Richard (ed.) (1984).

O'Sullivan, Tim, Hartley, John, Saunders, Danny and Fiske, John (1983) *Key Concepts in Communication* (London: Methuen).

Open University (1977) *Mass Communication and Society* (Milton Keynes: Open University).

Owusu, Kwesi (1986) *The Struggle for Black Arts in Britain – What Can We Consider Better than Freedom* (London: Comedia).

Padfield, A. (1976) 'Put Them in the Picture' *Cog*, no. 1, Summer 1976, Nottingham Teachers' Centre.

Pahl, R. and Winkler, J. (1974) 'The Economic Elite: Theory and Practice', in Stanworth, P. and Giddens, A. (eds) (1974).

Parker, Ros and Pollock, Griselda (1981) *Old Mistresses – Women, Art and Ideology* (London: Routledge & Kegan Paul).

Parliamentary Group Video Enquiry (1983) *Video Violence and Children* (London: Oasis Projects) November 1983.

Paterson, Richard (1980) 'Planning The Family: The Art of the Television Schedule', *Screen Education*, no. 35, Summer 1980.

—— (1982) *TV Globo: Brazilian Television in Context* (London: BFI).

—— (ed.) (1984) *Boys From the Blackstuff*, BFI Dossier No. 20 (London: BFI).

Pearson, Tony (1983) 'Teaching Television', *Screen*, vol. 24, no. 3, May–June 1983.

Perkins, V. F. (1972) *Film as Film – Understanding and Judging Movies* (Harmondsworth: Penguin).

Petley, Julian (1978) *BFI Distribution Library Catalogue 1978* (London: BFI).

—— (1979) *Capital and Culture – German Cinema 1933–45* (London: BFI).

Phillipson, Chris (1982) *Capitalism and the Construction of Old Age* (London: Macmillan).

Pilling, Jayne and Canham, Kingsley (ed.) (1983) *The Screen on the Tube: Filmed TV Drama* (Norwich: Cinema City Dossier No. 1).

Pines, Jim (1975) *Blacks in Films – A Survey of Racial Themes and Images in the American Film* (London: Studio Vista).

—— (1981) 'Blacks in Films – The British Angle', *Multiracial Education*, vol. 9, no. 2, Spring 1981.

Pirie, David (ed.) (1981) *Anatomy of the Movies* (New York: Macmillan).

Plummer, Ken (ed.) (1981) *Making of the Modern Homosexual* (London: Hutchinson).

Points, Chris (ed.) (1985) *Clwyd Working Papers for 16+ Media Studies*, Wales.

Polito, Ronald (1965) 'The History of Film Teaching in the American School System', *Screen Education*, no. 31, Sept–Oct 1965.

Poole, Mike and Wyver, John (1984) *Powerplays – Trevor Griffiths in Television* (London: BFI).

Porter, Vincent (1985) *On Cinema* (London: Pluto).

Poulantzas, Nicos (1978) *Political Power and Social Classes* (London: Verso).

Prendergast, Roy M. (1977) *A Neglected Art – A Critical Study of Music in Films* (New York: New York University Press).

Propp, Vladimir (1968) *Morphology of the Folktale* (University of Texas).

Quigley, Isabel (1961) *The Spectator*, 22 September 1961.

Ranson, Stewart (1984) 'Towards a Tertiary Tripartisan: New Codes of Social Control and the 17+', in Broadfoot, Patricia (ed.) (1984).

Rayns, Tony (ed.) (1976) *Fassbinder* (London: BFI) (revised edition 1979).

Reed, Stanley (1950a) 'Film Appreciation in the School', *The Bulletin* vol. 1, no. 1, December 1950.

—— (1950b) 'Teaching Film for Seven Years Without a Projector', *The Bulletin* (London: SFT).

Reeve, Andy and Stubbs, Paul (1981) 'Racism and the Mass Media: Revising Old Perspectives' *Multiracial Education*, vol. 9, no. 2, Spring 1981.

Robins, Kevin and Webster, Frank (1979) 'Mass Communications and Information Technology', *The Socialist Register* (London: Merlin).

Rodrigues, Chris and Stoneman, Rod (1981) 'The Use of Independent Film in Education' in Stoneman, Rod and Thompson, Hilary (eds) (1981).

Rogers, Rick (ed.) (1980) *Television and the Family* (London: IYC/University of London).

Root, Jane (1984) *Pictures of Women – Sexuality* (London: Pandora).

—— (1986) *Open the Box – A New Way of Looking at Television* (London: Comedia).

Rose, Jacqueline (1984) *The Case of 'Peter Pan'* (London: Macmillan).

Rosen, Marjorie (1973) *Popcorn Venus – Women, Movies and the American Dream* (London: Peter Owen).

Ryan, Trevor (1983) 'The New Road to Progress: The Use and Production of Films by the Labour Movement 1929–39' in Curran, James and Porter, Vincent (eds) (1983).

Said, Edward W. (1981) *Covering Islam – How the Media and the Experts Determine How We See the Rest of the World* (London: Routledge & Kegan Paul).

Schiller, Herbert I. (1976) *Communication and Cultural Domination* (New York: Sharpe).

Schlesinger, Philip (1978) *Putting 'Reality' Together – BBC News* (London: Constable).

—— (1980) 'Princes' Gate, 1980: The Media Politics of Siege Management', *Screen Education* no. 37, Winter 1980/81.

Schlesinger, Philip, Murdock, Graham and Elliott, Philip (1983) *Televising 'Terrorism': Political Violence in Popular Culture* (London: Comedia).

School Without Walls (1978) *Lunatic Ideas or A Lesson in what school is all about . . .* (London: Corner House Bookshop).

Scottish Curriculum Development Service *Brand X, King's Royal, Baxters: The Magic of Advertising* (Edinburgh: SCDS).

Shannon, C. and Weaver, W. (1949) *The Mathematical Theory of Communications* (University of Illinois Press).

Sheridan, Geoffrey (1982) 'CARM, race and the media: the story so far' in Cohen, Phil and Gardner, Carl (eds) (1982).

Sieghart, Paul (1982) *Micro-Chips with Everything – The Consequences of Information Technology* (London: Comedia).

Silverstone, Roger (1981) *The Message of Television – Myth and Narrative in Contemporary Culture* (London: Heinemann).

—— (1985) *Framing Science. The Making of a BBC Documentary* (London: BFI).

Simons, Michael *et al.* (1985) *Front Page News* (London: ILEA English Centre).

Simpson, Anne (1985) 'Charity Begins at Home', *Ten-8*, no. 19, Birmingham.

Sitney, P. Adams (ed.) (1970) *Film Culture – Reader* (New York: Praeger).

Sivanandan, A. (1982) *A Different Hunger – Writings on Black Resistance* (London: Pluto).

Smith, Anthony (1976) *The Shadow in the Cave – the Broadcaster, the Audience and the State* (London: Quartet).

—— (ed.) (1978) *The Politics of Information – Problems of Policy in Modern Media* (London: Macmillan).

—— (ed.) (1979) *Television and Political Life – Studies in Six European Countries* (London: Macmillan).

—— (1980) *The Geopolitics of Information – How Western Culture Dominates the World* (London: Faber).

Stanworth, P. and Giddens, A. (1974) *Elites and Power in British Society* (London: Cambridge University Press).

Stenhouse, Lawrence (1969) 'Open Minded Teaching', *New Society*, 24 July 1969.

Steven, Peter (ed.) (1985) *Jump Cut: Hollywood, Politics and Counter-Cinema* (Ontario: Between the Lines).

Steward, Sue and Garrett, Sheryl (1984) *Signed, Sealed and Delivered – True Life Stories of Women in Pop* (London: Pluto).

Stewart, John (1985) *The Films of Amos Gitai* (London: BFI).

Stoddard, Karen M. (1983) *Saints and Sirens: Women and Ageing in American Popular Film* (Connecticut: Greenwood Press).

Stonemen, Rod and Tompson, Hilary (eds) (1981) *The New Social Function of Cinema: Catalogue of British Film Institute Productions 1979–80* (London: BFI).

Swanson, Gillian (1981) '*Dallas*', *Framework*, no. 14, Spring 1981, and no. 15/16/17, Summer 1981.

Taylor, Laurie and Mullan, Bob (1986) *Uninvited Guests – The Intimate Secrets of Television and Radio* (London: Chatto & Windus).

Television Research Committee (1966) *Problems of Television Research: A Progress Report of the Television Research Committee* (Leicester: Leicester University Press).

Therborn, Göran (1983) 'Which Class Wins?', *New Left Review*, no. 138.

Thompson, Denys (1965) *Discrimination and Popular Culture* (Harmondsworth: Penguin).

Thompson, E. P. (1963) *The Making of the English Working Class* (Harmondsworth: Penguin).

Todorov, Tzvetan (1970) *The Fantastic – A Structural Approach to a Literary Genre* (New York: Cornell University Press).

Tomlinson, Alan and Whannel, Garry (eds) (1984) *Five Ring Circus – Money, Power and Politics at the Olympic Games* (London: Pluto).

—— (eds) (1986) *Off The Ball – The Football World Cup* (London: Pluto).

Tracey, Michael (1978) *The Production of Political Television* (London: Routledge & Kegan Paul).

—— (1985) 'The Poisoned Chalice? International Television and the Idea of Dominance' *Daedalus*, vol. 114, no. 4, Autumn 1985.

—— and Morrison, David (1979) *Whitehouse* (London: Macmillan).

TUC Media Working Group (1979a) *A Cause For Concern – Media Coverage of Industrial Disputes January and February 1979* (London: TUC).

—— (1979b) *How To Handle the Media – A Guide for Trade Unionists* (London: TUC).

—— (1984) *Images of Inequality – The Portrayal of Women in the Media and Advertising* (London: TUC).

Tuchman, Gaye, Daniels, Arlene, Kaplan, E. Ann and Benet, James (1978) *Hearth and Home – Images of Women in the Mass Media* (New York: OUP).

Tudor, Andrew (1974a) *Image and Influence – Studies in the Sociology of Film* (London: Allen & Unwin).

—— (1974b) *Theories of Film* (London: Secker & Warburg/BFI).

Tulloch, John (1976) 'Gradgrind's Heirs: The Quiz and the Presentation of "Knowledge" by British Television', in Whitty, Geoff and Young, Michael F. D. (eds) (1976).

Tulloch, John and Alvarado, Manuel (1983) *'Doctor Who' – The Unfolding Text* (London: Macmillan).

Tumber, Howard (1982) *Television and the Riots* (London: BFI).

Tunstall, Jeremy (ed.) (1970) *Media Sociology – A Reader* (London: Constable).

—— (1977) *The Media are American – Anglo-American Media in the World* (London: Constable).

—— (1983) *The Media in Britain* (London: Constable).

Turvey, Sarah (1982) *Barthes' 'S/Z' and the Analysis of Film Narrative: 'The Searchers'* (London: University of London Institute of Education).

UNESCO (1977) *Media Studies in Education* (Paris: UNESCO).
—— (1984) *Media Education* (Paris: UNESCO).
University of the Third Age (1984) *The Image of the Elderly on TV*, 8a Castle Street, Cambridge CB3 0AQ.
Vaughan, Dai (1974) 'The Space between Shots', *Screen*, vol. 15, no. 1, Spring 1974.
—— (1976) *Television Documentary Usage* (London: BFI).
—— (1983) *Portrait of an Invisible Man – The Working Life of Stewart McAllister, Film Editor* (London: BFI).
Veljanovski, C. G. and Bishop, W. D. (1983) *Choice by Cable – The Economics of a New Era in Television*, Hobart Paper 96 (London: IEA).
Vulliamy, Graham and Lee, Edward (1982) *Popular Music – A Teacher's Guide* (London: Routledge & Kegan Paul).
Waites, Bernard, Bennett, Tony and Martin, Graham (eds) (1982) *Popular Culture: Past and Present* (London: Croom Helm/Open University).
Wallis, Roger and Malm, Krister (1984) *Big Sounds from Small Peoples – The Music Industry in Small Countries* (London: Constable).
Walker, Alexander (1970) *Stardom – The Hollywood Phenomenon* (London: Michael Joseph).
Watts, A. G. (ed.) (1983) *Work, Experience and Schools* (London: Heinemann).
Whannel, Garry (1979) 'Football, Crowd behaviour and the Press', *Media, Culture and Society*, vol. 1, no. 4, October 1979.
—— (1983) *Blowing the Whistle* (London: Pluto).
Whannel, Paddy (1969) 'Film Education and Film Culture', *Screen*, vol. 10, no. 3, May –June 1969.
Wheare Report (1950) *The Report of the Departmental Committee on Children and the Cinema* (London: HMSO).
Whitfield, Stephen E. and Roddenberry, Gene (1968) *The Making of 'Star Trek'* (New York: Ballantine Books).
Whitty, Geoff and Young, Michael F. D. (1976) *Explorations in the Politics of School Knowledge* (Driffield: Nafferton).
Widdowson, Peter (ed.) (1982) *Re-Reading English* (London: Methuen).
Wigbold, Herman (1979) 'Holland: The Shaky Pillars of Hilversum' in Smith, Anthony (ed.) (1979).
Willeman, Paul and Gandhy, Behroze (ed.) (1980) *Indian Cinema*, BFI Dossier No. 5 (London: BFI).
Williams, Christopher (ed.) (1980) *Realism and the Cinema: A Reader* (London: Routledge & Kegan Paul/BFI).
Williams, Raymond (1962) *Communications* (Harmondsworth: Penguin).
—— (1973) 'Base and Superstructure in Marxist Cultural Theory', *New Left Review*, no. 82, Nov–Dec 1973.
—— (1974) *Television, Technology and Cultural Form* (London: Fontana).
—— (1976) *Keywords – A Vocabulary of Culture and Society* (London: Fontana) (revised edition 1983).

Williams, Raymond (1962) *Communications* (Harmondsworth: Penguin).
—— (1974) *Television: Technology and Cultural Form* (London: Fontana).
—— (1980) *Problems in Materialism and Culture* (London: Verso).
—— (1981) *Culture* (London: Fontana).
—— (1983) *Towards 2000* (London: Chatto & Windus).
—— and Orrom, Michael (1954) *Preface to Film* (London: Film Drama Ltd.).
Williamson, Judith (1978) *Decoding Advertisements: Ideology and Meaning in Advertising* (London: Marion Boyars).
Willis, Paul (1977) *Learning to Labour – How Working Class Kids Get Working Class Jobs* (Farnborough, Hants: Saxon House).
Wills, H. R. (1959) 'Editorial', *Screen Education*, no. 1, October 1959.
Wilson, David (ed.) (1982) *'Sight and Sound': A Fiftieth Anniversary Selection* (London: Faber/BFI).
Wolpe, Ann-Marie and Donald, James (eds) (1983) *Is There Anyone Here From Education?* (London: Pluto).
Wolff, Janet (1981) *The Social Production of Art* (London: Macmillan).
Wollen, Peter (undated) *Working Papers on the Cinema: Sociology and Semiology* (London: BFI).
—— (1969) *Signs and Meaning in the Cinema* (London: Secker & Warburg/BFI) (revised edition 1972).
—— (1976) 'North by Northwest: A Morphological Analysis', in Wollen, Peter (1982).
—— (1980) 'Manet: Modernism and the Avant-Garde', *Screen*, vol. 21, no. 2, Summer 1980.
—— (1982) *Readings and Writings – Semiotic Counter-Strategies* (London: Verso).
Wollen, Tana (1985a) *Memory: 'The Flame Trees of Thika'*, in Alvarado, Manuel and Stewart, John (1985).
—— (1985b) 'Teaching Television', *The English Programme 1985–86* (London: Thames).
—— (1985c) 'Television, Media Studies and Schooling', in Lusted, David and Drummond, Phillip (eds) (1985).
Women's Monitoring Network (undated) *Women and Ageism: A Woman's Place*, Hungerford House, Victoria Embankment, London WC2.
Women's Studies Group, Centre for Contemporary Cultural Studies (1978) *Women Take Issue – Aspects of Women's Subordination* (London: Hutchinson/CCCS).
Wren-Lewis, Justin (1981) 'The Story of a Riot: The Television Coverage of Civil Unrest in 1981', *Screen Education*, no. 40, Autumn 1981.
Yale French Studies (1980) 'Cinema/Sound', no. 60.
Young, Michael F. D. (ed.) (1971) *Knowledge and Control – New Directions for the Sociology of Education* (London: Collier-Macmillan).

Index